TEACHING LÉVI-STRAUSS

AMERICAN ACADEMY OF RELIGION
TEACHING RELIGIOUS STUDIES

Edited by
Susan Henking

Number 1
TEACHING LÉVI STRAUSS

Edited with an Introduction by
Hans Penner

Teaching Lévi-Strauss

Edited with an Introduction by

Hans Penner
Preston Kelsey Professor of Religion
Dartmouth College

Scholars Press
Atlanta, Georgia

TEACHING LÉVI-STRAUSS

Edited with an Introduction by
HANS PENNER
Preston Kelsey Professor of Religion
Dartmouth College

Library of Congress Cataloging in Publication Data
Teaching Lévi-Strauss / edited with an introduction by Hans Penner.
      p.   cm. — (Teaching religious studies series ; no. 1)
    Includes bibliographical references.
    ISBN 0-7885-0490-8 (paper : alk. paper)
    1. Lévi-Strauss, Claude. 2. Structural anthropology.
  3. Mythology. I. Penner, Hans, H., 1934–   . II. Series: Teaching religious studies series (American Academy of Religion) ; no. 1.
GN362.T43 1998
301–dc21   98-27126
                             CIP

Printed in the United States of America
on acid-free paper

TABLE OF CONTENTS

PART THREE: LÉVI-STRAUSS RESPONDS

SERIES PREFACE

As I sit writing this, I can hear conversations echoing in the hallway of the building. Colleagues and students mingle. "What do you think I should do about the student who talks constantly in class and won't let others speak at all?" "Have you ever taught this book? Does it teach well?" "What exactly is a comma splice?" "Can you help me with my paper topic?" "What did you think of the recent issue of JAAR?" "Have you tried putting students into groups to discuss the text?" "That was the worst teaching experience I have ever had. What did I do wrong?" "Do you know a good film on Zen?" "You should take this course. Wow, can that professor teach." "What do you mean you're a reductionist?" "Want a pretzel?" "Have you read your course evaluations yet?" As a senior colleague and friend told me during my very first year at the Colleges where I still teach, teaching is very much about interruption. Yet, as these samples hint, there is much that is important amidst the flotsam and jetsam of our daily lives as teachers and scholars. For it is here that we raise—in local and particular forms—the many topics which stand at the intersection of pedagogy and the substantive content of religious studies.

In recent years, our nation—and our discipline—has turned a critical eye toward our profession and higher education, asking an array of questions about the relation of teaching and other professorial duties. As this has happened, many newcomers have appeared in our metaphorical hallways, asking (and sometimes demanding) that we reflect anew upon such questions as: What is good teaching? How can teachers accomplish their aims in the context of this time and place? How are good teaching and good learning intertwined? What is—or should be—the relation of scholarship and teaching? Within the particular contexts of religious studies, we have tackled these and other more specific questions. We have asked, for example, what it means to teach religious studies in a secular setting or in a religious milieu, in a traditional liberal arts college or a community college, in a setting which is increasingly multicultural and/or one which is undergoing immense technological transformation. We have inquired how the texts, theories and phenomena of religious studies change as they move into (and out of) classrooms. And we have struggled with how best to introduce students to our field. In facing such questions, the everyday realities of pedagogical practice and the substantive concerns of religious studies come together. How we teach and what we teach, why we teach and how we know are intertwined. Put another way, situated teaching and scholarship are integral to our vitality as communities of inquiry.

These ongoing conversations about higher education and religious studies, like those which take place outside my office door and across the quad, are personal, political, epistemological, theoretical, and methodological. And they are ongoing—shifting and changing with historical and cultural circumstance, as interlocutors come and go, as we reach across disciplinary lines and speak within narrower confines, as novices and experienced teachers converse, and as we move between periods of fallowness and richness in our work. Such conversations must steer between naive idealism about teaching or scholarship which fails to recognize the difficult and complex nitty gritty of our work and the cynicism elicited by exhaustion, depleted budgets, or anti-intellectual cultural surrounds. Throughout it all, the central questions of religious studies are, it seems to me, the central questions of our teaching. And vice versa.

This series, then, seeks to join your hallway conversation—bringing to it some additional voices of teacher/scholars who combine classroom and scholarly expertise (and angst). By bringing these voices together, the series seeks to refresh us as teachers, to point us forward, and to teach us about the substance of our field in teacherly and scholarly ways. Whether attending to Freud or apocalypticism, to the Tao Te Ching or Durkheim, these volumes ask what good teaching is, in doing so, they remind us that such teaching is always informed by the best of scholarship. Moreover, the series challenges us to be reflexive and dialogical in our work, to listen and learn ....

"Oh excuse me. There's a student at my door wanting to discuss ... And I have that one more reference to check before my 1:20 class ...."

Susan E. Henking
Department of Religious Studies
Hobart and William Smith Colleges

VOLUME PREFACE

Durkheim wrote that, "men do not weep for the dead because they fear them, they fear them because they weep for them." I believe that Lévi-Strauss would agree with him, only instead of viewing fear and weeping solely as social facts Lévi-Strauss would transform the sense of the sentence into an oppositional relation between "nature is to culture as fear is to weeping." I have found the work of Lévi-Strauss as revolutionary as Durkheim's publications at the beginning of our century. The reaction to Lévi-Strauss' work on kinship and myth was immediate and swift. The study of myth after 1955 would never be the same again. Many scholars, especially British and American empiricist anthropologists and historians of religions found his thought to be simply wrong, or "reductionistic," if not off the wall.

I have taught Lévi-Strauss in a course on "Myth and Ritual" for many years. I usually introduce students to his thought by having them read his little book, *Totemism*, since it sums up his thought and his theory of structuralism very nicely—it also put an end to the subject of "totemism" as a religious institution! There are two passages in *Totemism* that are pure Lévi-Strauss and I quote them here as a compass or lighthouse should you feel lost as you move into and out of the primary and secondary sources in this anthology. Here they are:

"As affectivity is the most obscure side of man, there has been the constant temptation to resort to it, forgetting that what is refractory to explanation is *ipso facto* unsuitable for use in explanation. A datum is not primary because it is incomprehensible: this characteristic indicates that an explanation, if it exists, must be sought on another level. Otherwise, we shall be satisfied to attach another label to the problem, thus believing it to have been solved." (65)

And,

"Actually, impulses and emotions explain nothing: they are always *results*, either of the power of the body or of the impotence of the mind. In both cases they are consequences, never causes. The latter can be sought in the organism, which is the exclusive concern of biology, or the intellect, which is the sole way offered to psychology, and to anthropology as well." (71)

This anthology begins and ends with Lévi-Strauss. The first piece, his introduction to Marcel Mauss, gives us at least as much about Lévi-Strauss as it does Marcel Mauss.It is an excellent introduction to his thought. The"Finale"allows Lévi-Strauss to have the last word concerning criticism and misunderstanding of his work. From my own study of his thought I believe it is fair to say that the charges of "anti-history," "idealism" and the impossibility of verifying or falsifying his work are simply false. Nevertheless, these charges were leveled at the very beginning of his publications and as usual they were then used by many who seem not to have read his publications including the four volume work on mythology. For many in the study of religion he was simply put down as a "reductionist." I hope that this anthology will help put to rest such charges. This is not to deny that at times Lévi-Strauss is his own worst enemy in the many opaque passages and pranks of style found throughout his writings. The "Finale" is also one of the few places where Lévi-Strauss reflects upon a structural approach to ritual which remains an incomplete and much needed project.

Part II is a selection of secondary sources that are critical of his work. Some are more hostile than others and together they set the framework for what would become the criticism of structuralism as anti-empiricist. The critics are right but did not see that Lévi-Strauss was ahead of them in his resistance to the last legacies of positivism. Sperber's essay remains a classic in its perception that the fundamental problem with Lévi-Strauss' theory of structuralism is that he thinks he is dealing with semantics, with meaning, and does not apparently see that the structure of a myth is not synonymous with its meaning.

I am grateful to Dartmouth College for help in covering research and editorial assistance. Jennifer Walker-Johnson quickly became the editor, director and producer of the manuscript in the form of a photo-copy format ready for Scholars Press. I am deeply indebted to her competence and judgment. Finally, I am grateful to Terry Godlove, editor of this series for Scholars Press, for encouraging me to take on and complete this anthology. I appreciate the thought of Lévi-Strauss even more now that the manuscript is complete.

ACKNOWLEDGMENTS & REFERENCES TO REPRINTED ARTICLES

Burridge, K. O. L. "Lévi-Strauss and Myth," In Edmund Leach (ed.), *The Structural Study of Myth and Totemism*, pp. 91–114. London: Tavistock Publications, 1967. Reprinted by permission of the publisher.

Derrida, Jacques. "Structure, Sign, and Play." In Richard Macksey and Eugenio Donato (eds.), *The Structuralist Controversy*, pp. 247–265. Baltimore: Johns Hopkins Press, 1970. Reprinted by permission of the publisher.

Douglas, Mary. "The Meaning of Myth." In Edmund Leach (ed.), *The Structural Study of Myth and Totemism*, pp. 49–68. London: Tavistock Publications, 1967. Reprinted by permission of the publisher.

Lévi-Strauss, Claude. "Finale," *The Naked Man*, pp. 625–648, 667–675, 679–695. New York: Harper & Row, 1981. Reprinted by permission of the publisher.

Lévi-Strauss, Claude. "Four Winnebago Myths." In Stanley Diamond (ed.) *Culture In History, Essays in Honor of Paul Radin*, pp. 351–362. New York: Columbia University Press, 1960. Reprinted by permission of the publisher.

Lévi-Strauss, Claude. *Introduction To Marcel Mauss,* pp. 24–66. London: Routledge & Kegan Paul, 1987. Reprinted by permission of the publisher.

Lévi-Strauss, Claude. "The Meaning and Use of the Notion of Model," in *Structural Anthropology,* Vol. II, pp. 71–81. New York: Basic Books, 1976. Reprinted by permission of the publisher.

Lévi-Strauss, Claude. "The Story of Asdiwal," in *Structural Anthropology*, Vol. II, pp. 146–185. New York: Basic Books, 1976. Reprinted by permission of the publisher.

Lévi-Strauss, Claude. "The Structural Study of Myth," in *Structural Anthropology*, Vol. I, pp. 206–230. New York: Basic Books, 1963. Reprinted by permission of the publisher.

Lévi-Strauss, Claude. "Towards the Intellect," *Totemism*, pp. 72–91. Boston: Beacon Press, 1963. Reprinted by permission of the publisher.

Maybury-Lewis, David. "Science or Bricolage?" *American Anthropologist*, Vol. 71, No. 1, 1969, pp. 114–121. Reprinted by permission of the publisher.

Penner, Hans H. "Structuralism, Anthropology and Lévi-Strauss," *Impasse and Resolution: A Critique of the Study of Religion*, pp. 147–180. New York: Peter Lang, 1989. Reprinted by permission of the publisher.

Sperber, Dan. "Absent Meaning." In Alice Morton (trans.), *Rethinking Symbolism*, pp. 51–84. New York: Cambridge University Press, 1974. Reprinted by permission of Cambridge University Press.

INTRODUCTION

Hans H. Penner

1.1 The Theory Of Structuralism

The list of scholars who have changed the course of an academic discipline in their own lifetime is very short. Einstein and Chomsky are clearly on the list and so is Claude Lévi-Strauss, who made the words "structuralism" and "structural analysis" common terms in most newspapers and weekly magazines around the world. The terms were certainly used before Lévi-Strauss made them so popular. No one would deny that the term "structure" was used in physics, logic, and anthropology long before Lévi-Strauss began to lecture on "structural anthropology." This being so it is often claimed that there is really nothing new in what Lévi-Strauss has to say, his popularity was nothing more than one of the many vogues that arise and pass away in Paris. If this is true then it is hard to explain the explosive controversy that took place after Lévi-Strauss began to publish essays on something called "structural analysis." Structuralism simply cannot be separated from the thought of Lévi-Strauss. After Lévi-Strauss the study of kinship, totemism, myth and ritual would never be the same again. As one disgruntled scholar put it, "Yet it has been said that when one turns from Lévi-Strauss to any other attempt to analyze these myths, the results look old-fashioned and unconvincing; and I too find this to be so."[1] I agree.

The fundamental theme running through all of his writings is that it is a serious error to follow the thought of Lévy-Bruhl (as many do) and think that there is a fundamental difference between so-called "primitive" and "modern" societies. That "primitive mentality" is like the mentality of our children, or, that they are "mystical" and we are "logical" in our way of thinking, that there are two modes of thinking that are different in kind. The basic binary opposition, nature/culture (raw/cooked) can be found in all of his publications. It would be an error to think of this basic opposition as a dualism or as containing ontological significance. Nevertheless, the opposition nature/culture clearly marks what Lévi-Strauss thinks human nature is all about. We are rational creatures who says Lévi-Strauss must first of all know the world before it becomes useful to us. Lévi-Strauss is not a pragmatist. What fascinates Lévi-Strauss are such questions as, "since it is clearly not necessary for our existence, why do human beings cook food?" Why are there prohibitions on eating certain kinds of food? Perhaps the most significant question Lévi-Strauss asks is, "what is the significance of 'the other'?" "We/they?" Throughout all of the diverse material he studies Lévi-Strauss finds a logic, a structure. And for Lévi-Strauss where there is a logical structure there is also rationality.

Lévi-Strauss did not create this new kind of analysis out of the thin air. Some of his early essays make it clear that many of his new insights were taken from linguistics. Although he states that his primary intellectual debts are to Marx, Freud and Geology you will find very little from this trinity in his collected writings. What you will find is a consistent homage to Ferdinand de Saussure, the father of modern linguistics. To give just one example, "In formulating the above rule, [that contrasting signifiers have a signified/signifier relationship with each other] I am merely extending to the domain of mythic thought de Saussure's principle of the arbitrary character of the linguistic sign..."[2]

Although you do not need a full understanding of de Saussure's theory in order to understand Lévi-Strauss it might be helpful to know the meaning of certain theoretical terms that Lévi-Strauss borrows and sometimes simply assumes are self-evident.

After may years of intellectual despair concerning the study of language, de Saussure asked the following important question: "is a science of language, linguistics possible?" It is the same question many scholars of religion have raised for the past several decades. It comes to the forefront in the subtitle of Lévi-Strauss's massive four volume study of myth—"Introduction to a Science of Mythology." de Saussure begins his lectures with a critique of the study of language and quickly concludes that the historical-comparative study of language did not succeed in establishing a science of language. Why? Because, de Saussure replies, "they never took very great care to define exactly what it was they were studying. And until this elementary step is taken, no science can hope to establish its own methods."[3]

Defining the object of linguistics entailed the formation of such new concepts as the differentiation of language as a system from speech as individual utterance, form from substance, synchrony from diachrony, signified from signifier. Saussure concluded from all this that "language then has the strange and striking characteristic of not having entities that are perceptible at the outset and yet of not permitting us to doubt that they exist and that their functioning constitutes it," that "to avoid being misled, it is first of all important to realize that concrete linguistic entities do not present themselves for inspection on their own accord."[4] In brief, and this cannot be overemphasized for those interested in the study of religion, the object of linguistic study, according to de Saussure, is *not immediately given* in experience. Lévi-Strauss puts it this way; "Explanation begins only when we have succeeded in constituting our object." Now if this is also true for the study of religion we face a major revolution given the traditional approaches to the study of religion.

How then did de Saussure proceed to describe the object of linguistics? I believe we can summarize the procedure by highlighting four fundamental principles which when taken together provide a theoretical definition of de Saussure's answer to the question, "what is language?" These principles also provide the theoretical foundation and the constraints for what has become known as "structuralism" or structural analysis.

Before describing the four principles I cannot help but tell the well known story about *Course in General Linguistics*. Ferdinand de Saussure never wrote the book! (This is somewhat ironic since structuralism is well known for its overthrow of essences, the dissolution of elements, and individualism.) De Saussure was assigned to teach a course in general linguistics. He gave the lectures from 1907 to 1911, became ill in the summer of 1912 and died in February 1913 at the age of fifty-six. The famous text, published three years later in 1916, is a synthesis of his lectures made from the notes of his students by two editors (Bally and Sechehaye) who never attended the course!

What then is the object of language? First, it is a set of oppositions, or bi-polar entities that have no value in themselves. Each element in the system takes its value from the fact that it is in opposition to the other. Thus, the units of a language system, (sounds, words, sentences) are *constituted* by their relations with other units in the system. Linguistic units, phonemes, morphemes, lexemes, syntagms, as such have no prior or independent value (significance) apart from the relations which define them. This is the principle from which all others proceed. It may be called the principle of holism.

The second principle in de Saussure's course follows from the first. Language is a system of signs. A sign is a double entity. Here is how the *Course* states the principle: "A linguistic sign is not a link between a thing and a name, but between a concept and a sound pattern.... A sound pattern may thus be distinguished from the other element associated with it in a linguistic sign. This other element is generally of a more abstract kind: the concept." [5] Thus a sign is composed of signifier and signified and the relation between these two aspects of the sign is defined as the *signification* of the sign.

Clearly, de Saussure's concept of language entails the important conclusion that language is not a nomenclature, a naming process which somehow connects a list of words with things that words name. Moreover, it is important to notice that Saussure does not include the notion of "reference" to some external entity as a component of signification. The relation signifier/signified *excludes* reference!

Saussure's definition of sign as composed of the relation signifier/signified leads him to the conclusion that the nature of the sign is arbitrary. The relation between signifier/signified is not "natural" or a necessary relation. The very existence of different languages confirms this conclusion. What then does define a signifier or a signified? If you answered, "it is the relation between the two that defines them" you understand Saussure's theory of linguistics.

The third important principle to be found in *Course* is the distinction between language and speech.[6] We can easily see the difference when we reflect upon the statement, "I speak a language." Or, "I use language to communicate." One way of stressing the difference is to point out that "language" is a system; "speech" is "use" of the system, also called "pragmatics." Speech is an act, speaking presupposes language. Saussure's distinction between language and speech is compatible with Chomsky's well known separation of "competence" from "performance" as a means for specifying the proper object of linguistics.[7]

For de Saussure, linguistics concentrates on language as a system rather than speech. From a formal point of view we must first of all explain language before we can begin to analyze speech as performance or utterance. Once this is stressed we can immediately understand why de Saussure focused on synchronic rather than diachronic analysis. Synchronic analysis stresses an analysis of language as a system in a particular state rather than an analysis of the evolution or history of a language through time. Saussure was fond of using chess as his example. First, we do not need to know the history of chess, its evolution, in order to play chess. Secondly, we do not need to know the history of chess in order to analyze a particular state of a game in progress. What we do need to know is the system of chess that constitutes the relations between the elements (king, queen, rook, bishop, knight, pawn.) Once again, using this example, an examination of the empirical properties of the "elements" of chess will not help us at all in explaining chess as a "system." The elements are arbitrary, they can be wood, plastic, jade, or purely symbolic in a game played on E-mail.

Let us recall that de Saussure began his quest for a science of language as someone trained in the history and comparison of languages. Thus it is reasonable to assume that Saussure was well aware of the historicity of language. This awareness led him to the conclusion that it is necessary to draw a distinction between language as a system and the evolution of language. The arbitrary nature of the sign is clearly tied to the contingencies of history. Saussure was fully aware that language is subject to change. He also knew that there are no essential properties in the nature of the sign that stand "outside" history. Thus Saussure knew, we can be assured, that it is *because* language is an historical phenomenon that synchronic analysis becomes necessary.

The issue here is not synchronic analysis *vs* diachronic analysis. For Saussure, the relation synchronic/diachronic was as important as signifier/signified. If, however, we wish to establish a theory of language, we have no choice but to begin with synchronic analysis. Nevertheless, it must be said that the precise nature of the relation between the synchronic and diachronic remains a problem.

The fourth and final principle is a consequence of the first principle concerning the bi-polar nature of linguistic entities. As we can now see, the fundamental term in Saussurian linguistics is "relation." How does he define the term? The text provides us with two definitions. The first kind of relation is called "syntagmatic" and the second relation is defined as "associative" now usually called "paradigmatic." Saussure claimed that all relations in a language system can be explained as either syntagmatic or paradigmatic.

Although the analysis becomes complex and problematic the concepts themselves are easy to understand.

Syntagmatic relations define the possible combinations that a linguistic unit may enter with other units. For example, the lexeme "old' is syntagmatically related with the definite article "the" and the noun "cat" in the syntagm "the old cat." Moreover, the phoneme "e" is syntagmatically related with "l" and "d" in the lexeme "led." The task then is to discover the finite set of axioms or definitions that allow for just such combinations that produce well formed lexemes, or, syntagms in, for example, English. Saussure claimed that syntagmatic relations define all the possible combinatory relations on all levels of a linguistic system from the phoneme up through syntactic and semantic relations.

Paradigmatic relations define the possible oppositions between linguistic units that can be substituted for one another in a syntagm. In our first example, "The old cat," "young," "small," or "sick" are paradigmatically related to "old" since they can be substituted for "old" in the syntagm, "The old cat," producing, "The young cat," or "The small cat," etc. etc. Furthermore, "woman" is paradigmatically related to "cat," in, "The old woman." On the phonetic level /a/ and /i/ are in paradigmatic relation with /e/ in the lexeme "led." The task then, is to construct or discover the rules that constitute the syntagmatic and paradigmatic relations of a language. One thing should stand out very clearly—the task cannot succeed if we begin with experience, history, or surface empirical data of our study be it language or religion. It is this principle, I believe, that remains essential in the work of Lévi-Strauss.

The ultimate law of language, according to the *Course* "is dare we say, that nothing can ever reside in a single term. This is a direct consequence of the fact that linguistic signs are unrelated to what they designate, and that therefore *a* cannot designate anything without the aid of *b* and vice versa, in other words, that both have value only by the differences between them, or that neither has value, in any of its constituents, except through this same network of forever negative differences."[8]

What is essential to remember is that the foundation of Saussure's theory and the continuing development of structuralism is holistic. As the *Course* says, " A language might also be compared to a sheet of paper. Thought is one side of the sheet and sound the reverse side. Just as it is impossible to take a pair of scissors and cut one side of paper without at the same time cutting the other, so it is impossible in a language to isolate sound from thought, or thought from sound. To separate the two for theoretical purposes takes us into either pure psychology or pure phonetics, not linguistics."[9] Thus it would be "a great mistake to consider a sign as nothing more than the combination of a certain sound and a certain concept. To think of a sign as nothing more would be to isolate it from the system to which it belongs. It would be to suppose that a start could be made with individual signs, and a system constructed by putting them together. On the contrary, the system as a united whole is the starting point, from which it becomes possible, by a process of analysis, to identify its constituent elements."[10] In other words, "A language is a system in which all the elements fit together, and in which the value of any one element depends on the simultaneous coexistence of all the others."[11] All of this may be summed up as follows: "A language is a system of which all the parts can and must be considered as synchronically interdependent."[12]

These statements are excellent descriptions of the principle of holism. It is the foundation of the structuralist edifice that Lévi-Strauss built in his work on kinship, totemism, myth, and culture. Without going into the details and problems here are three examples that should illustrate the importance of this theoretical principle. Before presenting the examples I want to emphasize an important point—each of these examples represents a solution to a problem: the problem of the avunculate in kinship studies, the problem of the disintegration of studies on totemism, and the apparent chaos in the study of myth which in itself seems irrational. *Structuralism, like any other scientific theory, was developed in order to solve problems.*

In his response to criticism of his work on kinship Lévi-Strauss replies that his critics forgot a fundamental rule of structural analysis: "The rule is that the analysis can never consider the terms only, but must, beyond the terms, apprehend their interrelations. *These alone constitute its true object.*"[13] He then goes on to describe what he calls "the atom of kinship." The simplest unit consists of the quadrangular system of relationships between brother and sister, husband and wife, father and son, maternal uncle and nephew." Thus the atom of kinship " can never be constructed from the biological family made up of a father, a mother, and their children, but that it always implies a marriage relationship."[14]

The second example comes from his book on totemism. As you will recall both Freud and Durkheim, among many others, thought that totemism was the origin of religion and culture. Lévi-Strauss quotes a textbook published in 1950 that sums up the situation very nicely:

> "It will be seen that the term 'totemism' has been applied to a bewildering variety of relationships between human beings and natural species or phenomena. For this reason it is impossible to reach any satisfactory definition of totemism, though many attempts have been made to do so...All definitions of totemism are either so specific as to exclude a number of systems which are commonly referred to as 'totemic' or so general as to include many phenomena which cannot be referred to by this term."[15]

After studying the problem Lévi-Strauss demonstrates that this venerable institution is a figment of our imaginations. He calls it the "totemic illusion." The illusion is the result of extracting certain elements from a total system, "giving them an originality and a strangeness which they do not really possess; for they are made to appear mysterious by the very fact of abstracting them from the system of which, as transformations, they formed an integral part."[16] Lévi-Strauss then constructs a model consisting of a set of relations between "Nature" and "Culture" and goes on to demonstrate how the empirical data of what has been called "totemism" fits into this set of relations. In so doing he also creates a new principle—"*it is not the resemblances, but the differences, which resemble each other.*"[17] He concludes his analysis as follows: "Totemism is thus reduced to a particular fashion of formulating a general problem, viz., how to make opposition, instead of being an obstacle to integration serve rather to produce it." We then find the famous sentence, "...natural species are chosen not because they are 'good to eat' but because they are 'good to think.'"[18]

The third problem Lévi-Strauss solved was the study of myth. Here is what he has to say about it.

> "Of all the chapters of religious anthropology probably none has tarried to the same extent as studies in the field of mythology. From a theoretical point of view the situation remains very much the same as it was fifty years ago, namely, chaotic. Myths are still widely interpreted in conflicting ways: as collective dreams, as the outcome of a kind of esthetic play, or as the basis of ritual. Mythological figures are considered as personified abstractions, divinized heroes, or fallen gods.

Whatever the hypothesis, the choice amounts to reducing mythology either to idle play or to a crude kind of philosophic speculation."[19]

After this essay appeared the study of myth would never the be same again. You simply cannot write about mythology without somehow coming to grips with what Lévi-Strauss has to say. It is in this essay where we can clearly see the influence of Saussure. Lévi-Strauss makes explicit use of the diachronic and synchronic and his diagrams of the myths clearly follow Saussure's analysis of paradigmatic and syntagmatic relations. If you read the myths horizontally, left to right, line be line you are reading them syntagmatically. If you read the myth, vertically, row by row, from top to bottom you have the paradigmatic relations of the units of the myth. (Lévi-Strauss confuses his own analysis here by using the terms "synchronic" and "diachronic.")

In this essay Lévi-Strauss asserts that his theory of myth eliminates the quest for the "true" or "genuine" or "earliest" version of a myth, since the myth consists of all of its versions. It is in this essay where we also find his well-known definition of the purpose of myth. Since it is widely quoted but never explained I think it is best to pause, quote it and then provide you with a brief explanation of the definition. "The purpose of myth," says Lévi-Strauss, "is to provide a logical model capable of overcoming a contradiction (an impossible achievement if as it happens the contradiction is real.)"[20]

There are at least two interesting concepts in this definition. The first is the use of a semantic term—contradiction. The use of this term in his definition of myth confirms that Lévi-Strauss thinks he is explaining the meaning of myth by means of structural analysis. This is problematic since the structure or syntax of myth might well be necessary for the meaning of myth, but, as we well know syntax does not generate or produce semantics. As Chomsky once said, "Green ideas sleep furiously" is a well formed sentence but it is also meaningless. Myths, of course, may prove to be the exception, in myths syntax and semantics may be synonymous, neither Lévi-Strauss nor any other structuralist has argued the case.

The two terms, "opposition" and "contradiction," often seem to be confused or seem to be taken as synonymous in Lévi-Strauss's and other structuralist's work on myth. I would suggest a simple revision of the definition—"myths are stories about the lives of superhuman beings and provide a logical model capable of overcoming sets of oppositions." The revised definition stresses "opposition" thus reminding us that oppositions such as nature/culture, day/night, earth/sky are not contradictions.

The second item of interest in Lévi-Strauss's definition of myth is the statement in parenthesis "(an impossible achievement if as it happens the contradiction is real)". Given what Lévi-Strauss has published, "the real" in this statement refers to the political/economic infrastructure of a society. Thus if the content of a myth contradicts (or is in opposition to) the actual infrastructure of a society (as it usually does) then the myth will never resolve its purpose but will continue to transform itself into never ending sets of contradictions or oppositions. This is, of course, the classic formulation of ideology that we find in Marx.

The essay is also the first place where we find the "genetic law", algorithm, or logic of mythology. Although Lévi-Strauss calls it an "approximate formula at the present stage" one that will "certainly need to be refined," eleven years later he quotes it again calling it a "canonical relationship," and cites it as "proof of the fact that I have never ceased to be guided by it since that time,"[21] There is a slight improvement in the notation of the formula. It now reads:

$$fx_{(a)} : fy_{(b)} :: fx_{(b)} : f(a-1)_{(y)}$$

We may simplify the notation as follows:

$$A : B :: C : D$$

The revised notation is to be understood as follows: First, the sets A/B and C/D are to be understood as sets of oppositions. Secondly, A is to be taken as the inverse of D. Thus in the analysis of the Oedipus myth, (A) "overrating of blood relations" is the inverse of (D) "the persistence of the autochthonous origin of man." In the Zuni emergence myth, (A) "change" is the inverse of (D) "Permanence." (see "Structural Study of Myth" this volume.) In another essay Lévi-Strauss demonstrates that this transformational syntax is clearly at work in the Tsimshian Indian myth of Asdiwal. The "Story of Asdiwal" begins with a mother and daughter down in a valley and ends with a father and son up on a mountain.[22]

I have not come across a review that covers all four volumes of Lévi-Strauss's *Introduction to a Science of Mythology*. This is unfortunate because when you reach the end of volume four you begin to realize that this massive study of the mythology of South and North America has the same structure, viz. A (Vol.1) : B (Vol.2) : : C (Vol.3) : D (Vol. 4). Very briefly, Lévi-Strauss begins his study with a South American myth, "The Ge hero," a jaguar who is master of terrestrial fire and of cooked meat. Volume four ends with myths concerning a mythical wolverine who is the victim of cooking fire and the master of raw meat. Both myths are related to a bird-nester myth. At the beginning of *The Raw and the Cooked,* (Vol.1) we find a photograph of a rock formation where the Bororo look for macaw's nests. In volume four, *The Naked Man* we find a photograph of "Pillar Rock" in the sea on the Northwest coast of Cape Flattery! I hope you too will discover that reading Lévi-Strauss is always an adventure.

1.2 . The Critique Of The Theory.

The reactions to structuralism à la Lévi-Strauss was quick and often brutal. His theory was called "the lemon squeezer technique," and that to follow Lévi-Strauss is to be asked "to suspend our critical faculties." One expert wrote that "Unfortunately, a great deal of what Lévi-Strauss writes cannot be taken seriously." His work is described as "clever dialectics," or, "incredibly clever," "unwarranted speculation," the product of a mind drawn to the "delusions produced by reification." One scholar thought that as soon as we can come up with the right tests, they would show that the work of Lévi-Strauss "will be very much outdated." Most of these reactions come from scholars trained in the British-American functionalist tradition—a tradition that is diametrically opposed and opposite to holistic theories such as structuralism.

Once you pass by the reactions you will find that there are two basic criticisms of the theory. The first asserts that it is not replicable, verifiable or falsifiable. The second criticism accuses Lévi-Strauss of formalism of an Hegelian type. The volumes that have been written using structuralist theory simply proves the first criticism false. The second criticism is rejected by Lévi-Strauss himself. He says, "It was necessary to mention at least the concrete results achieved by structural analysis... to put the reader on his guard against the charge of formalism, and even of idealism, that has sometimes been leveled against me.... Such misgivings, which have often been expressed, seem to me to arise from a total misunderstanding of what I am trying to do."[23] Throughout his work Lévi-Strauss has repeatedly and consistently rejected all phenomenological notions of transcendental subjectivity or ego, mystical essences, and archetypes. In short he has rejected all forms of idealism.

I believe it is fair to say that the logical structure of myth has been vindicated. Anyone familiar with the work of Lévi-Strauss knows, however, that Lévi-Strauss consistently links the structure of a myth or myths with its meaning. It is this linkage that creates serious problems. Unless myths are exceptions, the semantics of myth cannot be reduced to its syntax or structure. Thus the structure of a myth or a ritual does not constitute it's meaning. Although this is a serious flaw it is not fatal to the theory. What would be fatal is a critique that would demonstrate that holism is invalid or false.

If all of this is true, then it would seem to be the case that we need to develop two important domains in the study of religion. First, we will need to develop a semantic theory that is consistently holistic and thus coherent with the structural foundations that are provided by Lévi-Strauss and other scholars. The development of such a theory would naturally included the semantics of religious belief. Secondly, we will need to develop a structural theory for ritual that will entail the holistic principles of structural analysis.

Whatever the outcome, when you review the writings of Lévi-Strauss and the criticism you will understand why it is the case that after Lévi-Strauss the study of myth, ritual and religion moved into an entirely new direction.

Notes

[1] G. S. Kirk, *Myth: Its Meaning and Function in Ancient and Other Cultures,* (Cambridge: Cambridge UP, 1973) 63.

[2] Claude Lévi-Strauss, *From Honey to Ashes,* (New York: Harper & Row, 1973), p. 421.

[3] Ferdinand de Saussure, *Course in General Linguistics,* eds. Charles Bally and Albert Sechehaye with Albert Reidlinger, trans. by Roy Harris, (La Salle, Ill: Open Court, 1986) p. 3.

[4] de Saussure, *Course,* p. 108.

[5] de Sausssure, *Course,* p. 66.

[6] These are technical terms in Saussure's theory. The differences between "langue" in French and "language " in English are well known in the on going scholarship on Saussure. See, R. Harris's "Introduction" to *Course* for a very good description of the difficulties and their resolution.

[7] As is the case in many academic disputes the controversy between American/British linguists and their European counterparts rests on a confusion about the meaning of "structuralist" or "structuralism." I suggest the following texts for those of you who are interested in this issue. John Lyons, *Semantics,* Vol. I, especially pages 230ff. Also, Ino Rossi, *From the Sociology of Symbols to the Sociology of Signs,* for an excellent analysis of what he calls, "transformational structuralism" in his comparison of Saussure, Lévi-Strauss, Chomsky and Althusser. Ricoeur only prolongs the confusion by equating structuralism of the Saussurian type with "taxonomies," when he makes the false distinction between "structural linguistics" and "generative linguistics." See, Paul Ricoeur, *The Conflict of Interpretation: Essays in Hermeneutics* (Evanston, Ill.: Northwestern UP, 1974).

[8] Quoted in Jonathan Culler, *Ferdinand de Saussure,* (New York: Penquin, 1976), p.49.

[9] *Course,* p. 111.

[10] *Course,* p. 112.

[11] *Course,* p. 113.

[12] *Course,* p.86.

[13] Lévi-Strauss, Claude, *Structural Anthropology,* Vol. II (New York: Basic Books, 1976) p. 83, italics mine.

[14] *Structural Anthropology,* Vol. II. p. 83.

[15] Piddington, R. quoted by Lévi-Strauss in *Totemism* (Boston: Beacon Press, 1962), p.9.

[16] *Totemism,* p. 18.

[17] *Totemism,* p.76.

[18] *Totemism,* p. 89.

[19] "The Structural Study of Myth," in *Structural Anthropology,* (New York: Basic Books, 1963). This essay was originally published in 1955. I have included it in this anthology rather than "The Story of Asdiwal." Although I think the analysis of "Asdiwal" is more elegant the revolution began with "The Structural Study of Myth." It remains a thought provoking study.

[20] "The Structural Study of Myth," (this vol.)

[21] *From Honey to Ashes: Introduction to a Science of Mythology,* Vol. 2 (New York: Harper & Row, 1973), p. 249.

[22] See, "The Story of Asdiwal," in *Structural Anthropology,* Vol. II, (New York: Basic Books, 1976), pp. 146-197.

[23] *The Raw and The Cooked,* (New York: Harper & Row, 1969), p. 9.

PART ONE:

ESSAYS BY LÉVI-STRAUSS

CHAPTER I

Introduction to Marcel Mauss

Claude Lévi-Strauss

It really would be a great mistake to isolate the *Essai sur le don* from the rest of [his] work, even though it is quite undeniably the masterwork of Marcel Mauss, his most justly famous writing, and the work whose influence has been the deepest. It is the *Essai sur le don* which introduced and imposed the notion of *total social fact*.... Now the social is only real when integrated in a system, and that is a first aspect of the notion of total fact: "After sociologists have, as they must, analysed and abstracted rather too much, they must then force themselves to recompose the whole." One might be tempted to apprehend the total fact through any one aspect of society exclusively: the familial aspect, the technical, economic, juridical or religious aspect; that would be an error; but the total fact does not emerge as total simply by reintegrating the discontinuous aspects. It must also be embodied in an individual experience, and that, from two different viewpoints: first, in an individual history which would make it possible to "observe the comportment of total beings, not divided up into their faculties"; and after that, in what I would like to call (retrieving the archaic meaning of a term whose applicability to the present instance is obvious) an *anthropology*, that is, a system of interpretation accounting for the aspects of all modes of behaviour simultaneously, physical, physiological, psychical and sociological, "Only to study that fragment of our life which is our life in society is not enough."

The total social fact therefore proves to be three-dimensional. It must make the properly sociological dimension coincide with its multiple synchronic aspects; with the historical or diachronic dimension; and finally, with the physiopsychological dimension. Only in individuals can these three dimensions be brought together. If you commit yourself to this "study of the concrete which is a study of the whole", you cannot fail to note that "what is true is not prayer or law, but the Melanesian of this or that island, Rome, Athens."

Consequently, the notion of total fact is in direct relation to the twofold concern (which until now we had encountered on its own), to link the social and the individual on the one hand, and the physical (or physiological) and the psychical on the other. But we are better able to understand the reason for it, which is also twofold. On the one hand, it is at the end of a whole series of reductive procedures that we can grasp the total fact, which includes: (1) different modes of the social (juridical, economic, aesthetic, religious and so on); (2) different moments of an individual history (birth, childhood, education, adolescence, marriage, and so on); (3) different forms of expression, from physiological phenomena such as reflexes, secretions, decreased and increased rates of movement, to unconscious categories and conscious representations, both individual and collective. All of that is definitely social, in one sense, since it is only in the form of a social fact that these elements, so diverse in kind, can acquire a global signification and become a whole. But the converse is no less true, for the only guarantee we can have that a total fact corresponds to reality, rather than being an arbitrary accumulation of more or less true details, is that it can be grasped in a concrete experience: first, in that of a society localised in space or time, "Rome, Athens"; but also, in that of any individual at all in any one at all of the societies thus localised, "the Melanesian of this or that island." So it really is true that, in one sense, any psychological phenomenon is a sociological phenomenon; that the mental is identified with the social. But on the other hand, in a different sense, it is all quite the reverse: the proof of the social cannot be other than mental; to put it another way, we can never be sure of having reached the meaning and the function of an institution, if we are not in a position to relive its impact on an individual consciousness. As that impact is an integral part of the institution, any valid interpretation must bring together the objectivity of historical or comparative analysis and the subjectivity of lived experience. When I followed, earlier, what seemed to me to be one of the directions of Mauss's thinking, I arrived at the hypothesis that the psychical and the social are complementary. That complementarity is not static, as would be that of two halves of a puzzle; it is dynamic and it arises from the fact that the psychical is both at once a simple *element of* signification for a symbolic system which transcends it, and the only *means of verification* of a reality whose manifold aspects can only be grasped as a synthesis inside it.

There is much more to the notion of total social fact, therefore, than a recommendation that investigators remember to link agricultural techniques and ritual, or boat-building, the form of the family agglomeration and the rules of distribution of fishing hauls. To call the social fact *total is* not merely to signify that *everything observed is part of the observation,* but also, and above all, that in a science in which the observer is of the same nature as his object of study, *the observer himself is a part of his observation.* I am not alluding, here, to the modifications which ethnological observation inevitably produces in the functioning of the society where it occurs, for that difficulty is not peculiar to the social sciences; it is encountered wherever anyone sets out to make fine measures, that is, wherever the observer (either he himself, or else his means of observation) is of the same order of magnitude as the observed object. In any case, it was physicians who brought that difficulty to light, and not sociologists; it merely imposes itself on sociologists in the same way. The situation particular to the social sciences is different in nature; the difference is to do with the intrinsic character of the object of study, which is that it is object and subject both at once; or both "thing" and "representation", to speak the language of Durkheim and Mauss. It could doubtless be said that the physical and natural sciences are in the same circumstance, since any element of the real is an object, and yet it triggers representations; and that a full explanation of the object should account simultaneously for its structure and for the representations through which our grasp of its properties is mediated. In theory, that is true; a total chemistry should explain not just the form and the distribution of a strawberry's molecules, but how there results from the arrangement a unique flavour. However, history can prove that a satisfactory science does not need to go so far, and that for centuries on end, and even millennia perhaps (since we do not know when it will complete its work), it can progress in the knowledge of its object by virtue of an eminently unstable distinction between qualities pertaining to the object which are the only ones that the science seeks to explain, and other qualities which are a function of the subject, and which need not be taken into consideration.

When Mauss speaks of total social facts, he implies, on the contrary, (if I am interpreting him correctly) that that easy and effective dichotomy is denied to the sociologist, or at least, that it could only correspond to a temporary and transient state of the development of the science. An appropriate understanding of a social fact requires that it be grasped totally, that is, from outside, like a thing; but like a thing which comprises within itself the subjective understanding (conscious or unconscious) that we would have of it, if, being inexorably human, we were living the fact as indigenous people instead of observing it as ethnographers. The problematic thing is to know how it is possible to fulfil that ambition, which does not consist only of grasping an object from outside and inside simultaneously, but also requires much more; for the insider's grasp (that of the indigenous person, or at least that of the observer reliving the indigenous person's experience) needs to be transposed into the language of the outsider's grasp, providing certain elements of a whole which, to be valid, has to be presented in a systematic and coordinated way.

The task would not be feasible if the distinction between the objective and the subjective, rejected by the social sciences, were as rigorous as it has to be when the physical sciences provisionally allow it. But that is precisely the difference: the physical sciences bow (temporarily to a distinction that they intend shall be rigorous, whereas the social sciences reject (permanently) a distinction which could only be a hazy one. I should like to explain further what I mean by that. I mean that, in so far as the distinction is, as a theoretical distinction, an impossible one, it can in practice be pushed much further, to the point where one of its terms becomes negligible, at least relative to the order of magnitude of the observation. The subject itself—once the object-subject distinction is posited—can then be split and duplicated in the same way, and so on without end, without ever being reduced to nothing. Sociological observation, seemingly sentenced by the insurmountable antinomy that we isolated in the last paragraph, extricates itself by dint of the subject's capacity for indefinite self-objectification, that is to say (without ever quite abolishing itself as subject) for projecting outside itself ever-diminishing fractions of itself. Theoretically, at least, this fragmentation is limitless, except for the persistent implication of the existence of the two extremes as the condition of its possibility.

The prominent place of ethnography in the sciences of man, which explains the role it already plays in some countries, under the name of social and cultural anthropology, as inspirer of a new humanism, derives from the fact that it offers this unlimited process of objectification of the subject, which is so difficult for the individual to effect; and offers it in a concrete, experimental form. The thousands of societies which exist or have existed on the earth's surface are human, and on that basis we share in them in a subjective way; we could have been born into them, and so we can seek to understand them as if we were. But at the same time, all of them taken together (as compared to any one of them on its own) attest the subject's capacity to objectify himself in practically unlimited proportions, since the society which is the reference group, which constitutes only a tiny fraction of the given, is itself always exposed to being subdivided into two different societies, one of which promptly joins the enormous mass of that which, for the other one, has and always will have the status of object; and so it goes on indefinitely. Any society different from our own has the status of object; any group of our own society, other than the group we come from ourselves, is object; and even every custom of our own group to which we do not adhere. That limitless series of objects constitutes, in ethnography, the Object, and is something that the individual subject would have to pull painfully away from himself, if the diversity of mores and customs did not present him with a prior fragmenting. But never could the historical and geographical closing of gaps induce him to forget (at the risk of annihilating the results of his efforts) that all those objects proceed from him, and that the most objectively conducted analysis of them could not fail to reintegrate them inside the analyst's subjectivity.

The ethnographer, having embarked on that work of identification, is always threatened by the tragic risk of falling victim to a misunderstanding; that is, the subjective grasp he reaches has nothing in common with that of the indigenous individual, beyond the bald fact of being subjective. That difficulty would be insoluble, subjectivities being, in hypothetical terms, incomparable and incommunicable, if the opposition of self and other could not be surmounted on a terrain which is also the meeting place of the objective and the subjective; I mean the unconscious. Indeed, on the one hand, the laws of unconscious activity are always outside the subjective grasp (we can reach conscious awareness of them, but only as an object); and yet, on the other hand, it is those laws that determine the modes of their intelligibility.

So it is not surprising that Mauss, imbued with a sense of the necessity for a close collaboration between sociology and psychology, referred constantly to the unconscious as providing the common and specific character of social facts: "In magic, as in religion, it is the unconscious ideas which are the active ones." In the essay on magic from which that quotation is taken, we can see an effort, doubtless still hesitant, to formulate ethnological problems by other means than through "rigid, abstract categories of our language and our thinking"; to do so in terms of a "non-intellectualist psychology" foreign to our "adult European understanding." It would be quite mistaken to perceive that as concordant (before the fact) with Lévy-Bruhl's idea of a prelogical mentality, an idea that Mauss was never to accept. We must rather seek its meaning in the attempt he himself made, in connection with the notion of *mana*, to reach a sort of "fourth dimension" of the mind, a level where the notions of "unconscious category" and "category of collective thinking" would be synonymous.

Mauss's perception was accurate, therefore, when from 1902 he affirmed that "in sum, as soon as we come to the representation of magical properties, we are in the presence of phenomena similar to those of language." For it is linguistics, and most particularly structural linguistics, which has since familiarised us with the idea that the fundamental phenomena of mental life, the phenomena that condition it and determine its most general forms, are located on the plane of unconscious thinking. The unconscious would thus be the mediating term between self and others. Going down into the givens of the unconscious, the extension of our understanding, if I may put it thus, is not a movement towards ourselves; we reach a level which seems strange to us, not because it harbours our most secret self, but (much more normally) because, without requiring us to move outside ourselves, it enables us to coincide with forms of activity which are both at once *ours* and *other*: which are the condition of all the forms of mental life of all men at all times. Thus, the grasp (which can only be objective) of the unconscious forms of mental activity leads, nevertheless, to subjectivisation; since, in a word, it is the same type of operation which in psychoanalysis allows us to win back our most estranged self, and in ethnological inquiry gives us access to the most foreign other as to another self. In both cases, the same problem is posed; that of a communication sought after, in the one instance between a subjective and an objective self, and in the other instance between an objective self and a subjective other. And, in both cases also, the condition of success is the most rigorously positive search for the unconscious itineraries of that encounter; itineraries traced once and for all in the innate structure of the human mind and in the particular and irreversible history of individuals or groups.

In the last analysis, therefore, the ethnological problem is a problem of communication; and that realization must be all that is required to show the radical separation of the path Mauss follows when he identifies *unconscious* with *collective*, from the path of Jung, which one might be tempted to define the same way. For it is not the same thing, to define the unconscious as a category of collective thinking, and to divide it up into sectors according to the individual or collective character of the content attributed to it. In both cases, the unconscious is conceived as a symbolic system; but for Jung, the unconscious is not reduced to the system; it is filled full of symbols, and even filled with symbolized things which form a kind of substratum to it. But that substratum is either innate or acquired. If it is innate, one must object that, without a theological hypothesis, it is inconceivable that the content coming from experience should precede it; if it is acquired, the problem of the hereditary character of an acquired unconscious would be no less awesome than that of acquired biological features. In fact, it is not a matter of translating an extrinsic given into symbols, but of reducing to their nature as a symbolic system things which never fall outside that system except to fall straight into incommunicability. Like language, the social is an autonomous reality (the same one, moreover); symbols are more real than what they symbolise, the signifier precedes and determines the signified. We will encounter this problem again in connection with *mana*....

.   .   .

What happened in that essay [*"The Gift"*], for the first time in the history of ethnological thinking, was that an effort was made to transcend empirical observation and to reach deeper realities. For the first time, the social ceases to belong to the domain of pure quality— anecdote, curiosity, material for moralising description or for scholarly comparison—and becomes a system, among whose parts connections, equivalences and interdependent aspects can be discovered. First, it is the products of social activity, whether technical, economic, ritual, aesthetic or religious (tools, manufactured products, foodstuffs, magical formulae, ornaments, chants, dances and myths), which are made comparable to one another through that common character they all have of being transferable; the modes of their transferability can be analysed and classified, and even when they seem inseparable from certain types of values, they are reducible to more fundamental forms, which are of a general nature. Furthermore, these social products are not only comparable, but often substitutable, in so far as different values can replace one another in the same operation. And, above all, it is the operations themselves which admit reduction to a small number. However diverse the operations may seem when seen through the events of social life—birth, initiation, marriage, contract, death or succession, and however arbitrary they may seem in the number and distribution of the individuals that they involve as members-elect, intermediaries or donors—it is these operations, above all else, which always authorise a reduction to a smaller number of operations, groups or persons, in which there finally remain only the fundamental terms of an equilibrium, diversely conceived and differently realised according to the type of society under scrutiny. So the types become definable by these intrinsic characteristics; and they become comparable to one another, since those characteristics are no longer located in a qualitative order, but in the number and the arrangement of elements which are themselves constant in all the types....

The *Essai sur le don* therefore inaugurates a new era for the social sciences, just as phonology did for linguistics. The importance of that double event (in which Mauss's part unfortunately remained in the outline stage) can best be compared to the discovery of combinatorial analysis for modern mathematical thinking. It is one of the great misfortunes of contemporary ethnology that Mauss never undertook to exploit his discovery, and that he thus unconsciously incited Malinowski (of whom we may, without prejudice to his memory, acknowledge that he was a better observer than theorist) to launch out alone upon the elaboration of the corresponding system, on the basis of the same facts and analogous conclusions, which the two men had reached independently.

It is difficult to know in what direction Mauss would have developed his doctrine, if he had been willing. The principal interest of one of his last works, *La Notion de personne* (1938), also published in *Sociologie et anthropologie,* is not so much in the argumentation, which we can find cursory and at times careless, as in the tendency which emerges in it to extend to the diachronic order a technique of permutations which the *Essai sur le don* had rather conceived as a function of synchronic phenomena. In any event, Mauss would probably have encountered some difficulties if he had tried to take the system to a further level of elaboration; we will shortly see why. But he certainly would not have given it the regressive form that Malinowski was to give it; for while Mauss construed the notion of function following the example of algebra, implying, that is, that social values are knowable *as functions of* one another, Malinowski transforms the meaning along the lines of what could seem to be a naive empiricism, in that it no longer designates anything more than the practiced usefulness for society of its customs and institutions. Whereas Mauss had in mind a constant *relation* between phenomena, which would be the site of their explanation, Malinowski merely wonders *what they are useful* for, to seek a justification for them. Such a posing of the problem annihilates all the previous advances, since it reintroduces an apparatus of assumptions having no scientific value.

The most recent developments in the social sciences, on the other hand, attest that Mauss's was the only way of posing the problem that was well founded; these new developments give us cause to hope for the progressive mathematisation of the field. In certain essential domains such as that of kinship, the analogy with language, so strongly asserted by Mauss, could enable us to discover the precise rules by which, in any type of society, cycles of reciprocity are formed whose automatic laws are henceforth known, enabling the use of deductive reasoning in a domain which seemed subject to the total arbitrariness. On the other hand, by associating more and more closely with linguistics, eventually to make a vast science of communications, social anthropology can hope to benefit from the immense prospects opened up to linguistics itself, through the application of mathematical reasoning to the study of phenomena of communication. Already, we know that a large number of ethnological and sociological problems, some on the level of morphology, some even on the level of art or religion, are only waiting upon the goodwill of mathematicians who could enable ethnologists collaborating with them to take decisive steps forward, if not yet to a solution of those problems, at least to a preliminary unification of them, which is the condition of their solution....

·   ·   ·

Whatever may have been the moment and the circumstances of its appearance in the ascent of animal life, language can only have arisen all at once. Things cannot have begun to signify gradually. In the wake of a transformation which is not a subject of study for the social sciences, but for biology and psychology, a shift occurred from a stage when nothing had a meaning to another stage when everything had meaning. Actually, that apparently banal remark is important, because that radical change has no counterpart in the field of knowledge, which develops slowly and progressively. In other words, at the moment when the entire universe all at once became *significant,* it was none the better known for being so, even if it is true that the emergence of language must have hastened the rhythm of the development of knowledge. So there is a fundamental opposition, in the history of the human mind, between symbolism, which is characteristically discontinuous, and knowledge, characterised by continuity. Let us consider what follows from that. It follows that the two categories of the signifier and the signified came to be constituted simultaneously and interdependently, as complementary units; whereas knowledge, that is, the intellectual process which enables us to identify certain aspects of the signifier and certain aspects of the signified, one by reference to the other—we could even say the process which enables us to choose, from the entirety of the signifier and from the entirety of the signified, those parts which present the most satisfying relations of mutual agreement—only got started very slowly. It is as if humankind had suddenly acquired an immense domain and the detailed plan of that domain, along with a notion of the reciprocal relationship of domain and plan; but had spent millenia learning which specific symbols of the plan represented the different aspects of the domain. The universe signified long before people began to know what it signified; no doubt that goes without saying. But, from the foregoing analysis, it also emerges that from the beginning, the universe signified the totality of what humankind can expect to know about it. What people call the progress of the human mind and, in any case, the progress of scientific knowledge, could only have been and can only ever be constituted out of processes of correcting and recutting of patterns, regrouping, defining relationships of belonging and discovering new resources, inside a totality which is closed and complementary to itself.

We appear to be far removed from *mana*, but in reality we are extremely close to it. For, although the human race has always possessed an enormous mass of positive knowledge, and although the different societies have devoted more or less effort to maintaining and developing it, it is nonetheless in very recent times that scientific thinking became established as authority and that forms of societies emerged in which the intellectual and moral ideal, at the same time as the practical ends pursued by the social body, became organised around scientific knowledge, elected as the centre of reference in an official and deliberate way. The difference is one of degree, not of nature, but it does exist. We can therefore expect the relationship between symbolism and knowledge to conserve common features in the non-industrial societies and in our own, although those features would not be equally pronounced in the two types of society. It does not mean that we are creating a gulf between them, if we acknowledge that the work of equalizing of the signifier to fit the signified has been pursued more methodically and rigorously from the time when modern science was born, and within the boundaries of the spread of science. But everywhere else, and still constantly in our own societies, and no doubt for a long time to come, a fundamental situation perseveres which arises out of the human condition: namely, that man has from the start had at his disposition a signifier-totality which he is at a loss to know how to allocate to a signified, given as such, but no less unknown for being given. There is always a non-equivalence or "inadequation" between the two, a non-fit and overspill which divine understanding alone can soak up;

this generates a signifier-surfeit relative to the signifieds to which it can be fitted. So, in man's effort to understand the world, he always disposes of a surplus of signification (which he shares out among things in accordance with the laws of the symbolic thinking which it is the task of ethnologists and linguists to study). That distribution of a supplementary ration—if I can express myself thus—is absolutely necessary to ensure that, in total, the available signifier and the mapped-out signified may remain in the relationship of complementarity which is the very condition of the exercise of symbolic thinking....

CHAPTER II

Toward the Intellect

Claude Lévi-Strauss

I.

The Tallensi of the northern Gold Coast are divided into patrilineal clans observing distinctive totemic prohibitions. They share this feature with the peoples of the upper Volta, and even with the generality of those of the western Sudan. It is not only a matter of formal resemblance, for the animal species most commonly prohibited are the same over the entire extent of this vast territory, as also are the myths which are invoked to account for the prohibitions.

The objects of the totemic prohibitions of the Tallensi comprise birds such as the canary, turtle-dove, domestic hen; reptiles such as the crocodile, snake, turtle (land and water); certain fish; the large grasshopper; rodents such as the squirrel and hare; ruminants such as the goat and sheep; carnivores such as the cat, dog, and leopard; and, finally, other animals such as the monkey, wild pig, etc.

It is impossible to find any common trait among this variety of creatures. Some play an important part in the economic life and the food-supply of the natives, but the majority are negligible in this respect. Many are prized as delicacies by those who are permitted to eat them; and, on the other hand, some are despised as food. No adult would willingly eat grasshopper, canaries, or small edible snakes, though little children, who eat almost any small animals they can lay their hands on, quite often do so. Several of these animal species are regarded as always potentially dangerous in the magical as well as the physical sense. Such are the crocodile, snakes, the leopard, and other wild carnivores. But many, on the contrary, are entirely innocent both in the magical and the physical sense. Some have a place in the meager folk-lore of the Tallensi, including such diverse creatures as the monkey, the turtle-dove, and the cat.... Incidentally, clans that have the cat as totem show no particular respect towards household cats, nor are household dogs treated differently by people who may and people who may not eat the dog.

The totemic animals of the Tallensi thus comprise neither a zoological nor a utilitarian nor a magical class. All that can be said of them is that they are generally fairly common domestic or wild creatures.

This takes us far from Malinowski. But, above all, Fortes brings out a problem which, since Boas, may be glimpsed behind the illusions created by totemism. To understand beliefs and prohibitions of this order it is not enough to attribute a general function to them, viz., as constituting a simple and concrete procedure which is easily transmissible in the form of habits contracted in childhood, in order to display the complex structure of a society. For yet another question presents itself, and one that is probably fundamental, viz., why the animal symbolism? Above all, and seeing that it has been established, at least negatively, that the choice of certain animals is not explicable from a utilitarian point of view, why such a particular symbolism rather than any other?

Let us take the Tallensi case by stages. There are individual animals, or even sometimes geographically localized species, which are the objects of tabus because they are met with in the neighborhood of shrines dedicated to particular ancestor cults. There is no question of totemism here, in the meaning normally given to the word. "Tabus of the Earth" form an intermediate category between these sacred animals or species and the totems, such as the large reptiles—crocodile, python, tree-lizard or water-lizard—which may not be killed near an Earth shrine. They are "the people of the Earth," in the same sense as men are described as people of such and such a village, and they symbolize the power of the Earth, which may be beneficent or maleficent. The question immediately arises why certain terrestrial creatures have been selected and not others. The python, for example, is particularly sacred in the territory guarded by a certain clan. Moreover, the animal is more than simple object of a prohibition; it is an ancestor, and to kill it would be almost as bad as murder. This is not because the Tallensi believe in metempsychosis, but because the ancestors, their human descendants, and the resident animals are all united by a territorial link: "The ancestors... are spiritually present in the social life of their descendants in the same way as the sacred animals are present in sacred pools or in the locality with which the group is identified."

Tallensi society is thus comparable to a fabric in which the warp and the woof correspond respectively to localities and to lineages. Intimately connected as they are, these elements nonetheless constitute distinct realities, accompanied by particular sanctions and ritual symbols, within the general framework of the ancestor cult. The Tallensi know that an individual, in his social capacity, combines multiple roles, each of which corresponds to an aspect or a function of the society, and that he is continually confronted by problems of orientation and selection: "Totemic and other ritual symbols are the ideological landmarks that keep an individual on his course." As a member of a large clan, a man is related to common and distant ancestors, symbolized by sacred animals; as member of a lineage, to closer ancestors, symbolized by totems; and lastly, as an individual, he is connected with particular ancestors who reveal his personal fate and who may appear to him through an intermediary such as a domestic animal or certain wild game:

> But what is the common psychological theme in those different categories of animals symbolized? The relations between men and their ancestors among the Tallensi are a never ceasing struggle. Men try to coerce and placate their ancestors by means of sacrifices. But the ancestors are unpredictable. It is their power to injure and their sudden attacks on routine well-being that make men aware of them rather than their beneficent guardianship. It is by their aggressive intervention in human affairs that they control the social order. Do what they will men can never control the ancestors. Like the animals of the bush and the river, they are restless, elusive, ubiquitous, unpredictable, aggressive. The relations of men with animals in the world of common-sense experience are an apt symbolism of the relations of men with their ancestors in the sphere of mystical causation.

Fortes finds in this comparison the explanation for the predominant place assigned to carnivorous animals, those which the Tallensi group together under the term "teeth-bearers," which exist and protect themselves by attacking other animals and sometimes even men: "their symbolic link with the potential aggressiveness of the ancestors is patent." Because of their vitality, these animals are also a convenient symbol for immortality. That this symbolism is always of the same type, viz., animal, is due to the fundamental character of the social and moral code, embodied in the ancestor cult; that different animal symbols should be employed is explained by the fact that this code has different aspects.

In his study of totemism in Polynesia, Firth had already tended toward this type of explanation:

> It is a feature of Polynesian totemism that the natural species concerned are generally animals, either land or marine, and that plants, though occasionally included in the list, never predominate. The reason for this preference for animals, it seems to me, lies in the fact that the behavior of the totem is usually held to give an indication as to the actions or intentions of the god concerned. Plants, because of their immobility, are not of much interest from this point of view, and the tendency is then for the more mobile species, endowed with locomotion and versatility of movement, and often with other striking characteristics in the matter of shape, colour, ferocity, or peculiar cries, to be represented in greater measure in the list of media which serve as outlet for the supernatural beings.

These interpretations by Firth and Fortes are much more satisfactory than those of the classical adherents of totemism, or of its first adversaries such as Goldenweiser, because they escape the double danger of recourse either to some arbitrary explanation or to factitious evidence. It is clear that in so-called totemic systems the natural species do not serve as any old names for social units which might just as well have been designated in another way; and it is no less clear that in adopting a plant or animal eponym a social unit does not make an implicit affirmation of an affinity of substance between it and itself, e.g., that the group is descended from it, that it participates in its nature, or that it is sustained by it. The connection is not arbitrary neither is it a relation of contiguity. There remains the possibility, which Firth and Fortes have glimpsed, that the relation is based on a perception of a resemblance. We then have to find out in what this resemblance consists, and on what level it is apprehended. Can we say, with the authors whom we have just quoted, that it is of a physical or moral order, thus transposing Malinowski's empiricism from the organic and affective plane to that of perception and judgment?

We may first note that the interpretation is conceivable only in the case of societies which separate the totemic from the genealogical series: though an equal importance is assigned to them, one may evoke the other because they are not connected. But in Australia they are merged, and the intuitively perceived resemblance which Fortes and Firth call into consideration would be inconceivable by the very fact of this contiguity. In very many of the tribes of North and South America, on the other hand, no resemblance at all is postulated, either implicitly or explicitly; the connection between ancestors and animals is external and historical, they came to be known, encountered, fought against, or associated with. The same is related in many African myths, including the Tallensi. All these facts lead one to search for a connection on a far more general level, a procedure which the authors we have been discussing could scarcely object to, since the connection which they themselves suggest is purely inferential.

In the second place, the hypothesis has a very restricted field of application. Firth adopts it for Polynesia because of the reported preference there for animal totems; and Fortes admits that it holds primarily for certain animals with fangs. But what is to be done with the others, and what about plants, where it is these that are more important? What, finally, of natural phenomena or objects, normal or pathological states, or manufactured objects, all of which may serve as totems and which play a part which is certainly not negligible, and is sometimes even essential, in certain Australian and Indian forms of totemism?

In other words, the interpretation offered by Firth and by Fortes is narrow in two senses. Firstly, it is limited to cultures with a highly developed ancestor cult, as well as a social structure of totemic type; secondly, among these, it is limited to mainly animal forms of totemism, or is even restricted to certain types of animals. Now we shall never get to the bottom of the alleged problem of totemism— and on this point we are in agreement with Radcliffe-Brown—by thinking up a solution having only a limited field of application and then manipulating recalcitrant cases until the facts give way, but by reaching directly a level so general that all observed cases may figure in it as particular modes.

Lastly and above all, Fortes's psychological theory is based on an incomplete analysis. It is possible that the animals, from a certain point of view, are roughly comparable to the ancestors. But this is not a necessary condition, nor is it a sufficient condition If we may be allowed the expression, *it is not the resemblances, but the differences, which resemble each other.* By this we mean that there are not, first, animals which resemble each other (because they all share animal behavior), then ancestors which resemble each other (because they all share ancestral behavior), and lastly an overall resemblance between the two groups; but on the one hand there are animals which differ from each other (in that they belong to distinct species, each of which has its own physical appearance and mode of life), and on the other there are men—among whom the ancestors form a particular case— who also differ from each other (in that they are distributed among different segments of the society, each occupying a particular position in the social structure). The resemblance presupposed by so-called totemic representations is *between these two systems of differences*. Firth and Fortes have taken a great step in passing from a point of view centered on *subjective utility* to one of *objective analogy*. But, this progress having been made, it remains to effect the passage from external analogy to *internal homology*.

II.

The idea of an objectively perceived resemblance between men and totems would constitute problem enough in the case of the Azande, who include among their totems imaginary creature such as the crested water-snake, rainbow snake, water leopard and the thunder beast. But even among the Nuer, all of whose totems correspond to real objects, it has to be recognized that the list forms a rather bizarre assortment: lion, waterbuck, monitor lizard, crocodile, various snakes, tortoise, ostrich, cattle, egret, durra-bird, various trees, papyrus, gourd, various fish, bee, red ant, river and stream, cattle with certain markings, monorchids, hide, rafter, rope, parts of beasts, and some diseases. Taking them as a whole, "we may say that there is no marked utilitarian element in their selection. The animals and birds and fish and plants and artifacts which are of the most use to the Nuer are absent from the list of their totems. The facts of Nuer totemism do not, therefore, support the contention of those who see in totemism chiefly, or even merely, a ritualization of empirical interests."

The argument is expressly directed against Radcliffe-Brown, and Evans-Pritchard recalls that it had previously been formulated by Durkheim with regard to similar theories. What follows may be applied to the interpretation offered by Firth and by Fortes: "Nor in general are Nuer totems such creatures as might be expected, on account of some striking peculiarities, to attract particular attention. On the contrary, those creatures which have excited the mythopoeic imagination of the Nuer and which figure most prominently in their folk-tales do not figure, or figure rarely and insignificantly, among their totems."

The author declines therefore to answer the question—constantly encountered like a *Leitmotiv* from the beginning of our exposition—why it is that mammals, birds, reptiles, and trees should be symbols of the relationships between spiritual power and the lineages. The farthest he goes is to observe that certain widely held beliefs might prepare certain things to fill this function: e.g., birds fly, and are thus better able to communicate with the supreme spirit who lives in the sky. The argument does not apply to snakes, even though they are also, in their way, manifestations of Spirit. Trees, rare on the Savannah, are regarded as divine favors, because of the shade they afford; rivers and streams are related to water spirits. As for monorchids and animals with certain markings, it is believed that they are visible signs of an exceptionally powerful spiritual activity.

Unless we return to an empiricism and a naturalism which Evans-Pritchard rightly rejects, it has to be recognized that these indigenous ideas are not very significant. For if we exclude the possibility that streams are the objects of ritual attitudes because of their biological or economic function, their supposed relationship with the water spirits is reduced to a purely verbal manner of expressing the spiritual value which is attributed to them, which is not an explanation. The same applies to the other cases. On the other hand, Evans-Pritchard has been able to make profound analyses which allow him to dismantle bit by bit, as it were, the relations which, in Nuer thought, unite certain types of men to certain species of animals.

In order to characterize twins, the Nuer employ expressions which at first sight seem contradictory. On the other one hand, they say that twins are "one person" *(ran)*; on the other, they state that twins are not "persons" *(ran)*, but "birds" *(dit)*. To interpret these expressions correctly, it is necessary to envisage, step by step, the reasoning involved. As manifestations of spiritual power, twins are firstly "children of God" *(gat kwoth)*, and since the sky is the divine abode they may also be called "persons of the above" *(ran nhial)*. In this context they are opposed to ordinary humans, who are "persons of below" *(ran piny)*. As birds are themselves "of the above," twins are assimilated to them.

However, twins remain human beings: although they are "of the above," they are relatively "of below." But the same distinction applies to birds, since certain species fly less high and less well than others: in their own sphere, consequently, while remaining generally "of the above," birds may also be divided according to above and below. We may thus understand why twins are called by the names of "terrestrial" birds: guinea fowl, francolin, etc.

The relation thus postulated between twins and birds is explained neither by a principle of participation after the manner of Lévy-Bruhl, nor by utilitarian considerations such as those adduced by Malinowski, nor by the intuition of perceptible resemblances proposed by Firth and by Fortes. What we are presented with is a series of logical connections uniting mental relations. Twins "are birds," not because they are confused with them or because they look like them, but because twins, in relation to other men, are as "persons of the above" to "persons of below," and, in relation to birds, as "birds of below" are to "birds of the above." They thus occupy, as do birds, an intermediary position between the supreme spirit and human beings.

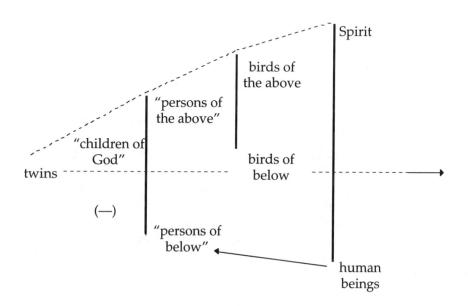

Although it is not explicitly set out by Evans-Pritchard, this reasoning leads him to an important conclusion. For this kind of inference is applicable not only to the particular relationships which the Nuer establish between twins and birds (which are closely paralleled, moreover, by those which the Kwakiutl of British Columbia conceive of between twins and salmon, a comparison which in itself suggests that in both cases the process is leased on a more general principle), but to every relationship postulated between human groups and animal species. As Evans-Pritchard himself says, this relation is metaphorical. The Nuer speak about natural species by analogy with their own social segments such as lineages, and the relation between a lineage and a totemic species is conceptualized on the model of what they call *buth,* the relationship between collateral lineages descended from a common ancestor. The animal world is thus thought of in terms of the social world. There is the community *(cieng) of* carnivorous animals—lion, leopard, hyena, jackal, wild dog and domestic dog—which includes as one of its lineages *(thok dwiel)* the mongooses, which are subdivided into a number of smaller lineages of little animals (several varieties of mongooses and the lesser felines, etc.). Another collectivity or class or kind *(bab)* is formed of graminivorous animals: antelopes, gazelles, buffaloes, and cows, and also hares, sheep, goats, etc. That of "the feetless people" groups the lineages of snakes, and "the river people" unites all animals which live in streams and marshes, such as crocodiles, monitor lizards, all fish, marsh birds and fisher-birds, as well as, furthermore, the Anuak and Balak Dinka peoples, who for the most. part are without cattle and are riverain cultivators and fishermen Birds form a vast community subdivided into a number of lineages: "children of God," "sister's sons of the children of God," and "sons or daughters of aristocrats."

These theoretical classifications are the basis of the totemic ideas:

> An interpretation of the totemic relationship is here, then, not to be sought in the nature of the totem itself but in an association it brings to the mind.

Evans-Pritchard has recently reformulated this view more rigorously:

On to the creatures are posited conceptions and sentiments derived from elsewhere than from them.

However fertile these views may be, they are nevertheless subject to reserve in two respects. In the first place, the native theory of twins is too strictly subordinated to Nuer theology: "The formula [assimilating twins to birds] does not express a dyadic relationship between twins and birds but a triadic relationship between twins, birds, and God. With respect to God twins and birds have a similar character."

But a belief in a supreme deity is not necessary to the establishment of relations of this type, and we have ourselves demonstrated them for societies much less theologically minded than the Nuer. In formulating his interpretation in this way, Evans-Pritchard thus runs the risk of restricting it: like Firth and Fortes (though to a lesser degree), he presents a general interpretation in the language of a particular society, thus limiting its scope.

In the second place, Evans-Pritchard seems not to have appreciated the importance of the revolution achieved by Radcliffe-Brown, some years before the publication of *Nuer Religion*, with his second theory of totemism. The latter differs from the first far more radically than English anthropologists seem to realize. In our opinion, it not only completes the liquidation of the problem of totemism, but it brings out the real problem, one which is posed at another level and in different terms and which until then had not been clearly perceived, though in the final analysis its presence may be taken to be the fundamental cause of the intense eddies produced by totemism in anthropological thought. It would scarcely be credible, indeed, that numerous and capable minds should have been so exercised without a reasonable motive, even if the state of knowledge and tenacious prejudices prevented them from realizing what it was, or revealed it to them only in a deformed aspect. We have now to turn our attention, therefore, to Radcliffe-Brown's second theory.

III.

This theory appeared twenty-two years after the first, without the author emphasizing its novelty, in the Huxley Memorial Lecture for 1951 entitled "The Comparative Method in Social Anthropology."

In fact, Radcliffe-Brown offers it as an example of this comparative method which alone will permit anthropology to formulate "general propositions." This is the same way in which the first theory was introduced. There is thus a methodological continuity between the one and the other. But the resemblance ends there.

The Australian tribes of the Darling River, in New South Wales, are divided into matrilineal exogamous moieties called Eaglehawk and Crow. A historical explanation for such a social System may be sought, e.g., that two hostile peoples once decided to make peace, and to secure it agreed that thenceforth the men of one group should marry women of the other, and reciprocally. But as we know nothing about the past of the tribes in question, this kind of explanation is condemned to remain gratuitous and conjectural.

Let us see rather whether similar institutions exist elsewhere. The Haida, of the Queen Charlotte Islands in British Columbia, are divided into matrilineal exogamous moieties called Eagle and Raven. A Haida myth tells how, at the beginning of time, the eagle was the master of all the water on the earth which he kept in a water-tight basket. The raven stole the basket but as he flew with it over the island the water spilled on to the earth, thus creating the lakes and rivers from which the birds have since drunk and where came the salmon on which men chiefly live.

The eponymous birds of these Australian and American moieties thus belong to very similar, and symmetrically opposed, species. Moreover, there is an Australian myth which very much resembles the one just related. In this, the eaglehawk formerly kept the water in a well that he kept closed with a large stone, and which he lifted when he wanted to drink. The crow discovered this subterfuge, and, wanting to have a drink himself, lifted the stone: he scratched his head, which was full of lice, over the water, and forgot to replace the stone. All the water ran away, forming the rivers of eastern Australia, and the lice changed into the fish which the natives eat. Ought we then to imagine, in the spirit of historical reconstruction, that there were formerly connections between Australia and America, in order to explain these analogies?

This would be to forget that Australian exogamous moieties— both matrilineal and patrilineal—are frequently designated by the names of birds, and that consequently, in Australia itself, the Darling River tribes are merely an illustration of a general situation. The white cockatoo is opposed to the crow in Western Australia, and white cockatoo to black cockatoo in Victoria. Bird totems are also very widespread in Melanesia, e.g., the moieties of certain tribes of New Ireland are named after the sea-eagle and the fish-hawk. To generalize further, we may compare the facts recounted earlier in connection with sexual totemism (and no longer with moieties), which also employs bird or animal designations: in eastern Australia the bat is the masculine totem, the night owl the feminine; in the northern part of New South Wales the totems are respectively the bat and the tree-creeper (*Climacteris sp.*). Finally, it happens that the Australian dualism is also applied to generations, i.e., an individual is placed in the same category as his grandfather his grandson, while his father and his son are assigned to the opposite category. The moieties by generations thus formed are usually not given names. But where they are, they may be known by the names of birds, e.g., in western Australia, as kingfisher and bee-eater, or little red bird and little black bird.

> Our question "Why all these birds?" is thus widened in its scope. It is not only the exogamous moieties, but also dual divisions of other kinds that are identified by connection with a pair of birds. It is, however, not always a question of birds In Australia the moieties nay be associated with other pairs of animals, with two species of kangaroo in one part, with two species of bee in another. In California one moiety is associated with the coyote and the other with the wild cat.

The comparative method consists precisely in integrating a particular phenomenon into a larger whole, which the progress of the comparison makes more and more general. In conclusion, we are confronted with the following problem: how may it be explained that social groups, or segments of society, should be distinguished from each other by the association of each with a particular natural species? This, which is the very problem of totemism, includes two others: how does each society see the relationship between human beings and the other natural species (a problem which is external to totemism, as the Andaman example shows); and how does it come about, on the other hand, that social groups should be identified by means of emblems or symbols, or by emblematic or symbolic objects? This second problem lies equally outside the framework of totemism, since in this regard the same role may be vested, according to the type of community considered, in a flag, a coat of arms, a saint, or an animal species.

So far, Radcliffe-Brawn's analysis has reproduced that which he formulated in 1929, which corresponds closely, as we have seen, with that of Boas. But his address of 1951 makes an innovation in declaring that this is not enough, for there remains an unresolved problem. Even if we assume that we can offer a satisfactory explanation of the "totemic" predilection for animal species, we still have to try to why any particular species is selected rather than another:

> What is the principle by which such pairs as eaglehawk and crow, eagle and raven, coyote and wild cat are chosen as representing the moieties of the dual division? The reason for asking this question is not idle curiosity. We may, it can be held, suppose that an understanding of the principle in question will give us an important insight into the way in which the natives themselves think about the dual division as a part of their social structure. In other words instead of asking 'Why all those birds?" we can ask 'Why particularly eaglehawk and crow, and other pairs?''

This step is decisive. It brings about a reintegration of content with form, and thus opens the way to a genuine structural analysis, equally far removed from formalism and from functionalism. For it is indeed a structural analysis which Radcliffe-Brown undertakes, consolidating institutions with representations on the one hand, and interpreting in conjunction all the variants of the same myth on the other.

This myth, which is known from many parts of Australia, has to do with two protagonists, whose conflicts are the principal theme of the story. One version from Western Australia is about Eaglehawk and Crow. The former is mother's brother to Crow, and his potential father-in-law also because of the preferential marriage with the mother's brother's daughter. A father-in-law, real or potential, has the right to demand presents of food from his son-in-law and nephew, and Eaglehawk accordingly tells Crow to bring him a wallaby. After a successful hunt, Crow succumbs to temptation: he eats the animal and pretends to return empty-handed. But the uncle refuses to believe him, and questions him about his distended belly. Crow answers that to stay the pangs of his hunger he had filled his belly with the gum from the acacia. Still disbelieving him, Eaglehawk tickles his nephew until he vomits the meat. As a punishment, he throws him into the fire and keeps him there until his eyes are red and his feathers are blackened, while he emits in his pain the cry which is henceforth to be characteristic. Eaglehawk pronounces that Crow shall never again be a hunter, and that he will be reduced to stealing game. This is the way things have been ever since.

It is impossible, Radcliffe-Brown continues, to understand this myth without reference to the ethnographic context. The Australian aborigine thinks of himself as a "meat-eater," and the eaglehawk and crow, which are carnivorous birds, are his main rivals. When the natives go hunting by lighting bush-fires, the eaglehawks quickly appear and join in the hunt: they also are hunters. Perching not far from the camp fires, the crows await their chance to steal from the feast.

Myths of this type may be compared with others, the structure of which is similar, although they are concerned with different animals. For example, the aborigines who inhabit the region where South Australia joins Victoria say that the kangaroo and the wombat (another marsupial, but smaller), which are the principal game, were once friends. One day Wombat began to make a "house" for himself (the animal lives in a burrow in the ground), and Kangaroo jeered at him and thus annoyed him. But when, for the very first time, rain began to fall, and Wombat sheltered in his house, he refused to make room for Kangaroo, claiming that it was too small for two. Furious, Kangaroo struck Wombat on the head with a big stone, flattening his skull; and Wombat, in riposte, threw a spear at Kangaroo which fixed itself at the base of the backbone. This is the way things have been ever since: the wombat has a flat skull and lives in a burrow; the kangaroo has a tail and lives in the open: "This is, of course, a 'just-so' story which you may think is childish. It amuses the listeners when it is told with the suitable dramatic expressions. But if we examine some dozens of these tales we find that they have a single theme. The resemblances and differences of animal species are translated into terms of friendship and conflict, solidarity and opposition. In other words the world of animal life is represented in terms of social relations similar to those of human society."

To arrive at this end, the natural species are classed in pairs of opposites, and this is possible only on condition that the species chosen have in common at least one characteristic which permits them to be compared.

The principle is clear in the case of the eaglehawk and crow, which are the two main carnivorous birds, though they differ from each other in that one is a bird of prey and the other a carrion-eater. But how are we to interpret the pair bat/night owl? Radcliffe-Brown admits that at first he was misled by the fact that both fly about at night. However, in one part of New South Wales it is the tree-creeper, a diurnal bird, which is opposed to the bat; it is the feminine totem, and a myth relates that it is this bird which taught women to climb trees.

Encouraged by this first explanation supplied by his informant, Radcliffe-Brown then asked, "What resemblance is there between the bat and the tree-creeper?" The native, obviously surprised by such ignorance, answered, "But of course they both live in holes in trees." This is also the case with the night owl and the nightjar. To eat meat, or to live in trees, is the common feature of the pair considered and presents a point of comparison with the human condition. But there is also an opposition within the pair, underlying the similarity: while both of the birds are carnivorous, one is a "hunter" and the other is a "thief." While they are members of the same species, cockatoos differ in color, being white or black; birds which similarly live in holes in trees are distinguished as diurnal and nocturnal, and so on.

Consequently, the division eaglehawk/crow among the Darling River tribes, with which we began, is seen at the end of the analysis to be no more than "one particular example of a widespread type of the application of a certain structural principle," a principle consisting of the union of opposites. The alleged totemism is no more than a particular expression, by means of a special nomenclature formed of animal and plant names (in a certain code, as we should say today), which is its sole distinctive characteristic, of correlations and oppositions which may be formalized in other ways, e.g., among certain tribes of North and South America, by oppositions of the type sky/earth, war/peace, upstream/downstream, red/white, etc. The most general model of this and the most systematic application, is to be found perhaps in China, in the opposition of the two principles of Yang and Yin, as male and female, day and night, summer and winter, the union of which results in an organized totality (tao) such as the conjugal pair, the day, or the year. Totemism is thus reduced to a particular fashion of formulating a general problem, viz., how to make opposition, instead of being an obstacle to integration, serve rather to produce it.

IV.

Radcliffe-Brown's demonstration ends decisively the dilemma in which the adversaries as well as the proponents of totemism have been trapped because they could assign only two roles to living species, viz., that of a natural stimulus, or that of an arbitrary pretext. The animals in totemism cease to be solely or principally creatures which are feared, admired, or envied: their perceptible reality permits the embodiment of ideas and relations conceived by speculative thought on the basis of empirical observations. We can understand, too, that natural species are chosen not because they are "good to eat" but because they are "good to think."

The gap between this thesis and its predecessor is so great that we should like to know whether Radcliffe-Brown appreciated it. The answer is perhaps to be found in the notes of lectures he delivered in South Africa, and in the unpublished manuscript of an address on Australian cosmology, the last occasions for the expression of his thought before he died in 1953. He was not the man to admit with good grace that he might change his mind, or to recognize possible influences. Yet it is difficult not to remark, in this respect, that the ten years which preceded his Huxley Memorial Lecture were marked by the drawing together of anthropology and structural linguistics. For those who took part in this enterprise it is tempting at least to think that this may have found an echo in Radcliffe-Brown's thought. The ideas of opposition and correlation, and that of pair of opposites, have a long history; but it is structural linguistics and subsequently structural anthropology which rehabilitated them in the vocabulary of the humane sciences. It is striking to meet them, with all their implications, in the writings of Radcliffe-Brown, who, as we have seen, was led by them to abandon his earlier positions, which were still stamped with the mark of naturalism and empiricism. This departure, nevertheless, was not made without hesitation, and at one point Radcliffe-Brown seems uncertain about the scope of his thesis and the extent of its application beyond the area of the Australian facts: "The Australian idea of what is here called 'opposition' is a particular application of that association by contrariety that is a universal feature of human thinking, so that we think by pairs of contraries, upwards and downwards, strong and weak, black and white. But the Australian conception of 'opposition' combines the idea of a pair of contraries with that of a pair of opponents."

It is certainly the case that one consequence of modern structuralism (not, however, clearly enunciated) ought to be to rescue associational psychology from the discredit into which it has fallen. Associationism had the great merit of sketching the contours of this elementary logic, which is like the least common denominator of all thought, and its only failure was not to recognize that it was an original logic, a direct expression of the structure of the mind (and behind the mind, probably, of the brain), and not an inert product of the action of the environment on an amorphous consciousness. But, contrary to what Radcliffe-Brown tends still to believe, it is this logic of oppositions and correlations, exclusions and inclusions, compatibilities and incompatibilities, which explains the laws of association, not the reverse. A renovated associationism would have to be based on a system of operations which would not be without similarity to Boolean algebra. As Radcliffe-Brown's very conclusions demonstrate, his analysis of Australian facts guides him beyond a simple ethnographic generalization—to the laws of language, and even of thought.

Nor is this all. We have already remarked that Radcliffe-Brown understood that in a structural analysis it is impossible to dissociate form from content. The form is not outside, but inside. In order to perceive the rationale of animal designations they must be envisaged concretely, for we are not free to trace a boundary on the far side of which purely arbitrary considerations would reign. Meaning is not decreed: if it is not everywhere it is nowhere. It is true that our limited knowledge often prevents us from pursuing it to its last retreats; for instance, Radcliffe-Brown does not explain why certain Australian tribes conceptualize the affinity between animal life and the human condition by analogy with carnivorous tastes while other tribes frame it in terms of common habitat. But his analysis implicitly presupposes that this difference itself is also meaningful, and that if we were better informed we should be able to correlate it with other differences, to be discovered between the respective beliefs of two groups, between their techniques, or between the relations of each to its environment.

In fact, the method adopted by Radcliffe-Brown is as sound as the interpretations which it suggests to him. Each level of social reality appears to him as an indispensable complement, without which it would be impossible to understand the other levels. Customs lead to beliefs, and these lead to techniques, but the different levels do not simply reflect each other. They react dialectically among themselves in such a way that we cannot hope to understand one of them without first evaluating, through their respective relations of opposition and correlation, *institutions, representations,* and *situations.* In every one of its practical undertakings, anthropology thus does no more than assert a homology of structure between human thought in action and the human object to which it is applied. The methodological integration of essence and form reflects, in its own way, a more necessary integration—that between method and reality.

CHAPTER III

Structural Study of Myth

Claude Lévi-Strauss

"It would seem that mythological worlds have been built up only to be shattered again, and that new worlds were built from the fragments."
—Franz Boas

Despite some recent attempts to renew them, it seems that during the past twenty years anthropology has increasingly turned from studies in the field of religion. At the same time, and precisely because the interest of professional anthropologists has withdrawn from primitive religion, all kinds of amateurs who claim to belong to other disciplines have seized this opportunity to move in, thereby turning into their private playground what we had left as a wasteland. The prospects for the scientific study of religion have thus been undermined in two ways.

The explanation for this situation lies to some extent in the fact that the anthropological study of religion was started by men like Tylor, Frazer, and Durkheim, who were psychologically oriented although not in a position to keep up with the progress of psychological research and theory. Their interpretations, therefore, soon became vitiated by the outmoded psychological approach which they used as their basis. Although they were undoubtedly right in giving their attention to intellectual processes, the way they handled these remained so crude that it discredited them altogether. This is much to be regretted, since, as Hocart so profoundly noted in his introduction to a posthumous book recently published, psychological interpretations were withdrawn from the intellectual field only to be introduced again in the field of affectivity, thus adding to "the inherent defects of the psychological school... the mistake of deriving clear-cut ideas... from vague emotions." Instead of trying to enlarge the framework of our logic to include processes which, whatever their apparent differences, belong to the same kind of intellectual operation, a naïve attempt was made to reduce them to inarticulate emotional drives, which resulted only in hampering our studies.

Of all the chapters of religious anthropology probably none has tarried to the same extent as studies in the field of mythology. From a theoretical point of view the situation remains very much the same as it was fifty years ago, namely, chaotic. Myths are still widely interpreted in conflicting ways: as collective dreams, as the outcome of a kind of esthetic play, or as the basis of ritual. Mythological figures are considered as personified abstractions, divinized heroes, or fallen gods. Whatever the hypothesis, the choice amounts to reducing mythology either to idle play or to a crude kind of philosophic speculation.

In order to understand what a myth really is, must we choose between platitude and sophism? Some claim that human societies merely express, through their mythology, fundamental feelings common to the whole of mankind, such as love, hate, or revenge or that they try to provide some kind of explanations for phenomena which they cannot otherwise understand—astronomical, meteorological, and the like. But why should these societies do it in such elaborate and devious ways, when all of them are also acquainted with empirical explanations? On the other hand, psychoanalysts and many anthropologists have shifted the problems away from the natural or cosmological toward the sociological and psychological fields. But then the interpretation becomes too easy: If a given mythology confers prominence on a certain figure, let us say an evil grandmother, it will be claimed that in such a society grandmothers are actually evil and that mythology reflects the social structure and the social relations; but should the actual data be conflicting, it would be as readily claimed that the purpose of mythology is to provide an outlet for repressed feelings. Whatever the situation, a clever dialectic will always find a way to pretend that a meaning has been found.

Mythology confronts the student with a situation which at first sight appears contradictory. On the one hand it would seem that in the course of a myth anything is likely to happen. There is no logic, no continuity. Any characteristic can be attributed to any subject; every conceivable relation can be found. With myth, everything becomes possible. But on the other hand, this apparent arbitrariness is belied by the astounding similarity between myths collected in widely different regions. Therefore the problem: If the content of a myth is contingent, how are we going to explain the fact that myths throughout the world are so similar?

It is precisely this awareness of a basic antinomy pertaining to the nature of myth that may lead us toward its solution. For the contradiction which we face is very similar to that which in earlier times brought considerable worry to the first philosophers concerned with linguistic problems; linguistics could only begin to evolve as a science after this contradiction had been overcome. Ancient philosophers reasoned about language the way we do about mythology. On the one hand, they did notice that in a given language certain sequences of sounds were associated with definite meanings, and they earnestly aimed at discovering a reason for the linkage between those *sounds* and that *meaning*. Their attempt, however, was thwarted from the very beginning by the fact that the same sounds were equally present in other languages although the meaning they conveyed was entirely different. The contradiction was surmounted only by the discovery that it is the combination of sounds, not the sounds themselves, which provides the significant data.

It is easy to see, moreover, that some of the more recent interpretations of mythological thought originated from the same kind of misconception under which those early linguists were laboring. Let us consider, for instance, Jung's idea that a given mythological pattern—the so-called archetype—possesses a certain meaning. This is comparable to the long-supported error that a sound may possess a certain affinity with a meaning: for instance, the "liquid" semi-vowels with water, the open vowels with things that are big, large, loud, or heavy, etc., a theory which still has its supporters. Whatever emendations the original formulation may now call for, everybody will agree that the Saussurean principle of the *arbitrary character of linguistic signs* was a prerequisite for the accession of linguistics to the scientific level.

To invite the mythologist to compare his precarious situation with that of the linguist in the prescientific stage is not enough. As a matter of fact we may thus be led only from one difficulty to another.

There is a very good reason why myth cannot simply be treated as language if its specific problems are to be solved; myth is language: to be known, myth has to be told; it is a part of human speech. In order to preserve its specificity we must be able to show that it is both the same thing as language, and also something different from it. Here, too, the past experience of linguists may help us. For language itself can be analyzed into things which are at the same time similar and yet different. This is precisely what is expressed in Saussure's distinction between *langue* and *parole*, one being the structural side of language, the other the statistical aspect of it, *langue* belonging to a reversible time, *parole* being non-reversible. If those two levels already exist in language, then a third one can conceivably be isolated.

We have distinguished *langue* and *parole* by the different time referents which they use. Keeping this in mind, we may notice that myth uses a third referent which combines the properties of the first two. On the one hand, a myth always refers to events alleged to have taken place long ago. But what gives the myth an operational value is that the specific pattern described is timeless; it explains the present and the past as well as the future. This can be made clear through a comparison between myth and what appears to have largely replaced it in modern societies, namely, politics. When the historian refers to the French Revolution, it is always as a sequence of past happenings, a non-reversible series of events the remote consequences of which may still be felt at present. But to the French politician, as well as to his followers, the French Revolution is both a sequence belonging to the past—as to the historian—and a timeless pattern which can be detected in the contemporary French social structure and which provides a clue for its interpretation, a lead from which to infer future developments. Michelet, for instance, was a politically minded historian. He describes the French Revolution thus: "That day... everything was possible.... Future became present... that is, no more time, a glimpse of eternity." It is that double structure, altogether historical and ahistorical, which explains how myth, while pertaining to the realm of *parole* and calling for an explanation as such, as well as to that of *langue* in which it is expressed, can also be an absolute entity on a third level which, though it remains linguistic by nature, is nevertheless distinct from the other two.

A remark can be introduced at this point which will help to show the originality of myth in relation to other linguistic phenomena. Myth is the part of language where the formula *traduttore, tradittore* reaches its lowest truth value. From that point of view it should be placed in the gamut of linguistic expressions at the end opposite to that of poetry, in spite of all the claims which have been made to prove the contrary. Poetry is a kind of speech which cannot be translated except at the cost of serious distortions; whereas the mythical value of the myth is preserved even through the worst translation. Whatever our ignorance of the language and the culture of the people where it originated, a myth is still felt as a myth by any reader anywhere in the world. Its substance does not lie in its style, its original music, or its syntax, but in the *story* which it tells. Myth is language, functioning on an especially high level where meaning succeeds practically at "taking off" from the linguistic ground on which it keeps on rolling.

To sum up the discussion at this point, we have so far made the following claims: (1) If there is a meaning to be found in mythology, it cannot reside in the isolated elements which enter into the compositions of a myth, but only in the way those elements are combined. (2) Although myth belongs to the same category as language, being, as a matter of fact, only part of it, language in myth exhibits specific properties. (3) Those properties are only to be found above the ordinary linguistic level, that is, they exhibit more complex features than those which are to be found in any other kind of linguistic expression.

If the above three points are granted, at least as a working hypothesis, two consequences will follow: (1) Myth, like the rest of language, is made up of constituent units. (2) These constituent units presuppose the constituent units present in language when analyzed on other levels—namely, phonemes, morphemes, and sememes—but they, nevertheless, differ from the latter in the same way as the latter differ among themselves; they belong to a higher and more complex order. For this reason, we shall call them *gross constituent units.*

How shall we proceed in order to identify and isolate these gross constituent units or mythemes? We know that they cannot be found among phonemes, morphemes, or sememes, but only on a higher level; otherwise myth would become confused with any other kind of speech. Therefore, we should look for them on the sentence level. The only method we can suggest at this stage is to proceed tentatively, by trial and error, using as a check the principles which serve as a basis for any kind of structural analysis: economy of

52 Teaching Lévi-Strauss

explanation; unity of solution; and ability to reconstruct the whole from a fragment, as well as later stages from previous ones.

The technique which has been applied so far by this writer consists in analyzing each myth individually, breaking down its story into the shortest possible sentences, and writing each sentence on an index card bearing a number corresponding to the unfolding of the story.

Practically each card will thus show that a certain function is, at a given time, linked to a given subject. Or, to put it otherwise, each gross constituent unit will consist of a *relation*.

However, the above definition remains highly unsatisfactory for two different reasons. First it is well known to structural linguists that constituent units on all levels are made up of relations, and the true difference between our *gross* units and the others remains unexplained; second, we still find ourselves in the realm of a non-reversible time, since the numbers of the cards correspond to the unfolding of the narrative. Thus the specific character of mythological time, which as we have seen is both reversible and non-reversible, synchronic and diachronic, remains unaccounted for. From this springs a new hypothesis, which constitutes the very core of our argument: The true constituent units of a myth are not the isolated relations, but *bundles of such relations*, and it is only as bundles that these relations can be put to use and combined so as to produce a meaning. Relations pertaining to the same bundle may appear diachronically at remote intervals, but when we have succeeded in grouping them together we have reorganized our myth according to a time referent of a new nature, corresponding to the prerequisite of the initial hypothesis, namely a two dimensional time referent which is simultaneously diachronic and synchronic and which accordingly integrates the characteristics of *langue* on the one hand, and those of *parole* on the other. To put it in even more linguistic terms, it is as though a phoneme were always made up of all its variants.

Two comparisons may help to explain what we have in mind.

Let us first suppose that archaeologists of the future coming from another planet would one day, when all human life had disappeared from the earth, excavate one of our libraries. Even if they were at first ignorant of our writing, they might succeed in deciphering it—an undertaking which would require, at some early stage, the discovery that the alphabet, as we are in the habit of printing it, should be read from left to right and from top to bottom. However, they would soon discover that a whole category of books did not fit the usual pattern—these would be the orchestra scores on the shelves of the music division. But after trying, without success, to decipher staffs one after the other, from the upper down to the lower, they would probably notice that the same patterns of notes recurred at intervals, either in full or in part, or that some patterns were strongly reminiscent of earlier ones. Hence the hypothesis: What if patterns showing affinity, instead of being considered in succession, were to be treated as one complex pattern and read as a whole? By getting at what we call *harmony*, they would then see that an orchestra score, to be meaningful, must be read diachronically along one axis—that is, page after page, and from left to right—and synchronically along the other axis, all the notes written vertically making up one gross constituent unit, that is, one bundle of relations.

The other comparison is somewhat different. Let us take an observer ignorant of our playing cards, sitting for a long time with a fortune-teller. He would know something of the visitors: sex, age, physical appearance, social situation, etc., in the same way as we know something of the different cultures whose myths we try to study. He would also listen to the séances and record them so as to be able to go over them and make comparisons—as we do when we listen to myth-telling and record it. Mathematicians to whom I have put the problem agree that if the man is bright and if the material available to him is sufficient, he may be able to reconstruct the nature of the deck of cards being used, that is, fifty-two or thirty-two cards according to the case, made up of four homologous sets consisting of the same units (the individual cards) with only one varying feature, the suit.

Now for a concrete example of the method we propose. We shall use the Oedipus myth, which is well known to everyone. I am well aware that the Oedipus myth has only reached us under late forms and through literary transmutations concerned more with esthetic and moral preoccupations than with religious or ritual ones, whatever these may have been. But we shall not interpret the Oedipus myth in literal terms, much less offer an explanation acceptable to the specialist. We simply wish to illustrate—and without reaching any conclusions with respect to it—a certain technique, whose use is probably not legitimate in this particular instance, owing to the problematic elements indicated above. The "demonstration" should therefore be conceived, not in terms of what the scientist means by this term, but at best in terms of what is meant by the street peddler, whose aim is not to achieve a concrete result, but to explain, as succinctly as possible, the functioning of the mechanical toy which he is trying to sell to the onlookers.

The myth will be treated as an orchestra score would be if it were unwittingly considered as a unilinear series; our task is to reestablish the correct arrangement. Say, for instance, we were confronted with a sequence of the type: 1,2,4,7,8,2,3,4,6,8, 1,4,5,7,8,1,2,5,7,3,4,5,6,8... , the assignment being to put all the 1's together, all the 2's, the 3's, etc.; the result is a chart:

1	2		4			7	8
	2	3	4		6		8
1			4	5		7	8
	1	2		5		7	
		3	4	5	6		8

We shall attempt to perform the same kind of operation on the Oedipus myth, trying out several arrangements of the mythemes until we find one which is in harmony with the principles enumerated above. Let us suppose, for the sake of argument, that the best arrangement is the following (although it might certainly be improved with the help of a specialist in Greek mythology):

Cadmos seeks his sister Europa, ravished by Zeus			
		Cadmos kills the dragon	
	The Spartoi kill one another		
			Labdacos (Laios' father) =*lame (?)*
	Oedipus kills his father, Laios		Laios (Oedipus' father) = *left-sided (?)*

		Oedipus kills the Sphinx	
			Oedipus = *swollen-foot (?)*
Oedipus marries his mother, Iocasta			
	Eteocles kills his brother, Polynices		
Antigone buries her brother, Polynices, despite prohibition			

We thus find ourselves confronted with four vertical columns, each of which includes several relations belonging to the same bundle. Were we to *tell* the myth, we would disregard the columns and read the rows from left to right and from top to bottom. But if we want to *understand* the myth, then we will have to disregard one half of the diachronic dimension (top to bottom) and read from left to right, column after column, each one being considered as a unit.

All the relations belonging to the same column exhibit one common feature which it is our task to discover. For instance, all the events grouped in the first column on the left have something to do with blood relations which are overemphasized, that are more intimate than they should be. Let us say, then, that the first column has as its common feature the *overrating of blood relations.* It is obvious that the second column expresses the same thing, but inverted: *underrating of blood relations.* The third column refers to monsters being slain. As to the fourth, a few words of clarification are needed. The remarkable connotation of the surnames in Oedipus' father-line has often been noticed. However, linguists usually disregard it, since to them the only way to define the meaning of a term is to investigate all the contexts in which it appears, and personal names, precisely because they are used as such, are not accompanied by any context. With the method we propose to follow the objection disappears, since the myth itself provides its own context. The significance is no longer to be sought in the eventual meaning of each name, but in the fact that all the names have a common feature: All the hypothetical meanings (which may well remain hypothetical) refer to *difficulties in walking straight and standing upright.*

What then is the relationship between the two columns on the right? Column three refers to monsters. The dragon is a chthonian being which has to be killed in order that mankind be born from the Earth; the Sphinx is a monster unwilling to permit men to live. The last unit reproduces the first one, which has to do with the *autochthonous origin* of mankind. Since the monsters are overcome by men, we may thus say that the common feature of the third column is denial of the *autochthonous origin of man.*

This immediately helps us to understand the meaning of the fourth column. In mythology it is a universal characteristic of men born from the Earth that at the moment they emerge from the depth they either cannot walk or they walk clumsily. This is the case of the chthonian beings in the mythology of the Pueblo: Muyingwu, who leads the emergence, and the chthonian Shumaikoli are lame ("bleeding-foot," "sore-foot"). The same happens to the Koskimo of the Kwakiutl after they have been swallowed by the chthonian monster, Tsiakish: When they returned to the surface of the earth "they limped forward or tripped sideways." Thus common feature of the fourth column *is the persistence of the autochthonous origin of man.* It follows that column four is to column three as column one is to column two. The inability to connect two kinds of relationships is overcome (or rather replaced) by the assertion that contradictory relationships are identical inasmuch as they are both self-contradictory in a similar way. Although this is still a provisional formulation of the structure of mythical thought, it is sufficient at this stage.

Turning back to the Oedipus myth, we may now see what it means. The myth has to do with the inability, for a culture which holds the belief that mankind is autochthonous (see, for instance, Pausanias, VIII, xxix, 4: plants provide a *model* for humans), to find a satisfactory transition between this theory and the knowledge that human beings are actually born from the union of man and woman. Although the problem obviously cannot be solved, the Oedipus myth provides a kind of logical tool which relates the original problem—born from one or born from two?—to the derivative problem: born from different or born from same? By a correlation of this type, the overrating of blood relations is to the underrating of blood relations as the attempt to escape autochthony is to the impossibility to succeed in it. Although experience contradicts theory, social life validates cosmology by its similarity of structure. Hence cosmology is true.

Two remarks should be made at this stage.

In order to interpret the myth, we left aside a point which has worried the specialists until now, namely, that in the earlier (Homeric) versions of the Oedipus myth, some basic elements are lacking, such as Jocasta killing herself and Oedipus piercing his own eyes. These events do not alter the substance of the myth although they can easily be integrated, the first one as a new case of autodestruction (column three) and the second as another case of crippledness (column four). At the same time there is something significant in these additions, since the shift from foot to head is to be correlated with the shift from autochthonous origin to self-destruction.

Our method thus eliminates a problem which has, so far, been one of the main obstacles to the progress of mythological studies namely, the quest for the *true* version, or the *earlier* one. On the contrary, we define the myth as consisting of all its versions; or to put it otherwise, a myth remains the same as long as it is felt as such. A striking example is offered by the fact that our interpretation may take into account the Freudian use of the Oedipus myth and is certainly applicable to it. Although the Freudian problem has ceased to be that of autochthony *versus* bisexual reproduction, it is still the problem of understanding how *one* can be born from *two*: is it that we do not have only one procreator, but a mother plus a father? Therefore, not only Sophocles, but Freud himself, should be included among the recorded versions of the Oedipus myth on a par with earlier or seemingly more "authentic" versions.

An important consequence follows. If a myth is made up of all its variants, structural analysis should take all of them into account. After analyzing all the known variants of the Theban version, we should thus treat the others in the same way: first, the tales about Labdacos' collateral line including Agave, Pentheus, and Jocasta herself; the Theban variant about Lycos with Amphion and Zetos as the city founders; more remote variants concerning Dionysus (Oedipus' matrilateral cousin) and Athenian legends where Cecrops takes the place of Cadmos, etc. For each of them a similar chart should be drawn and then compared and reorganized according to the findings: Cecrops killing the serpent with the parallel episode of Cadmos; abandonment of Dionysus with abandonment of Oedipus; "Swollen Foot" with Dionysus' loxias, that is, walking obliquely; Europa's quest with Antiope's; the founding of Thebes by the Spartoi or by the brothers Amphion and Zetos; Zeus kidnapping Europa and Antiope and the same with Semele; the Theban Oedipus and the Argian Perseus, etc. We shall then have several two-dimensional charts, each dealing with a variant, to be organized in a three-dimensional order, ... so that three different readings become possible: left to right, top to bottom, front to back (or vice versa). All of these charts cannot be expected to be identical; but experience shows that any difference to be observed may be correlated with other differences, so that a logical treatment of the whole will allow simplifications, the final outcome being the structural law of the myth.

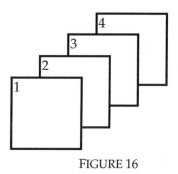

FIGURE 16

At this point the objection may be raised that the task is impossible to perform, since we can only work with known versions. Is it not possible that a new version might alter the picture? This is true enough if only one or two versions are available, but the objection becomes theoretical as soon as a reasonably large number have been recorded. Let us make this point clear by a comparison. If the furniture of a room and its arrangement were known to us only through its reflection in two mirrors placed on opposite walls, we should theoretically dispose of an almost infinite number of mirror images which would provide us with a complete knowledge. However, should the two mirrors be obliquely set, the number of mirror images would become very small; nevertheless, four or five such images would very likely give us, if not complete information, at least a sufficient coverage so that we would feel sure that no large piece of furniture is missing in our description.

On the other hand, it cannot be too strongly emphasized that all available variants should be taken into account. If Freudian comments on the Oedipus complex are a part of the Oedipus myth, then questions such as whether Cushing's version of the Zuni origin myth should be retained or discarded become irrelevant. There is no single "true" version of which all the others are but copies or distortions. Every version belongs to the myth.

The reason for the discouraging results in works on general mythology can finally be understood. They stem from two causes. First, comparative mythologists have selected preferred versions instead of using them all. Second, we have seen that the structural analysis of one variant of *one* myth belonging to *one* tribe (in some cases, even *one* village) already requires two dimensions. When we use several variants of the same myth for the same tribe or village, the frame of reference becomes three-dimensional, and as soon as we try to enlarge the comparison, the number of dimensions required increases until it appears quite impossible to handle them intuitively. The confusions and platitudes which are the outcome of comparative mythology can be explained by the fact that multidimensional frames of reference are often ignored or are naively replaced by two- or three-dimensional ones. Indeed, progress in comparative mythology depends largely on the cooperation of mathematicians who would undertake to express in symbols multidimensional relations which cannot be handled otherwise.

To check this theory, an attempt was made from 1952 to 1954 toward an exhaustive analysis of all the known versions of the Zuni origin and emergence myth: Cushing, 1883 and 1896; Stevenson, 1904; Parsons, 1923; Bunzel, 1932; Benedict, 1934. Furthermore, a preliminary attempt was made at a comparison of the results with similar myths in other Pueblo tribes, Western and Eastern. Finally, a test was undertaken with Plains mythology. In all cases, it was found that the theory was sound; light was thrown, not only on North American mythology, but also on a previously unnoticed kind of logical operation, or one known so far only in a wholly different context. The bulk of material which needs to be handled practically at the outset of the work makes it impossible to enter into details, and we shall have to limit ourselves here to a few illustrations.

A simplified chart of the Zuni emergence myth would read:

CHANGE　　　　　　　　　　　　　　　　　　**DEATH**

CHANGE		DEATH	
mechanical value of plants (used as ladders to emerge from lower world)	emergence led by Beloved Twins	sibling incest (origin of water)	gods kill children of men (by drowning)
food value of wild plants	migration led by the two Newekwe (ceremonial clowns)		magical contest with People of the Dew (collecting wild food *versus* cultivation)
		brother and sister sacrificed (to gain victory)	
food value of cultivated plants		brother and sister adopted (in exchange for corn)	
periodical character of agricultural work			war against the Kyanakwe (gardeners *versus* hunters)
food value of game (hunting)	war led by the two War-Gods		
inevitability of warfare			salvation of the tribe center of the World found)
		brother and sister sacrificed (to avoid the Flood)	

DEATH　　　　　　　　　　　　　　　　　　**PERMANENCE**

As the chart indicates, the problem is the discovery of a life-death mediation. For the Pueblo, this is especially difficult; they understand the origin of human life in terms of the model of plant life (emergence from the earth). They share that belief with the ancient Greeks, and it is not without reason that we chose the Oedipus myth as our first example. But in the American Indian case, the highest form of plant life is to be found in agriculture which is periodical in nature, that is, which consists in an alternation between life and death. If this is disregarded, the contradiction appears elsewhere: Agriculture provides food, therefore life; but hunting provides food and is similar to warfare which means death. Hence there are three different ways of handling the problem. In the Cushing version, the difficulty revolves around an opposition between activities yielding an immediate result (collecting wild food) and activities yielding a delayed result—death has to become integrated so that agriculture can exist. Parsons' version shifts from hunting to agriculture, while Stevenson's version operates the other way around. It can be shown that all the differences between these versions can be rigorously correlated with these basic structures.

Thus the three versions describe the great war waged by the ancestors of the Zuni against a mythical population, the Kyanakwe, by introducing into the narrative significant variations which consist (1) in the friendship or hostility of the gods; (2) in the granting of final victory to one camp or the other; (3) in the attribution of the symbolic function to the Kyanakwe, described sometimes as hunters (whose bows are strong with animal sinews) and sometimes as gardeners (whose bows are strung with plant fibers) .

CUSHING		PARSONS	STEVENSON	
Gods,	allied, use fiber	Kyanakwe, alone,	Gods,	allied, use
Kyanakwe	string on their	use fiber string	Men	fiber string
	bows			
	(gardeners)			
VICTORIOUS OVER		VICTORIOUS OVER	VICTORIOUS OVER	
Men, alone, use sinew (until		God's, allied, use	Kyanakwe, alone, use	
they shift to fiber)		Men sinew string	sinew string	

Since fiber string (agriculture) is always superior to sinew string (hunting), and since (to a lesser extent) the gods' alliance is preferable to their antagonism, it follows that in Cushing's version, men are seen as doubly underprivileged (hostile gods, sinew string); in the Stevenson version, doubly privileged (friendly gods, fiber string) while Parsons' version confronts us with an intermediary situation (friendly gods, but sinew strings, since men begin by being hunters). Hence:

OPPOSITIONS	CUSHING	PARSONS	STEVENSON
gods/men	—	+	+
fiber/sinew	—	—	+

Bunzel's version is of the same type as Cushing's from a structural point of view. However, it differs from both Cushing's and Stevenson's, inasmuch as the latter two explain the emergence as the result of man's need to evade his pitiful condition, while Bunzel's version makes it the consequence of a call from the higher powers— hence the inverted sequences of the means resorted to for the emergence: In both Cushing and Stevenson, they go from plants to animals; in Bunzel, from mammals to insects, and from insects to plants.

Among the Western Pueblo the logical approach always remains the same; the starting point and the point of arrival are simplest, whereas the intermediate stage is characterized by ambiguity:

LIFE (= INCREASE)

(Mechanical) value of the plant kingdom, taking growth alone into account	ORIGINS
Food value of the plant kingdom, limited to wild plants	FOOD GATHERING
Food value of the plant kingdom, including wild plants and cultivated plants	AGRICULTURE
Food value of the animal	*(but there is a contradiction* HUNTING

kingdom, limited to	*here, owing to the negation*	
animals	*of life = destruction, hence:)*	
Destruction of the animal		**WARFARE**
kingdom, extended to		
human beings		

DEATH (= DECREASE)

The fact that the contradiction appears in the middle of the dialectical process results in a double set of dioscuric pairs, the purpose of which is to mediate between conflicting terms:

I.	2 divine messengers	2 ceremonial clowns		2 war-gods
2.	homogenous pair: dioscuri (2 brothers)	siblings (brother and sister)	couple (husband and wife)	heterogeneous pair: (grandmother and grandchild)

We have here combinational variants of the same function in different contexts (hence the war attribute of the clowns, which has given rise to so many queries).

The problem, often regarded as insoluble, vanishes when it is shown that the clowns—gluttons who may with impunity make excessive use of agricultural products—have the same function in relation to food production as the war-gods. (This function appears, in the dialectical process, as *overstepping the boundaries of hunting*, that is, hunting for men instead of for animals for human consumption.)

Some Central and Eastern Pueblos proceed the other way around. They begin by stating the identity of hunting and cultivation (first corn obtained by Game-Father sowing deer-dewclaws), and they try to derive both life and death from that central notion. Then, instead of extreme terms being simple and intermediary ones duplicated as among the Western groups, the extreme terms become duplicated (i.e., the two sisters of the Eastern Pueblo) while a simple mediating term comes to the foreground (for instance, the Poshaiyanne of the Zia), but endowed with equivocal attributes. Hence the attributes of this "messiah" can be deduced from the place it occupies in the time sequence: good when at the beginning (Zuni, Cushing), equivocal in the middle (Central Pueblo), bad at the end

(Zia), except in Bunzels version, where the sequence is reversed as has been shown.

By systematically using this kind of structural analysis it becomes possible to organize all the known variants of a myth into a set forming a kind of permutation group, the two variants placed at the far ends being in a symmetrical, though inverted, relationship to each other.

Our method not only has the advantage of bringing some kind of order to what was previously chaos; it also enables us to perceive some basic logical processes which are at the root of mythical thought. Three main processes should be distinguished.

The trickster of American mythology has remained so far a problematic figure. Why is it that throughout North America his role is assigned practically everywhere to either coyote or raven? If we keep in mind that mythical thought always progresses from the awareness of oppositions toward their resolution, the reason for these choices becomes clearer. We need only assume that two opposite terms with no intermediary always tend to be replaced by two equivalent terms which admit of a third one as a mediator; then one of the polar terms and the mediator become replaced by a new triad, and so on. Thus we have a mediating structure of the following type:

INITIAL PAIR	FIRST TRIAD	SECOND TRIAD
Life		
	Agriculture	
		Herbivorous animals
		Carrion-eating animals
		(raven; coyote)
	Hunting	
		Beasts of prey
	Warfare	
Death		

The unformulated argument is as follows: carrion-eating animals are like beasts of prey (they eat animal food), but they are also like food-plant producers (they do not kill what they eat). Or to put it otherwise, Pueblo style (for Pueblo agriculture is more "meaningful" than hunting): ravens are to gardens as beasts of prey are to herbivorous animals. But it is also clear that herbivorous animals may be called first to act as mediators on the assumption that they are like collectors and gatherers (plant-food eaters), while they can be used as animal food though they are not themselves hunters. Thus we may have mediators of the first order, of the second order, and so on (where each term generates the next by a double process of opposition and correlation.

This kind of process can be followed in the mythology of the Plains, where we may order the data according to the set:

> Unsuccessful mediator between Earth and Sky
> (Star-Husband's wife)
>
> Heterogeneous pair of mediators
> (grandmother and grandchild)
>
> Semi-homogeneous pair of mediators
> (Lodge-Boy and Thrown-away)

While among the Pueblo (Zuni) we have the corresponding set:

> Successful mediator between Earth and Sky
> (Poshaiyanki)
>
> Semi-homogeneous pair of mediators
> (Uyuyewi and Matsailema)
>
> Homogeneous pair of mediators
> (the two Ahaiyuta)

On the other hand, correlations may appear on a horizontal axis (this is true even on the linguistic level; see the manifold connotation of the root pose in Tewa according to Parsons: coyote, mist, scalp, etc.). Coyote (a carrion-eater) is intermediary between herbivorous and carnivorous just as mist between Sky and Earth; as scalp between war and agriculture (scalp is a war crop); as corn smut between wild and cultivated plants; as garments between "nature" and "culture"; as refuse between village and outside; and as ashes (or soot) between roof (sky vault) and hearth (in the ground). This chain of mediators, if one may call them so, not only throws light on entire parts of North American mythology - why the Dew-God may be at the same time the Game-Master and the giver of raiments and be personified as an "Ash-Boy"; or why scalps are mist-producing; or why the Game-Mother is associated with corn smut; etc.—but it also probably corresponds to a universal way of organizing daily experience. See, for instance, the French for plant smut (*nielle*, form Latin *nebula*); the luck-bringing power attributed in Europe to refuse (old shoe) and ashes (kissing chimney sweeps); and compare the American Ash-Boy cycle with the Indo-European Cinderella: Both are phallic figures (mediators between male and female); masters of the dew and the game; owners of fine raiments; and social mediators (low class marrying into high class); but they are impossible to interpret through recent diffusion, as has been contended, since Ash-Boy and Cinderella are symmetrical but inverted in every detail (while the borrowed Cinderella tale in America-Zuni Turkey-Girl—is parallel to the prototype). Hence the chart:

	EUROPE	AMERICA
Sex	female	male
Family Status	double family (remarried father)	no family (orphan)
Appearance	pretty girl	ugly boy
Sentimental status	nobody likes her	unrequited love for girl
Transformation	luxuriously clothed with supernatural help	stripped of ugliness with supernatural help

Thus, like Ash-Boy and Cinderella, the trickster is a mediator. Since his mediating function occupies a position halfway between two polar terms, he must retain something of that duality—namely an ambiguous and equivocal character. But the trickster figure is not the only conceivable form of mediation; some myths seem to be entirely devoted to exhausting all the possible to the problem of bridging the gap between *two* and *one*. For instance, a comparison between all the variants of the Zuni emergence myth provides us with a series of mediating devices, each of which generates the next one by a process of opposition and correlation:

messiah > dioscuri > trickster > bisexual being > sibling pair > married couple > grandmother-grandchild > four-term group > triad

In Cushing's version this dialectic is associated with a change from a spatial dimension (mediation between Sky and Earth) to a temporal dimension (mediation between summer and winter, that is, between birth and death). But while the shift is being made from space and time, the final solution (triad) reintroduces space, since a triad consists of a dioscuric pair *plus* a messiah, present simultaneously; and while the point of departure was ostensibly formulated in terms of a space referent (Sky and Earth), this was nevertheless implicitly conceived in terms of a referent (first the messiah calls, *then* the dioscuri descend). Therefore the logic of myth confronts us with a double, reciprocal exchange of functions to which we shall return shortly.

Not only can we account for the ambiguous character of the trickster, but we can also understand another property of mythical figures the world over, namely, that the same god is endowed with contradictory attributes—for instance, he may be good and bad at the same time. If we compare the variants of the Hopi myth of the origin of Shalako, we may order then in terms of the following structure:

(Masauwu: x) ~ (Muyingwu: Masauwu) ~ (Shalako: Muyingwu)

~ (y: Masauwu)

where x and y represent arbitrary values corresponding to the fact that in the two "extreme" variants the god Masauwu, while appearing alone rather than associated with another god, as in variant two, or being absent, as in variant three, still retains intrinsically a relative value. In variant one, Masauwu (alone) is depicted as helpful to mankind (though not as helpful as he could be), and in version four, harmful to mankind (though not as harmful as he could be). His role is thus defined—at least implicitly—in contrast with another role which is possible but not specified and which is represented here by the values x and y. In version two, on the other hand, Muyingwu is relatively more helpful than Masauwu, and in version three, Shalako more helpful than Muyingwu. We find an identical series when ordering the Keresan variants.

(Poshaiyanki: x) ~ (Lea: Poshaiyanki) ~ (Poshaiyanki: Tiamoni)

~ (y: Poshaiyanki)

This logical framework is particularly interesting, since anthropologists are already acquainted with it on two other levels— first, in regard to the problem of the pecking order among hens, and second, to what this writer has called *generalized exchange* in the field of kinship. By recognizing it also on the level of mythical thought, we may find ourselves in a better position to appraise its basic importance in anthropological studies and to give it a more inclusive theoretical interpretation.

Finally, when we have succeeded in organizing a whole series of variants into a kind of permutation group, we are in a position to formulate the law of that group. Although it is not possible at the present stage to come closer than an approximate formulation which will certainly need to be refined in the future, it seems that every myth (considered as the aggregate of all its variants) corresponds to a formula of the following type:

$$F_x(a): F_y (b) \sim F_x (b): F_{a-1} (y)$$

Here, with two terms, *a* and *b*, being given as well as two functions, *x* and *y*, of these terms, it is assumed that a relation of equivalence exists between two situations defined respectively by an inversion of *terms* and *relations*, under two conditions: (1) that one term be replaced by its opposite (in the above formula, a and a-1); (2) that an inversion be made between the *function value* and the *term value* of two elements (above, *y* and *a*).

This formula becomes highly significant when we recall that Freud considered that *two traumas* (and not one, as is so commonly said) are necessary in order to generate the individual myth in which a neurosis consists. By trying to apply the formula to the analysis of these traumas (and assuming that they correspond to conditions 1 and 2 respectively) we should not only be able to provide a more precise and rigorous formulation of the genetic law of the myth, but we would find ourselves in the much desired position of developing side by side the anthropological and the psychological aspects of the theory; we might also take it to the laboratory and subject it to experimental verification.

At this point it seems unfortunate that with the limited means at the disposal of French anthropological research no further advance can be made. It should be emphasized that the task of analyzing mythological literature, which is extremely bulky, and of breaking it down into its constituent units, requires team work and technical help. A variant of average length requires several hundred cards to be properly analyzed. To discover a suitable pattern of rows and columns for those cards, special devices are needed, consisting of vertical boards about six feet long and four and a half feet high, where cards can be pigeonholed and moved at will. In order to build up three-dimensional models enabling one to compare the variants, several such boards are necessary, and this in turn requires a spacious workshop, a commodity particularly unavailable in Western Europe nowadays. Furthermore, as soon as the frame of reference becomes multidimensional (which occurs at an early stage, as has been shown above) the board system has to be replaced by perforated cards, which in turn require IBM equipment, etc.

Three final remarks may serve as conclusion.

First, the question has often been raised why myths, and more generally oral literature, are so much addicted to duplication, triplication, or quadruplication of the same sequence. If our hypotheses are accepted, the answer is obvious: The function of repetition is to render the structure of the myth apparent. For we have seedy that the synchronic-diachronic structure of the myth permits us to organize it into diachronic sequences (the rows in our tables) which should be read synchronically (the columns). Thus, a myth exhibits a "slated" structure, which comes to the surface, so to speak, through the process of repetition.

However, the slates are not absolutely identical. And since the purpose of myth is to provide a logical model capable of overcoming a contradiction (an impossible achievement if, as it happens, the contradiction is real), a theoretically infinite number of slates will be generated, each one slightly different from the others. Thus, myth grows spiral-wise until the intellectual impulse which has produced it is exhausted. Its *growth* is a continuous process, whereas its *structure* remains discontinuous. If this is the case, we should assume that it closely corresponds, in the realm of the spoken word, to a crystal in the realm of physical matter. This analogy may help us to better understand the relationship of myth to both *langue* on the one hand and *parole* on the other. Myth is an intermediary entity between a statistical aggregate of molecules and the molecular structure itself.

Prevalent attempts to explain alleged differences between the so-called primitive mind and scientific thought have resorted to qualitative differences between the working processes of the mind in both cases, while assuming that the entities which they were studying remained very much the same. If our interpretation is correct, we are led toward a completely different view—namely, that the kind of logic in mythical thought is as rigorous as that of modern science, and that the difference lies, not in the quality of the intellectual process, but in the nature of the things to which it is applied. This is well in agreement with the situation known to prevail in the field of technology: What makes a steel ax superior to a stone ax is not that the first one is better made than the second. They are equally well made, but steel is quite different from stone. In the same way we may be able to show that the same logical processes operate in myth as in science, and that man has always been thinking equally well; the improvement lies, not in an alleged progress of man's mind, but in the discovery of new areas to which it may apply its unchanged and unchanging powers.

CHAPTER IV

The Story of Asdiwal

Claude Lévi-Strauss

This study of a native myth from the Pacific coast of Canada has two aims. First, to isolate and compare the *various levels* on which the myth evolves: geographic, economic, sociological, and cosmological—each one of these levels, together with the symbolism proper to it, being seen as a transformation of an underlying logical structure common to all of them. And, second, to compare the *different versions* of the myth and to look for the meaning of the discrepancies between them, or between some of them; for, since they all come from the same people (but are recorded in different parts of their territory), these variations cannot be explained in terms of dissimilar beliefs, languages, or institutions.

The story of Asdiwal, which comes from the Tsimshian Indians, is known to us in four versions, collected some sixty years ago by Franz Boas and published in the following books: *Indianische Sagen van der Nord-Pacifischen Küste Amerikas* (Berlin, 1895); *Tsimshian Texts,* Smithsonian Institution, Bureau of American Ethnology, Bulletin No. 27 (Washington, 1902); *Tsimshian Texts* (G. Hunt, co-author) Publications of the American Ethnological society, n.s., III, (Leyden, 1912); and *Tsimshian Mythology,* Smithsonian Institution, Bureau of American Ethnology 31st Annual Report, 1909–1910, (Washington; 1916).

We shall begin by calling attention to certain facts which must be known if the myth is to be understood.

The Tsimshian Indians, with the Tlingit and the Haida, belong to the northern group of cultures on the Northwest Pacific coast. They live in British Columbia, immediately south of Alaska, in a region which embraces the basins of the Nass and Skeena rivers, the coastal region stretching between their estuaries, and, further inland, the land drained by the two rivers and their tributaries. Both the Nass in the north and the Skeena in the south flow in a northeast-southwesterly direction, and they are approximately parallel. The Nass, however, is slightly nearer north-south in orientation, a detail which, as we shall see, is not entirely devoid of importance.

This territory was divided among three local groups, distinguished by their different dialects: in the upper reaches of the Skeena, the Gitskan; in the lower reaches and the coastal region, the Tsimshian themselves; and in the valleys of the Nass and its tributaries, the Nisqa. Three of the versions of the myth of Asdiwal were recorded on the coast and in Tsimshian dialect (Boas 1895a, pp. 285–288; Boas and Hunt 1912, pp. 71–146; Boas and Hunt 1916, pp. 243–245, and the comparative analysis, pp. 792–824) the fourth was recorded at the mouth of the Nass, in Nisqa dialect (Boas and Hunt 1902, pp. 225–228). It is this last which, when compared with the other three, reveals the most marked differences.

Like all the people on the northwest Pacific Coast, the Tsimshian had no agriculture. During the summer, the women's work was to collect fruit, berries, plants, and wild roots, while the men hunted bears and goats in the mountains and sea lions on the coastal reefs. They also practiced deep-sea fishing, catching mainly cod and halibut, but also herring nearer the shore. It was, however, the complex rhythm of river fishing that made the deepest impression upon the life of the tribe. Whereas the Nisqa were relatively settled, the Tsimshian moved, according to the seasons, between their winter villages, which were situated in the coastal region, and their fishing places, either on the Nass or the Skeena.

At the end of the winter, when the stores of smoked fish, dried meat, fat, and preserved fruits were running low, or were even completely exhausted, the natives would undergo periods of severe famine, an echo of which is found in the myth. At such times they anxiously awaited the arrival of the candlefish, which would go up the Nass (which was still frozen to start with) for a period of about six weeks in order to spawn (Goddard 1935, p. 68). This would begin about March 1, and the entire Skeena population would travel along the coast in boats as far as the Nass in order to take up position on the fishing grounds, which were family properties. The period from February 15 to March 15 was called, not without reason the "month when Candlefish is Eaten," and that which followed, from March 15 to April 15, the "Month when Candlefish is Cooked" (to extract its oil). This operation was strictly taboo to men, whereas the women were obliged to use their naked breasts to press the fish. The oil-cake residue had to be left to become rotten from maggots and putrefaction and, despite the pestilential stench, it had to be left in the immediate vicinity of the dwelling houses until the work was finished (Boas and Hunt 1916, pp 44–45, 398–399) .

Then everyone would return by the same route to the Skeena for the second major event, which was the arrival of the salmon fished in June and July (the "Salmon Months"). Once the fish was smoked and stored away for the year, the families would go up to the mountains, where the men would hunt while the women laid up stocks of fruit and berries. With the coming of the frost in the ritual "Month of the Spinning Tops" (which were spun on the ice), people settled down in permanent villages for the winter. During this period, the men sometimes went off hunting again for a few days or a few weeks. Finally, toward November 15, came the "Taboo Month," which marked the inauguration of the great winter ceremonies, in preparation for which the men were subjected to various restrictions.

Let us remember, too, that the Tsimshian were divided into four nonlocalized matrilineal clans, which were strictly exogamous and divided into lineages, descent lines, and households: the Eagles, the Ravens, the Wolves, and the Killer Whales; also, that the permanent villages were the seat of chiefdoms (generally called "tribes" by native informants); and, finally, that Tsimshian society was divided into three hereditary castes with bilateral inheritance of caste status (each individual was supposed to marry according to his rank): the "Real People" or reigning families, the "Nobles," and the "People," which comprised all those who (failing a purchase of rank by generous potlatches) were unable to assert an equal degree of nobility in both lines of their descent (Boas and Hunt 1916, pp. 478–5 14; Garfield 1939, pp. 173–174; Garfield, Wingert, and Barbeau 1951, p. 134; Garfield and Wingert 1966).

Now follows a summary of the story of Asdiwal taken from Boas and Hunt (1912) which will serve as a point of reference. This version was recorded on the coast at Port Simpson in Tsimshian dialect. Boas published the native text together with an English translation.

Famine reigns in the Skeena valley; the river is frozen and it is winter. A mother and her daughter, both of whose husbands have died of hunger, both remember independently the happy times when they lived together and there was no dearth of food. Released by the death of their husbands, they simultaneously decide to meet, and they set off at the same moment. Since the mother lives down-river and the daughter upriver, the former goes eastwards and the latter westwards. They both travel on the frozen bed of the Skeena and meet halfway.

Weeping with hunger and sorrow, the two women pitch camp on the bank at the foot of a tree, not far from which they find, poor pittance that it is, a rotten berry, which they sadly share.

During the night, a stranger visits the young widow. It is soon learned that his name is Hatsenas, a term which means, in Tsimshian, a bird of good omen. Thanks to him, the women start to find food regularly, and the younger of the two becomes the wife of their mysterious protector and soon gives birth to a son, Asdiwal (Asiwa, Boas 1895a; Asi-hwil, Boas 1902). His father speeds up his growth by supernatural means and gives him various magic objects: a bow and arrows, which never miss, for hunting, a quiver, a lance, a basket, snowshoes, a bark raincoat, and a hat—all of which will enable the hero to overcome all obstacles, make himself invisible, and procure an inexhaustible supply of food. Hatsenas then disappears and the elder of the two women dies.

Asdiwal and his mother pursue their course westward and settle down in her native village, Gitsalasert, in the Skeena Canyon (Boas and Hunt 1912, p. 83). One day a white she-bear comes down the valley.

Hunted by Asdiwal, who almost catches it thanks to his magic objects, the bear starts to climb up a vertical ladder. Asdiwal follows it up to the heavens, which he sees as a vast prairie, covered with grass and all kinds of flowers. The bear lures him into the home of its father, the sun, and reveals itself to be a beautiful girl, Evening-Star. The marriage takes place, though not before the Sun has submitted Asdiwal to a series of trials, to which all previous suitors had succumbed (hunting wild goat in mountains which are rent by earthquakes, drawing water from a spring in a cave whose walls close in on each other, collecting wood from a tree which crushes those who try to cut it down, a period in a fiery furnace). But Asdiwal overcomes them all, thanks to his magic objects and the timely intervention of his father. Won over by his son-in-law's talents, the Sun finally approves of him.

Asdiwal, however, pines for his mother. The Sun agrees to allow him to go down to earth again with his wife, and gives them, as provisions for the journey, four baskets filled with inexhaustible supplies of food, which earn the couple a grateful welcome from the villagers, who are in the midst of their winter famine.

In spite of repeated warnings from his wife, Asdiwal deceives her with a woman from his village. Evening-Star, offended, departs, followed by her tearful husband. Halfway up to heaven, Asdiwal is struck down by a look from his wife, who disappears. He dies, but his loss is at once regretted and he is brought back to life by his celestial father-in-law.

For a time, all goes well. Then, Asdiwal once again feels a twinge of nostalgia for earth. His wife agrees to accompany him as far as the earth, and there bids him a final farewell. Returning to his village, the hero learns of his mother's death. Nothing remains to hold him back, and he sets off again on his journey downstream.

When he reaches the Tsimshian village of Ginaxangioget, he seduces and marries the daughter of the local chief. To start with, the marriage is a happy one, and Asdiwal joins his four brothers-in-law on wild goat hunts which, thanks to his magic objects, are crowned with success. When spring approaches, the whole family moves, staying first at Metlakatla, and then setting off by boat for the river Nass, going up along the coast. A head wind forces them to a halt and they camp for a while at Ksemaksén. There, things go wrong because of a dispute between Asdiwal and his brothers-in-law over the respective merits of mountain-hunters and sea-hunters. A competition takes place— Asdiwal returns from the mountain with four bears that he has killed, while the brothers-in-law return empty-handed from their sea expedition. Humiliated and enraged, they break camp, and, taking their sister with them, abandon Asdiwal.

He is picked up by strangers coming from Gitxatla, who are also on their way to the Nass for the candlefish season.

As in the previous case, they are a group of four brothers and a sister, whom Asdiwal wastes no time in marrying. They soon arrive together at the River Nass, where they sell large quantities of fresh meat and salmon to the Tsimshian, who have already settled there and are starving.

Since the catch that year is a good one, everyone goes home: the Tsimshian to their capital at Metlkatla and the Gitxatla to their town Laxalan, where Asdiwal, by this time rich and famous, has a son. One winter's day, he boasts that he can hunt sea lions better than his brothers-in-law. They set out to sea together. Thanks to his magic objects, Asdiwal has a miraculously successful hunt on a reef, but is left there without food or fire by his angry brothers-in-law. A storm gets up and waves sweep over the rock. With the help of his father, who appears in time to save him, Asdiwal, transformed into a bird, succeeds in keeping himself above the waves, using his magic objects as a perch.

After two days and two nights the storm is calmed, and Asdiwal falls asleep exhausted. A mouse wakes him and leads him to the subterranean home of the sea lions whom he has wounded, but who imagine (since Asdiwal's arrows are invisible to them) that they are victims of an epidemic. Asdiwal extracts the arrows and cures his hosts, whom he asks, in return, to guarantee his safe return. Unfortunately, the sea lions' boats, which are made of their stomachs, are out of use, pierced by the hunter's arrows. The king of the sea lions therefore lends Asdiwal his own stomach as a canoe and instructs him to send it back without delay.

When he reaches land, the hero discovers his wife and his son inconsolable. Thanks to the help of this good wife (but bad sister, for she carries out the rites which are essential to the success of the operation), Asdiwal makes killer whales out of carved wood and brings them to life. They break open the boats with their fins and bring about the shipwreck and death of the wicked brothers-in-law.

But once again Asdiwal feels an irrepressible desire to revisit the scenes of his childhood. He leaves his wife and returns to the Skeena valley. He settles in the town of Ginadâos, where he is joined by his son, to whom he gives his magic bow and arrows, and from whom he receives a dog in return.

When winter comes, Asdiwal goes off to the mountains to hunt, but forgets his snowshoes. Lost, and unable to go either up or down without them, he is turned to stone with his lance and his dog, and they can still be seen in that form at the peak of the great mountain by the lake of Ginadâos (Boas and Hunt 1912, pp 71–146).

Let us keep provisionally to this version alone in order to attempt to define the essential points of its structure. The narrative refers to facts of various orders: first, the physical and political geography of the Tsimshian country, since the places and towns mentioned really do exist; second, the economic life of the natives which, as we have seen, governs the great seasonal migrations between the Skeena and Nass valleys during the course of which Asdiwal's adventures take place; third, the social and family organizations, for we witness several marriages, divorces, widowhoods, and other connected events; and lastly, the cosmology, for, unlike the others, two of Asdiwal's visits, one to heaven and the other below the earth, are of a mythological and not of an experiential order.

First of all, let us consider the geographical aspects.

The story begins in the Skeena Valley, when the two heroines leave their villages, one upstream, the other downstream, and meet halfway. In the version that Boas recorded at the Nass estuary, it is stated that the meeting place, this time on the Nass, is called Hwil-lê-ne-hwada,"Where-They-Meet-Each-Other" (Boas 1902 p. 225).

After her mother's death, the young woman and her son settle in her native village (i.e., her father's, where her mother had lived from the time of her marriage until her husband's death, the downstream village. It is from there that the visit to heaven takes place. This village, called Gitsalasert, "People of the [Skeena] Canyon," is situated not far from the modern town of Usk (Garfield 1939, p. 175; Boas and Hunt 1912, pp. 71, 276; cf. Krause 1956, pp.

214–215: "Kîtselassin," on the Skeena River). Although the Tsimshian dialect was spoken there, it was outside the "nine towns" which, strictly speaking, formed the Tsimshian province (Boas and Hunt 1912, p.225).

On his mother's death, Asdiwal continues his journey downstream, that is to say, westward. He settles in the town of Ginaxangioget, where he marries. This is in Tsimshian country proper on the lower reaches of the Skeena. Ginaxangioget is, in fact, a term formed from the root of *git* = *"people"* and *gi.k* = "hemlock tree," from which comes *Ginax-angi.k,* "the people of the firs" (Garfield 1939, p. 175). Ginaxangioget was one of the nine principal towns of the Tsimshian (Boas and Hunt 1916, pp.482–483).

When Asdiwal leaves with his in-laws for the Nass to fish candlefish there, they go first to the Skeena estuary, then take to the sea and stop at the capital city of the Tsimshian, Metlakatla. A recent town of the same name, founded by natives converted to Christianity, is to be found on Annette Island in Alaska (Beynon 1941; Garfield, Wingert, and Barbeau 1951, pp.33–34). Old Metlakatla is on the coast, north of Prince Rupert and halfway between the Skeena and the Nass estuaries. Ksemaksén, where the first quarrel takes place, and where Asdiwal is first abandoned by his brothers-in-law, is also on the coast, a little further north.

The Tsimshian-speaking tribe called Gitxatla, which is independent of those centers around Metlakatla, forms a group of islanders living on McCauley, Porcher, and Dolphin islands, across and south of the Skeena estuary. Their name comes from *git,* "people," and *qxatla,* "channel" (Garfield 1939, p. 175; Boas and Hunt 1916, p. 483). Having traveled from east to west, Asdiwal accompanies them to the Nass, that is to say in a south-north direction, then in the opposite direction, to "their town," offshore from which (and probably to the west, since it was a deep-sea expedition) the visit to the sea lions takes place.

From there, Asdiwal returns to the Skeena—this time from west to east. The story ends at Ginadâos (or perhaps Ginadoiks from *git,* "people," *na,* "of," *doiks,* "rapid current"; the name of a torrent which flows into the Skeena. (Garfield 1939, p.176).

Let us now consider the economic aspect. The economic activities brought to notice by the myth are no less real than the geographical places and the populations evoked in the preceding paragraphs. Everything begins with a period of winter famine such as was well known to the natives in the period between mid-December and mid-January, before the moment when, theoretically, the spring salmon arrived, which was just before the arrival of the candlefish, the period called the interval" (Boas and Hunt 1916, pp. 398–399). After his visit to the heavens, Asdiwal takes part in the spring migration to the Nass for the candlefish season; then we are told of the return of the families to the Skeena in the salmon season.

These seasonal variations—to use Marcel Mauss's expression—are on a par with other, no less real differences emphasized by the myth, notably that between the land hunter (personified by Asdiwal, born on the river and upstream, i.e., inland) and the sea hunter (personified first by the People of the Firs who live downstream on the estuary, and then, still more clearly, by the inhabitants of Porcher and Dolphin islands.)

When we move on to the sociological aspects, there is a much greater freedom of interpretation. It is not a question of an accurate documentary picture of the reality of native life, but a sort of counterpoint which seems sometimes to be in harmony with this reality, and sometimes to part from it in order to rejoin it again.

The initial sequence of events evokes clearly defined sociological conditions. The mother and daughter have been separated by the latter's marriage, and since that time each has lived with her own husband in his village. The elder woman's husband was also the father of the younger woman, who left her native village to follow her own husband upstream. We can recognize this as a society in which, while having a system of matrilineal filiation, residence is patrilocal, the wife going to live in her husband's village; and one in which the children, although they belong to their mother's clan, are brought up in their father's home and not in that of their maternal kin.

Such was the situation among the Tsimshian. Boas emphasizes it several times: "In olden times it was customary for a great chief to take a princess from each tribe to be his wife. Some had as many as sixteen or eighteen wives. . . ," which would clearly be impossible if a man had to live in his wife's native village. More generally, says Boas, "There is ample evidence showing that the young married people lived with the young man's parents," so that "the children grew up in their fathers home" (Boas and Hunt 1916, pp. 355, 529, 426; cf. p. 420, 427, 441, 499–500).

But, in the myth, this patrilocal type of residence is quickly undermined by famine, which frees the two women from their respective obligations and allows them, upon the death of their husbands, to meet (significantly enough) halfway. Their camping at the foot of the tree on the bank of the frozen river, equidistant from up-river and down-river, presents a picture of a matrilocal type of residence reduced to its simplest form, since the new household consists only of a mother and her daughter.

This reversal, which is barely hinted at, is all the more remarkable because all the subsequent marriages are going to be matrilocal, and thus contrary to the type found in reality.

First, Hatsenas's marriage with the younger woman. Fleeting though this union between a human being and a supernatural being may be, the husband still lives in his wife's home, and therefore in her mother's home. The matrilocal trend is even more apparent in the version recorded on the Nass. When his son Asi-hwil has grown up, Hatsenas (who here is called Hôux) says to his wife: "Your brothers are coming to look for you. Therefore I must hide in the woods." Shortly thereafter, the brothers come, and leave again, laden with supplies of meat given to the women by their protector. "As soon as they left, Hôux returned. The [women] told him that their brothers and uncles had asked them to return home. Then Hôux said, 'Let us part. You may return to your home; I will return to mine.' On the following morning, many people came to fetch the women and the boy. They took them to Gitxaden. The boy's uncles gave a feast and his mother told them the boy's name, Asi-hwil..." (Boas 1902, p. 227).

Not only does the husband seem an intruder—regarded with suspicion by his brothers-in-law and afraid that they might attack him—but, contrary to what happens among the Tsimshian and in other societies characterized by the association of matrilineal filiation and patrilocal residence (Boas and Hunt 1916, p. 423; Malinowski 1922) the food gifts go from the sister's husband to the wife's brothers.

Matrilocal marriage, accompanied by antagonism between the husband and his in-laws, is further illustrated by Asdiwal's marriage to Evening-Star; they live in her father's home, and the father-in-law shows so much hostility toward his son-in-law that he sets him trials which are deemed to be fatal.

Matrilocal, too, is Asdiwal's second marriage in the land of the People of the Firs; which is accompanied by hostility between the husband and his brothers-in-law because they abandon him and persuade their sister to follow them.

The same theme is expressed in the third marriage in the land of the People of the Channel, at any rate to start with. After Asdiwal's visit to the sea lions, the situation is reversed: Asdiwal recovers his wife, who has refused to follow her brothers and was wandering in search of her husband. What is more, she collaborates with him to produce the "machination"—in the literal and the figurative sense—by means of which he takes revenge on his brothers-in-law. Finally, patrilocality triumphs when Asdiwal abandons his wife (whereas in the previous marriages it had been his wife who had abandoned him) and returns to the Skeena where he was born, and where his son comes alone to join him. Thus, having begun with the story of the *reunion of a mother and her daughter,* freed from their affines or *paternal kin,* the myth ends with the story of the *reunion of a father and his son,* freed from their affines or *maternal kin.*

But if the initial and final sequences on the myth constitute, from a sociological point of view, a pair of oppositions, the same is true, from a cosmological point of view, of the two supernatural voyages which interrupt the hero's "real" journey. The first voyage takes him to the heavens and into the home of the Sun, who first tries to kill him and then agrees to bring him back to life. The second takes Asdiwal to the subterranean kingdom of the sea lions, whom he has himself killed or wounded, but whom he agrees to look after and to cure. The first voyage results in a marriage which, as we have seen, is matrilocal, and which, moreover, bears witness to a maximal exogamous separation (between an earthborn man and a woman from heaven). But this marriage will be broken up by Asdiwal's infidelity with a woman of his own village. This may be seen as a suggestion of a marriage which, if it really took place, would neutralize matrilocality (since husband and wife would come from the same place) and would be characterized by an endogamous proximity which would also be maximal (marriage within the village). It is true that the hero's second supernatural voyage, to the subterranean kingdom of the sea lions, does not lead to a marriage. But, as has already been shown, this visit brings about a reversal in the matrilocal tendency of Asdiwal's successive marriages, for it separates his third wife from her brothers, the hero himself from his wife, their son from his mother, and leaves only one relationship in existence: that between the father and his son.

In this analysis of the myth, we have distinguished four levels: the geographic, the techno-economic, the sociological, and the cosmological. The first two are exact transcriptions of reality; the fourth has nothing to do with it; and in the third real and imaginary institutions are interwoven. Yet in spite of these differences, the levels are not separated out by the native mind. It is rather that everything happens as if the levels were provided with different codes, each being used according to the needs of the moment, and according to its particular capacity, to transmit the same message. It is the nature of this message that we shall now consider.

Winter famines are a recurrent event in the economic life of the Tsimshian. But the famine that starts the story off is also a cosmological theme. All along the northwest PacificCoast, in fact, the present state of the universe is attributed to the havoc wrought in the original order by the demiurge Giant or Raven (Txamsen, or Tsimshian) during travels which he undertook in order to satisfy his irrepressible voracity. Thus Txamsen is perpetually in a state of famine, and famine, although a negative condition, is seen as the *primum mobile* of creation. In this sense we can say that the hunger of the two women in our myth has a cosmic significance. These heroines are not so much legendary persons as incarnations of principles which are at the origin of place names.

One may schematize the initial situation as follows:

mother	daughter
elder	younger
downstream	upstream
west	east
south	north

The meeting takes place at the halfway point, a situation which, as we have seen, corresponds to a neutralization of patrilocal residence and to the fulfillment of the conditions for a matrilocal residence which is as yet only hinted at. But since the mother dies on the very spot where the meeting and the birth of Asdiwal took place, the essential movement, which her daughter begins by leaving the village of her marriage "very far upstream" (Boas and Hunt 1912, p. 71), is in the direction east-west, as far as her native village in the

Skeena Canyon, where she in her turn dies, leaving the field open for
the hero.

Asdiwal's first adventure presents us with an opposition—that
of heaven and earth—which the hero is able to surmount by virtue of
the intervention of his father, Hatsenas, the bird of good omen. The
latter is a creature of the atmospheric or middle heaven and
consequently is well qualified to play the role of mediator between
the earth-born Asdiwal and his father-in-law the Sun, ruler of the
highest heaven. Even so, Asdiwal does not manage to overcome his
earthly nature, to which he twice submits, first in yielding to the
charms of a fellow countrywoman and then in yielding to nostalgia
for his home village. Thus there remains a series of unresolved
oppositions:

low	high
earth	heaven
man	woman
endogamy	exogamy

Pursuing his course westward, Asdiwal contracts a second
matrilocal marriage which generates a new series of oppositions:

| mountain hunting | sea hunting |
| land | water |

These oppositions, too, are insurmountable, and Asdiwal's
earthly nature carries him away a third time, with the result that he
is abandoned by his wife and his brothers-in-law.

Asdiwal contracts his last marriage not with the river dwellers,
but with islanders, and the same conflict is repeated. The opposition
continues to be insurmountable, although at each stage the terms are
brought closer together. This time it is in fact a question of a quarrel
between Asdiwal and his brothers-in-law on the occasion of a hunt
on a reef on the high seas; that is, on land and water at the same
time. In the previous incident, Asdiwal and his brothers-in-law had
gone their separate ways, one inland and on foot, the others out to
sea and in boats. This time they go together in boats, and it is only
when they land that Asdiwal's superiority is made manifest by the
use he makes of the magic objects intended for mountain hunting: "It
was a very difficult hunt on account of the waves which swept past
[the reef] in the direction of the open sea. While they were speaking
about this, [Asdiwal] said: 'My dear fellows, I have only to put on my

snowshoes and I'll run up the rocks you are talking about.' He succeeds in this way, whilst his brothers-in-law, incapable of landing, stay shamefacedly in their boats" (Boas and Hunt 1912, pp. 125–126).

Asdiwal, the earth-born master of the hunt finds himself abandoned on a reef in high seas. He has come to the furthest point in his westward journey; so much for the geographic and economic aspects. But from a logical point of view, his adventures can be seen in a different form—that of a series of impossible mediations between oppositions which are ordered in a descending scale: high and low, water and earth, sea hunting and mountain hunting, and so forth.

Consequently, on the spatial plane, the hero is completely led off his course, and his failure is expressed in this *maximal separation* from his starting point. On the logical plane, he has also failed because of his immoderate attitude toward his brothers-in-law, and because of his inability to play the role of a mediator, even though the last of the oppositions which had to be overcome—between the types of life led by the land hunters and sea hunters—is reduced to a *minimal separation*. There would seem to be a dead end at this point; but from neutral the myth goes into reverse and its machinery starts up again.

The king of the mountains (in Nass dialect, Asdiwal is called Asi-hwil, which means "Crosser of Mountains") is caught on a caricature of a mountain, one that is doubly so because, on the one hand, it is nothing more than a reef and, on the other, it is surrounded and almost submerged by the sea. The ruler of wild animals and killer of bears is to be saved by a she-mouse, a caricature of a wild animal. She makes him undertake a *subterranean journey*, just as the she-bear, the supreme wild animal, had imposed on Asdiwal a *celestial journey*. In fact, the only thing that is missing is for the mouse to change into a woman and to offer the hero a marriage which would be symmetrical to the other, but opposite to it. Although this element is not to be found in any of the versions, we know at least that the mouse is a fairy: Lady Mouse-Woman, as she is called in the texts, where the word *ksem,* a term of respect addressed to a woman, is prefixed to the word denoting a rodent. Following through the inversion more systematically than had been possible under the preceding hypothesis, this fairy is an old woman incapable of procreation—an "inverse wife."

And that is not all. The man who had killed animals by the hundreds goes this time to heal them and win their love. The bringer of food (who repeatedly exercises the power he received from his father in this respect for the benefit of his family) becomes food, since he is transported in the sea lion's stomach.

Finally, the visit to the subterranean world (which is also, in many respects, an "upside-down world") sets the course of the hero's return; for from then onward he travels from west to east, from the sea toward the mainland, from the salt water of the ocean to the fresh water of the Skeena.

This overall reversal does not affect the development of the plot, which unfolds up to the final catastrophe. When Asdiwal returns to his people and to the initial patrilocal situation, he takes up his favorite occupation again, helped by his magic objects. But he *forgets* one of them, and this mistake is fatal. After a successful hunt, he finds himself trapped halfway up the mountain side: "Where might he go now? He could not go up, he could not go to either side" (Boas and Hunt 1912, p. 145). And on the spot he is changed to stone, that is to say, paralyzed, reduced to his earthborn nature in the stony and unchangeable form in which he has been seen "for generations."

The above analysis leads us to draw a distinction between two aspects of the construction of a myth: the sequences and the schemata.

The sequences form the apparent content of the myth, the chronological order in which things happen: the meeting of the two women, the intervention of the supernatural protector, the birth of Asdiwal, his childhood, his visit to heaven, his successive marriages, his hunting and fishing expeditions, his quarrels with his brothers-in-law, and so forth.

But these sequences are organized on planes at different levels of abstraction in accordance with schemata, which exist simultaneously, superimposed one upon the other; just as a melody composed for several voices is held within bounds by two-dimensional constraints: first by its own melodic line, which is horizontal, and second by the contrapuntal schemata, which are vertical. Let us then draw up an inventory of such schemata for this present myth.

1. *Geographic schema.* The hero goes from east to west, then returns from west to east.

This return journey is modulated by another one, from the south to the north and then from the north to the south, which corresponds to the seasonal migrations of the Tsimshian (in which the hero takes part) to the River Nass for the candlefish season in the spring, then to the Skeena for the salmon fishing in the summer.

```
                    North
    East ─────────→ West ─────────→ East
                    South
```

2. *Cosmological schema.* Three supernatural visits establish a relationship between terms thought of respectively as "below" and "above": the visit to the young widow by Hatsenas, the bird of good omen associated with the atmospheric heavens; the visit by Asdiwal to the highest heavens in pursuit of Evening-Star; and his visit to the subterranean kingdom of the sea lions under the guidance of Lady Mouse-Woman. The end of Asdiwal, trapped in the mountain, then appears as a *neutralization* of the intermediate mediation established at his birth but which even so does not enable him to bring off two further extreme mediations (the one between heaven and earth considered as the opposition low/high and the other between the sea and the land considered as the opposition east/west).

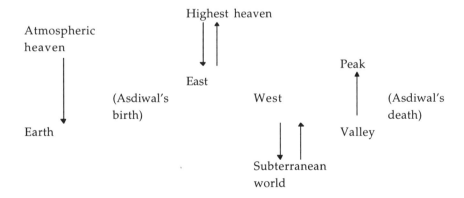

3. *Integration schema.* The above two schemata are integrated in a third consisting of several binary oppositions, none of which the

hero can resolve, although the distance separating the opposed terms gradually dwindles. The initial and final oppositions, high/ low and peak/valley, are "vertical" and thus belong to the cosmological schema. The two intermediate oppositions, water/land and sea hunting/mountain hunting, are "horizontal" and belong to the geographic schema. But the final opposition, peak/valley, which is also the narrowest contrast, brings into association the essential characteristics of the two preceding schemata: it is "vertical" in form; but "geographical" in content. Asdiwal's failure (he is trapped half way up the mountain because he forgot his snowshoes) thus takes on a significance geographical, cosmological, and logical.

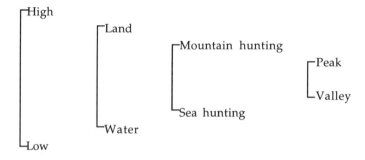

When the three schemata are reduced in this way to their bare essentials, retaining only the order and amplitude of the oppositions, their complementarily becomes apparent.

> *Schema 1* is composed of a sequence of oscillations of constantamplitude: east-north-west-south-east.
> *Schema 2* starts at a zero point (the meeting halfway between upstream and downstream) and is followed by an oscillation of medium amplitude (atmospheric heavens—earth), then by oscillations of maximum amplitude (earth-heaven, heaven-earth, earth-subterranean world, subterranean world-earth) which die away at the zero point (halfway up, between peak and valley).
> *Schema 3* begins with an oscillation of maximum amplitude (high-low) which dies away in a series of oscillations of decreasing amplitude (water-land; sea hunting-mountain hunting; valley-peak).

4. *Sociological schema.* To start with, the patrilocal residence prevails. It gives way progressively to the matrilocal residence (Hatsenas's marriage), which becomes deadly (Asdiwal's marriage in heaven), then merely hostile (the marriage in the land of the People of the Firs), before weakening and finally reversing (marriage among People of the Channel) to allow a return to patrilocal residence.

The sociological schema does not have, however, a closed structure like the geographic schema, since, at the beginning, it involves a mother and her daughter; in the middle, a husband, his wife, and his brothers-in-law; and, at the end, a father and his son.

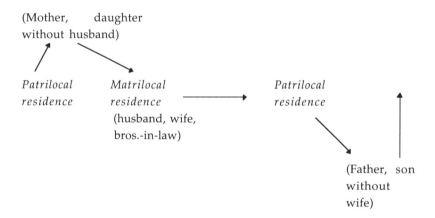

(Mother,   daughter without husband)

Patrilocal residence

Matrilocal residence (husband, wife, bros.-in-law)

Patrilocal residence

(Father, son without wife)

5. *Techno-economic schema.* The myth begins by evoking a winter famine; it ends with a successful hunt. In between, the story follows the economic cycle and the seasonal migrations of the native fishermen:

Famine ⟶ Fishing for candlefish ⟶ Salmon fishing ⟶ Successful hunt

6. *Global integration.* If the myth is finally reduced to its two extreme propositions, the initial state of affairs and the final, which together summarize its operational function, then we end up with a simplified diagram:

Having separated out the codes, we have analyzed the structure of the message. It now remains to decipher the meaning.

In Boas's *Tsimshian Mythology,* there is a version of the story of Asdiwal that is remarkable in several respects. First, it brings a new character into play: Waux, the son of Asdiwal's second marriage, who seems to be a double of his father, although his adventures take place after those of Asdiwal. In chronological order, they form supplementary sequences of events. But these *later* sequences are organized in schemata which are at the same time *homologous* to those which have been described before and more *explicit.* Everything seems to suggest that, as it draws to its close, the apparent narrative (the sequences) tends to approach the latent content of the myth (the schemata). It is a convergence which is not unlike that which the listener discovers in the final chords of a symphony.

> When Asdiwal's second wife (his first earth-born wife) bore him a son, he was called Waux. That means "very light," for this son used to fly away like a spark.
> The father and son loved each other very much and always hunted together. And thus it was a cause of great sorrow to Waux when his uncles forced him to follow them after they had left his father (Asdiwal) at Ksemaksén. The mother and son had even secretly tried to find Asdiwal and had only abandoned the attempt when they were convinced that he must have been devoured by some wild animal.
> Waux, following in his father's footsteps, became a great hunter. Before his mother died, she made him marry a cousin, and the young couple lived happily. Waux continued to hunt on his father's hunting grounds, sometimes in company with his wife who gave birth to twins. Soon Waux's children went hunting with him, as he had formerly done with his father. One day he went with them into an unexplored region. The children slipped on the mountain and were both killed. The following year, Waux returned to the same place to hunt, armed with all the magic objects he had inherited from his father, except the lance, which he forgot. Taken unawares by an earthquake, he tried in vain to make his wife (whom he saw in the valley) understand that he needed her ritual help. He shouted to her to sacrifice fat to the supernatural powers is order to appease them. But the wife could not hear and misunderstood, repeating not what her husband had said but

what she wanted to do herself: "You want me to eat fat?" Discouraged, Waux agreed, and his wife sated herself with fat and cold water. Satisfied, she lay down on an old log. Her body broke apart and was changed into a veined flint which is still found all over that place today.

Waux, because he had forgotten the lance which enabled him to split the rock and open a way through the mountain, and having lost his last chance of placating the elements because of the misunderstanding which had arisen between his wife and himself, was turned to stone, as were his dog and all his magic objects. They are still here to this day (Boas and Hunt 1916, pp. 243–245).

Several significant permutations will be noticed if this is compared with the version which we have taken as a point of reference.

Asdiwal had an only son (in fact, as we have seen, two only sons, born of consecutive marriages and confused into one single one in the story), whereas Waux has twins. We do not know much about these twins, but it is tempting to set up a parallel between them and the two magic dogs that Asi-hwil was given by his father in the River Nass version, one red, the other spotted; that is, marked by a contrast which suggests (when compared with the symbolic color systems so common among the North American Indians) divergent functions.

Moreover, the existence of twins already provides a pointer. In the American series of mediators, twins represent the weakest term, and come at the bottom of the list, after the Messiah (who unites opposites), and the trickster (in whom they are in juxtaposition). The pair of twins brings opposites into association but at the same time leaves them individually distinct.

The change from a single mediator to a pair of twins is thus a sign of a weakening in the function of the mediator. This is all the clearer from the fact that, only shortly after their appearance on the mystical scene, the twins die in unexplored territory without having played any part.

Like Asdiwal, Waux ends by being turned to stone as a result of forgetting a magic object. The identity of this object, however, changes from one version to another. In Asdiwal, it is the snowshoes, in Waux the lance. The magic objects are the instruments of mediation given to the hero by his supernatural father. Here again there is a gradation. The snowshoes make it possible to climb up and down the steepest slopes. The lance enables its owner to go straight through walls of rock. The lance is thus a more radical means than the snowshoes, which come to terms with the obstacle rather than doing away with it. Waux's omission seems more serious than Asdiwal's. The weaker mediator loses the stronger instrument of mediation and his powers are doubly diminished as a result.

Thus the story of Waux follows a dialectic regression. But, in another sense, it reveals a progression, since it is with this variant that a structure which had remained open in certain respects is finally closed.

Waux's wife dies of *repletion.* That is the end of a story which opened by showing Asdiwal's (or Asi-hwil's) mother a victim of *starvation.* It was this famine which set her in *motions,* just as, now, abuse of food brings Waux's wife to a *halt.*

Before leaving this point let us note that in fact two characters of the initial sequence were two women who were *single, unfed,* and *on the move,* whereas those of the final sequence were a *couple* composed of a husband and his wife, one a *bringer of food* (who is not understood) and the other *overfed* (because she does not understand), and both *paralyzed* in spite of this opposition (but also perhaps because of the negative complementarity that it expresses) .

The most important transformation is that represented by the marriage of Waux. It has been seen that Asdiwal contracted a series of marriages, all equally unsuccessful. He cannot choose between his supernatural bride and his fellow countrywoman; he is abandoned (though against her will, it is true) by his Tsimshian spouse. His Gitxatla wife remains faithful to him and even goes so far as to betray her brothers; it is he who abandons her. He ends his days, having joined forces with his son again, in a celibate state.

Waux, on the other hand, marries only once, but this marriage proves fatal to him. Here, however, it is a case of a marriage *arranged* by Waux's mother (unlike Asdiwal's *adventurous* marriages) and a marriage with a *cousin* (whereas Asdiwal marries complete *strangers*); or more precisely, with his cross-cousin, his mother's brother's daughter (which explains the intermediary role played by his mother).

As Boas explains in the text quoted in the footnote above, there was a preference for marriage with the mother's brother's daughter among Tsimshian, especially in the noble classes from which our heroes are drawn. Garfield doubts whether the practice was strictly in accordance with mythical models (1939, pp. 232–233), but the point is of secondary importance, since we are studying schemata with a normative function. In a society like that of the Tsimshian, there is no difficulty in seeing why this type of marriage could be thought ideal. Boys grew up in their fathers' homes, but sooner or later they had to go over to their maternal uncle when they inherited his titles, prerogatives, and hunting grounds. Marriage with the matrilineal cousin provided a solution to this conflict. Furthermore, as has often been found to be the case in other societies of the same type, such a marriage made it possible to overcome another conflict: that between the patrilineal and matrilineal tendencies of Tsimshian society, which, as we have seen above, is very deeply conscious of the two lines. By means of such a marriage, a man ensures the continued existence of his hereditary privileges and of such titles as he might have within the limits of a small family circle (Swanton 1909*a*; Wedgewood 1928; Richards 1914)

I have shown elsewhere that it is unlikely that this interpretation may be seen as the universal origin of cross-cousin marriage (Lévi-Strauss 1969*a*, pp. 123–124). But in the case of a society which has feudal tendencies, it certainly corresponds to real motives which contributed to the survival or the adoption of the custom. The final explanation of this custom must, however, be sought in those characteristics which are common to all societies which practiced it.

The Tsimshian myths provide, furthermore, a surprising commentary on the native theory of marriage with the matrilateral cross-cousin in the story of the princess who refused to marry her cousin (her father's sister's son).

> No less cruel than she was proud, the princess demands that her cousin prove his love by disfiguring himself. He slashes his face and then she rejects him because of his ugliness. Reduced to a state of despair, the young man seeks death and ventures into the land of Chief Pestilence, master of deformities. After the Hero has undergone rigorous trials, the chief agrees to transform him into a Prince Charming.
>
> Now his cousin is passionately attracted to him, and the young man, in his turn, demands that she sacrifice her beauty, but only in order to heap sarcasm upon her head. The now hideous princess tries to move Chief Pestilence to pity, and at once the maimed and deformed race of people who make up his court set upon the unfortunate woman, break her bones and tear her apart (Boas and Hunt 1916, pp.185–191).

Boas' informant sees in this tale the myth which lies at the origin of the rites and ceremonies celebrated at the marriages of cross-cousins.

> There was a custom among our people that the nephew of the chief had to marry the chief's daughter, because the tribe of the chief wanted the chief's nephew to be the heir of his uncle and to inherit his place after his death. This custom has gone on, generation after generation, all along until now, and the places of the head men have thus been inherited.

But, the informant goes on, it is because of the disaster that struck the rebellious princess that it was decided that on such occasions "no young woman should have any say about her marriage. . . . Even though the young woman does not want to marry the man, she has to consent when the agreement has been made on both sides to marry them" (that is to say, after negotiations between the maternal-descent groups of the young people):

> When the prince and princess have married, the tribe of the young man's uncle mobilize. Then the tribe of the young woman's uncle also mobilize and they have a fight. The two parties cast stones at each other, and the heads of many of those on each side are hit. The scars made by the stones on the heads of each chief's people are signs of the marriage pledge (Boas and Hunt 1916, pp. 185–191).

In his commentary Boas notes that this myth is not peculiar to the Tsimshian, but is found also among the Tlingit and the Haida, who are likewise matrilineal and likewise faithful to the same type of marriage. Thus it is clear that it portrays a fundamental aspect of the social organization of these peoples, which consists in a hostile equilibrium between the matrilineal lineages of the village chiefs. In a system of generalized exchange, such as results in these feudal families from the preferential marriage with the mother's brother's daughter, the families are, so to speak, ranged around a more or less stable circle, in such a way that each family occupies (at least temporarily) the position of "wife-giver" with respect to some other family and of "wife-taker" with respect to a third. Depending on the society, this lopsided structure (lopsided because there is no guarantee that in giving one will receive) can achieve a certain equilibrium—more apparent, however, than real—in any of several ways. It can achieve this democratically, by following the principle that all marriage exchanges are equivalent; or, on the contrary, by stipulating that one of the positions (wife-giver, wife-taker) is, by definition, superior to the other. But given a different social and economic context, this amounts in theory, if not in practice, to the same thing, since each family must occupy both positions (Lévi-Strauss 1949; *S.A.*, p. 305). The societies of the northwest Pacific Coast could not, or would not, choose one of these points of balance, and the respective superiority or inferiority of the groups involved was openly contested on the occasion of each marriage. Each marriage, along with the potlatches which accompanied and preceded it, and the tranfers of titles and property occasioned by it, provided the means by which the groups concerned might simultaneously gain an advantage over each other and end former disputes. French mediaeval society offers, in terms of patrilineal institutions, a symmetrical picture of a situation which had much in common with the one just described.

In such circumstances, is there anything amazing about the horrid little story in which the natives see the origin of their marriage institutions? Is there anything surprising in the fact that the ceremony of marriage between first cousins takes the form of a internecine battle? When we believe that, in bringing to light these antagonisms which are inherent in the structure of Tsimshian society, we are "reaching rock bottom" (in the words of Marcel Mauss), we express in this geological metaphor an approach that has many points of comparison with that of the myths of Asdiwal and Waux. All the paradoxes conceived by the native mind, on the most diverse planes—geographic, economic, sociological, and even cosmological—are, when all is said and done, assimilated to that less obvious yet so real paradox, the dilemma which marriage with the matrilateral cousin attempts but fails to resolve. But the failure is *admitted* in our myths, and there precisely lies their function.

Let us glance at them again in this light. The winter famine which kills the husbands of the two original heroines frees them from patrilocal residence and enables them first to meet and then to return to the daughter's native village, which corresponds, for her son, to a matrilocal type of residence. Thus a shortage of food is related to the sending out of young women, who return to their own descent groups when food is scarce. This is symbolic of an event which is illustrated in a more concrete fashion each year—even when there is no famine—by the departure of the candlefish from the Nassand then of the salmon from the Skeena. These fish come from the open sea, arrive from the south and the west, and go up the rivers in an easterly direction. Like the departing fish, Asdiwal's mother continues her journey westward and toward the sea, where Asdiwal discovers the disastrous effects of matrilocal marriage.

The first of his marriages is with Evening-Star, who is a supernatural being. The correlation of female heaven and male earth which is implicit in this event is interesting from two points of view.

First, Asdiwal is in a way fished up by the She-Bear who draws him up to heaven, and the myths often describe grizzly bears as *fishing for salmon* (Boas and Hunt 1916, p. 403). Like a salmon, too, Asdiwal is fished up in a net by the compassionate Sun after he has crashed to earth. (Boas and Hunt 1912:, pp. 112–113). But when Asdiwal returns from his symmetrically opposite visit to the subterranean kingdom of the sea lions, he travels in one of their stomachs, like food—comparable to the *candlefish* which are scooped up from the bed of the River Nass, the "Stomach River." Furthermore, the hero now goes in the opposite direction, no longer from the east to west like the food disappearing, but from west to east like the food returning.

Second, this reversal is accompanied by another: that from matrilocal to patrilocal residence. This latter reversal is in itself a variable of the replacement of a celestial journey by a subterranean one, which brings Asdiwal from the position of earth/male/dominated to that of earth/male/dominant.

Patrilocal residence is no more successful for Asdiwal. He gets his son back but loses his wife and his affines. Isolated in this new relationship and incapable of bringing together the two types of filiation and residence, he is stuck halfway at the end of a successful hunt: he has reconquered food but lost his freedom of movement. Famine, which causes movement, has given way to abundance, but at the price of paralysis.

We can now better understand how Waux's marriage with his matrilateral cousin, following that of his father, symbolizes the last futile attempts of Tsimshian thought and Tsimshian society to overcome their inherent contradictions. For this marriage fails as the result of a *misunderstanding* added to an *omission*. Waux had succeeded in staying with his maternal kin while at the same time retaining his father's hunting grounds. He had managed to inherit in both the maternal and paternal lines at the same time. But, although they are cousins, he and his wife remain alienated from one another, because cross-cousin marriage, in a feudal society, is a palliative and a decoy. In these societies, women are always objects of exchange, but property is also a cause of battle.

The above analysis suggests an observation of a different kind: it is always rash to undertake, as Boas wanted to do in his monumental *Tsimshian Mythology*, "a description of the life, social organization and religious ideas and practices of a people . . . as it appears from their mythology" (Boas and Hunt 1916, p. 32).

The myth is certainly related to given facts, but not as a *representation* of them. The relationship is of a dialectic kind, and the institutions described in the myths can be the very opposite of the real institutions. This will always be the case when the myth is trying to express a negative truth. As has already been seen, the story of Asdiwal has landed the great American ethnologist in no little difficulty, for there Waux is said to have inherited his father's hunting grounds. Other texts—as well as eyewitness observation—reveal that a man's property, including his hunting grounds, went to his sister's son, that is, from man to man in the maternal line.

But Waux's paternal inheritance no more reflects real conditions than do his father's matrilocal marriages. In real life, the children grew up in the patrilocal home. Then they went to finish their education at their maternal uncle's home. After marrying, they returned to live with their parents, bringing their wives with them, and they settled in their uncle's village only when they were called upon to succeed him. Such, at any rate, was the case among the nobility, whose mythology formed a real "court literature."

The comings and goings were some of the outward signs of the *tensions* lineages connected by marriage. Mythical speculations about types of residence which are exclusively patrilocal or matrilocal do not therefore have anything to do with the reality of the structure of Tsimshian society, but rather with its inherent possibilities and its latent potentialities. Such speculations, in the last analysis, do not seek to depict what is real, but to justify the shortcomings of reality, since the extreme positions are only *imagined* in order to show that they are *untenable.* This step, which is fitting for mythical thought, implies an admission (but in the veiled language of the myth) that the social facts when thus examined are marred by an insurmountable contradiction. A contradiction which, like the hero of the myth, Tsimshian society cannot understand and prefers to forget.

This conception of the relation of the myth to reality no doubt limits the use of the former as a documentary source. But it opens the way for other possibilities; for, in abandoning the search for a constantly accurate picture of ethnographic reality in the myth, we gain, on occasions, a means of reaching unconscious categories.

A moment ago it was recalled that Asdiwal's two journeys— from east to west and from west to east—were correlated with types of residence, matrilocal and patrilocal, respectively. But in fact the Tsimshian have patrilocal residence, and from this we can (and indeed must) draw the conclusion that one of the orientations corresponds to the direction implicit in a real-life "reading" of their institutions, the other to the opposite direction. The journey from west to east, the return journey, is accompanied by a return to patrilocality. Therefore the direction in which it is made is, for the native mind, the only real direction, the other being purely imaginary.

That is, moreover, what the myth proclaims. The move to the east assures Asdiwal's return to his element, the earth, and to his native land. When he went westward it was as a bringer of food, putting an end to starvation; he made up for the absence of food while at the same time traveling in the same direction as that taken by food when it departed. Journeying in the opposite direction, in the sea lion's stomach, he is symbolically identified with food, and he travels in the direction in which the food returns.

The same applies to matrilocal residence. It is introduced as a negative reality, to make up for the nonexistence of patrilocal residence caused by the death of the husbands.

What then is the west-east direction in native thought? It is the direction taken by the candlefish and the salmon when they arrive from the sea each year to enter the rivers and race upstream. If this orientation is also that which the Tsimshian must adopt in order to obtain an undistorted picture of their concrete social existence, is it not because they see themselves as being *sub specie piscis*; that they put themselves in the fishes' place—or rather, that they put the fish in their place?

This hypothesis, arrived at by a process of deductive reasoning, is indirectly confirmed by ritual institutions and mythology.

Fishing and the preparation of the fish are the occasion for all kinds of ritual among the natives of the northwest Pacific Coast. We have already seen that the women must use their naked breasts to press the candlefish in order to extract the oil from it, and that the remains must be left to rot near the dwellings in spite of the smell. The salmon does not rot, since it is dried in the sun or smoked. But there are other ritual conditions which must be observed; for instance, the salmon must be cut up with a primitive knife made of a mussel shell, and any kind of stone, bone, or metal blade is forbidden. Women set about this operation sitting on the ground with their legs apart (Boas and Hunt 1916, pp. 449–450, 919–932, Nootka).

These prohibitions and prescriptions seem to represent the same intention: to bring out the "immediacy" of the relationship between fish and man by treating fish as if it were man, or at any rate by ruling out, or limiting to the extreme, the use of manufactured objects which are part of culture; in other words, by denying or underestimating the differences between fish and men.

The myths, for their part, tell of the visit of a prince to the kingdom of the salmon, whence he returns—having won their alliance—himself transformed into a fish. All these myths have one incident in common: the hungry prince is welcomed by the salmon and learns that he may under no circumstances eat the same food as they. But he must not hesitate to kill and eat the fish themselves, regardless of the fact that they thenceforth appear to him in human form (Boas and Hunt 1916, pp. 192–206, 770–778, 919–932).

It is at this point that the mythical identification hits upon the only real relationship between fish and men: one of food. It persists, even in the myth, as an alternative: either to eat like salmon (although one is a man) or to eat salmon (although they are like men). This latter solution is the right one, provided that the ritual requested by the salmon is observed and thanks to it they are reborn from their bones, which had been carefully collected and then immersed or burned. But the first solution would be an *abuse of identification,* of man with salmon, not of salmon with man. The character in the myth who was guilty of this was transformed into a root or a rock—like Asdiwal—condemned to immobility and perpetually bound to the earth.

Starting with an initial situation characterized by irrepressible movement and ending in a final situation characterized by perpetual immobility, the myth of Asdiwal expresses in its own way a fundamental aspect of the native philosophy. The beginning presents us with the absence of food; and everything which has been said above leads us to think that the role of Asdiwal, as bringer of food, consists in a negation of this absence, but that is quite another thing from the presence of food. In fact, when this presence is finally obtained, with Asdiwal taking on the aspect of food itself (and no longer that of bringer of food), the result is a state of inertia.

But starvation is no more a tolerable human condition than is immobility. We must therefore conclude that for these natives the only positive form of existence is a *negation of nonexistence*. It is out of the question to develop this theory within the limits of the present work. But let us note in passing that it would shed new light on the *need for self-assertion*, which, in the potlatch, the feasts, the ceremonies, and the feudal rivalries, seems to be such a particular characteristic of the societies of the northwest Pacific Coast.

There is one last problem which remains to be solved: that posed by the differences between the Nass River version and those recorded on the coast, in which the action takes place on the Skeena. Up to now we have followed these latter ones. Let us now look at the Nass version.

> Famine reigns in the two villages of Laxqaltsap and Gitwunksilk—it is possible to place them: the first is the present Greenville on the Nass estuary, and the second is on the lower Nass, but farther upstream. Two sisters, separated by marriage, each live in one of the villages. They decide to join forces, and meet halfway in a place which is named in memory of this event. They have a few provisions. The sister from down-river has only a few hawberries, the one from up-river, a small piece of spawn. They share this and bewail their plight.
>
> One of the sisters—the one from up-river—has come with her daughter, who does not enter the story again. The one from down-river, the younger of the two, is still unmarried. A stranger visits her at night. He is called Hôux, which means "Good Luck." When he learns of the state of the women, he miraculously provides food for them, and the younger woman soon gives birth to a son, Asi-hwil, for whom his father makes a pair of snowshoes. At first they are useless; but once perfected, they bestow magic powers on their wearer. Asi-hwil's father also gives him two magic dogs, and a lance which can pass through rock. From then on the hero reveals himself to be a better hunter than other supernatural beings against whom he is matched.

Here follows the episode of Hoax's retreat from his brothers-in-law, which has been summarized above (see p. 156).

Then they carry off their sister and their nephew at Gitxaden, downstream from Nass Canyon. There the hero is drawn toward the sky by the slave of a supernatural being, disguised as a white bear. But he does not succeed in reaching the heavenly abode and returns to earth having lost track of the bear.

He then goes to Tsimshian country, where he marries the sister of the sea lion hunters. He humiliates them with his superiority, is abandoned by them, visits the sea lions in their subterranean kingdom, looks after them and cures them, and gets a canoe made of their intestines which brings him back to the coast, where he kills his brothers-in-law with artificial killer whales. He finds his wife and never leaves her again (Boas 1902, pp. 225–229).

Clearly, this version is very poor. It has very few episodes, and when compared with the version by Boas and Hunt 1912, which has been our point of reference up to now, the sequence of events seems very confused. It would be quite wrong, however, to treat the Nass version simply as a weakened echo of the Skeena ones. In the best-preserved part—the initial sequence of events—it is as if the richness of detail had been preserved, but at the cost of permutations which, without any doubt, form a system. Let us therefore begin by listing them, distinguishing the elements which are common to both versions from the elements which have been transformed.

In both cases, the story begins in a river valley: that of the Skeena, that of the Nass. It is winter and famine reigns. Two related women, one living upstream and the other downstream, decide to join forces, and meet halfway.

Already, several differences are apparent:

	Nass	Skeena
Place of the action	Nass	Skeena
State of the river	?	frozen
Situation of the two villages	not far apart	"very far apart"
Relationship between the women	sisters	mother and daughter
Civil status	{1 married} {1 unmarried}	2 widows

These differences, it is clear, are equivalent to a *weakening of all the oppositions* in the Nass version. This is very striking in the situations of the two villages and even more so in the relationship between the two women. In the latter there is a constant element, the relationship of elder to younger, which is manifested in the form *mother/daughter* in the one case, and *elder sister/younger sister* in the other. The first couple live *farther apart* from one another than the second and are brought together by a *more radical event* (the double simultaneous widowhood) than the second (of whom only one is married—it is not stated whether she has lost her husband).

One may also prove that the Nass version is a weakening of the Skeena version and that the Skeena version is not a strengthened form of the other. The proof lies in the vestigial survival of the original mother/daughter relationship in the form of the maternity of the elder sister, who is accompanied by her daughter. This is a detail which in every other respect has no function in the Nass version (the constant element being given by the opposition between *retrospective fertility* and *prospective fertility*), as seen in Formula a.

a. [mother: daughter] :: [(mother + daughter): nonmother]

But these differences, which one could consider in a "more" or "less" or quantitative sense, are accompanied by others which are genuine inversions.

In the Skeena versions, the elder of the two women comes from down-river, the younger from up-river. In the Nass variant, the contrary is true, since the pair (mother and daughter) comes from Gitwunksilk, upstream of the canyon, and the unmarried sister (who will marry the supernatural protector and is therefore identical with the daughter in the Skeena version) arrives from Laxqaltsap, which is downstream.

In the Skeena version, the women are completely emptyhanded, reduced to sharing a *single rotten berry*, found at their meeting place. Once again, the Nass version shows a weakening, since the women bring provisions, though they are in fact very meager—a handful of berries and a piece of spawn.

	Down-river		*Up-river*
Skeena version:	o ⟶	rotten berry	⟵ o
Nass version:	berries ⟶	⟵	spawn

It would be easy to show that on the northwest Pacific Coast and in other regions of America, decomposition is considered the borderline between food and excrement. If, in the Skeena version, a single berry *(quantitatively,* the minimal food) is the bearer of decomposition (*qualitatively*, the minimal food), then it is because berries in themselves are thought of *specifically* as a weak kind of food, in contrast with strong foods.

Without any doubt, in the Skeena version the two women are deliberately associated not with any particular food but with lack of any sort of food. But this "dearth of food," though a negative category, is not an empty category, for the development of the myth gives it, in retrospect, a content. The two women represent "absence of food," but they are also bound respectively to the east and to the west, to the land and to the sea. The myth of Asdiwal tells of an opposition between two types of life, also bound up with the same cardinal points and the same elements: mountain hunters on the one side, fishermen and sea hunters on the other. In the Skeena version the "alimentary" opposition is therefore double: (I) between animal food (at the extreme positions) and vegetable food (in the intermediate position); and (2) between sea animal (west) and land animal (east) as seen in Figure 10.

From this we obtain Figure l0. Formula b:

b. [land:sea] :: [(sea + land): middle]

Its analogy with Formula a is immediately obvious.

The alimentary system of the Nass version is based on a simplified structure (with two terms instead of three) and on weakened oppositions. From not being defined at all, vegetable food moves to a state of being weakly defined. From a borderline state

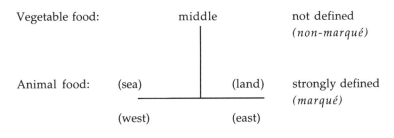

FIGURE 10

between food and absence of food, it becomes a positive food, both quantitatively (a handful of berries) and qualitatively (fresh berries). This vegetable food is now opposed not to animal food—a category which is strongly defined (and here distinguished by a minus sign - 1)—but to the weakest imaginable manifestation of this same animal food (to which we still assign a plus sign +1), and this is done in three ways:

> fish, and not meat
> fish spawn, and not fish
> a piece "as big as the finger"

Thus we have a system:

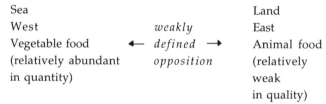

Sea		Land
West	*weakly*	East
Vegetable food	← *defined* →	Animal food
(relatively abundant	*opposition*	(relatively
in quantity)		weak
		in quality)

FIGURE 11

From the point of view of the alimentary system, the correlation between the two variants of the myth can thus be expressed by the following formulae:

c1. [(-meat) : (-fish)]

$$:: [\, dx \text{ (meat + fish)} : dx \text{ (vegetable food)}]$$

or, in simplified form (ignoring the minute quantity dx):

c2.   [meat : fish] :: [(meat + fish) : (vegetable food)]

where the sum of (meat + fish) constitutes the category of animal food. It will be noticed, once again, that there is an analogy between the three formulae a, b, and c1 = c2.

The two types of food in the Nass version are berries (downstream) and spawn (upstream). Spawn is an animal food from the river, berries a vegetable food from the land—and, of all earthgrown foods, this (in contrast to the game that is hunted in the mountains) is the one most commonly associated with the river banks.

Thus the transformation that has occurred in the process of transferring the story from the one version to the other can, from this point of view, be written as Formula d:

d. [west: east] :: [sea: land] :: [water: solid ground]:: [river: bank]

But the opposition between the river and its banks is not only a weakened form of the fundamental contrasts between east and west and between solid ground and water, which are most strongly defined in the opposition sea/land. It is also a *function* of this last opposition.

In fact, the opposition river/bank is more strongly defined inland (where the element "water" is reduced to "river") than toward the coast. There the opposition is no longer so pertinent because, in the category "water," the sea takes precedence over the river; and in the category "land," the coast takes precedence over the bank. One can thus understand the logic of the reversal whereby, *up-river*, we are led again to Formula d:

d. [water: solid ground] :: [river: bank]

where the combination (river + bank) has, by permutation, been assimilated into the category "land," this time in opposition to the category "sea"—we are led to Formula e:

e. [water solid ground] :: [sea (river+bank)]

where the combination (river + bank) has, by permutation, been moved into the position originally occupied by "land."

Since d. and e. can be recast in Formula f:

f. [land: water]:: [(river + bank): sea]

which is analogous to formulae a, b, and c, this example shows how a mythological transformation can be expressed by a series of equivalences, such that the two extremes are radically inverted (*S.A.*, pp.224–225).

In fact, in the last stage of the transformation, the (downstream, west) position is occupied by a vegetable food, that is, by an "earth-food"; the (upstream, east) position is occupied by an animal food, which, since it consists of fish spawn, comes from the river and is therefore a "water-food." The two women, reduced to their common denominator, which is the relationship elder/ younger, have thus, in coherent fashion, had their positions exchanged with respect to the relationship upstream/downstream.

Consequently, in the Skeena version, the weak opposition between river and bank is *neutralized* (this is expressed in the myth by specifying that the river is frozen and that the women walk on the ice) in favor of the strong opposition between sea and land which is, however, negatively evoked (since the women are defined by their lack of foods which are associated with their respective positions). In the Nass version it is the strong opposition which is neutralized, by weakening and inversion, in favor of the weak opposition between river and bank, which is positively evoked (since in this case the women are provided, albeit meagerly, with the appropriate foods).

Parallel transformations are to be found in the episode of the supernatural protector as related by the two versions. In that of the Skeena, he provides meat alone, in an ever-increasing quantity (in the order: little squirrel, grouse, porcupine, beaver, goat, black bear, grizzly bear, caribou). In the Nass version, he provides meat and fish at the same time in such large quantities that in that one case the hut is "full of meat and fish" but only "full of dried meat" in the other. In the Skeena version this balance between the two types of life is brought about only much later and in a transitory way: during Asdiwal's third marriage with the sister of the Gitxatla people, when, accompanied.by his brothers-in-law, he is abundantly provided with "salmon and fresh meat," which they sell to the starving Tsimshian (cf. Boas 1902, pp. 225–226; Boas and Hunt 1912,pp. 74–77, 120–123).

On the other hand, Asdiwal's father gives him magic objects which are immediately effective (Skeena version). Those given to Asi-hwil have to be gradually perfected (Ness version). In each case, the hero returns from the west like the food, transported in the insides of a sea lion. But in the second case the change from stomach (Skeena) to intestines (Ness) suggests a food that is nearer to putrefaction, a theme that is final here and no longer initial (a rotten berry was the women's first food in the Skeena version). Nor must it be forgotten that, from this point of view, the candlefish—the only hope of escaping from starvation (in Tsimshian, candlefish is called: *hale-mâ'tk*, which means "saviour")—must be tolerated up to the point of decomposition; otherwise the fish would be offended and would never return.

How can a concrete content be given to this double mechanism of the *weakening of oppositions,* accompanied by a *reversal of correlations* the formal coherence of which we have now established? It should first be noted that the inversion is given in the respective geographical positions of the two populations. The Nisqa, people of the Nass, are found in the north; the Tsimshian (whose name means: "inside the river Skeena" from *K-sia'n,* "Skeena") in the south. In order to marry on (relatively speaking) foreign territory, the Nass hero goes to the land of the Tsimshian—that is to say, toward the Skeena, in the south; and the last marriage of the Skeena-born Asdiwal shows him, up to the time of the break, camping with his in-laws on the Nass and thus in the north. Each population spontaneously forms symmetrical but inverse conceptions of the same country.

But the myths bear witness to the fact that the duality Skeena valley/Ness valley—which, with the region in between, forms the Tsimshian country (in the broadest sense)—is seen as an opposition, as are also the economic activities which are respectively associated with each of the two rivers.

A young man of miraculous birth decided to go up to heaven while night reigned on earth. Changed into a leaf, he impregnated the daughter of the Master of the Sun, who bore a son called Giant. The child seized the sun, made himself master of daylight, and went down to earth where he found himself a companion, Logobola, who was master of mist, water, and marshes. The two boys had a competition, and after several undecided contests they decided to shoot arrows and play for the River Skeena against the River Nass. Giant won by a trick and was so overjoyed that he spoke in Tsimshian—in the dialect of the lower reaches of the Skeena—to voice his feelings. And Logobola said, "You won, brother Giant. Now the candlefish will come to Nass River twice every summer." And Txamsem (Giant) said, "And the salmon of Skeena shall always be fat." Thus they divided what Txamsem had won at Nass River.... After which the two brothers parted.

One of the versions recorded by Boas says, "Txamsem went down to the ocean and Logobola went southward to the place he had come from" (Boas and Hunt 1916, p. 70; cf. Boas and Hunt 1912, p. 7ff.).

In any case, the symmetry of the geographical positions provides only the beginning of an explanation. We have seen that the reversal of correlations is itself the function of a general weakening of all the oppositions, which cannot be explained merely by a substitution of south for north and north for south. In passing from the Skeena to the Nass, the myth becomes distorted in two ways, which are structurally connected. First, it is reduced and, second, it is reversed. In order to be admissible, any interpretation must take account of both of these aspects.

The Skeena people and the Nass people speak similar dialects (Boas and Hunt, 1911). Their social organization is almost identical. But their modes of life are profoundly different. We have described the way of life on the Skeena and on the coast, characterized by a great seasonal movement which is in fact two-phased: between the winter towns and the spring camps on one hand, and then between the spring candlefish season on the Nass and the summer fishing of the salmon on the Skeena.

As for the Nass people, it does not seem that they made periodic visits to the Skeena. The most that we are told is that those who lived very far up the Nass were called kit'anwi'like, "people who left their permanent villages from time to time," because they came down toward the Nass estuary each year, but only for the candlefish season (Sapir 1915, p. 3). The largest seasonal migrations of the Nisqa seem thus to have been limited to the Nass, while those of the Tsimshian were based on a much more complex Skeena-Nass system. The reason is that in March the candlefish visit the Nass, which therefore becomes the meeting place of all the groups who anxiously await the arrival of their "savior." The salmon go up both rivers much later. Thus the Nisqa lived in one valley, and the Tsimshian in two.

Since this is so, all the natives are able to conceptualize the duality Nass/Skeena as an opposition which correlates with that of candlefish/salmon. There can be no doubt about it, since the myth that lays the foundations of this opposition was recorded by Boas in two practically identical versions, one in Nass dialect, the other in Skeena dialect. But an opposition that is recognized by all need not have the same significance for each group. The Tsimshian lived through the opposition in the course of each year; the Nisqa were content to know about it. Although a grammatical construction employing couplets of antithetical terms is present in the Tsimshian tongue as a very obvious model, and probably presents itself as such quite consciously to the speaker, its logical and philosophical implication would not be the same in each of the two groups. The Tsimshian use it to build up a system which is global and coherent but which is not communicable in its entirety to people whose concrete experiences are not stamped with the same duality; perhaps, also, the fact that the course of the Nass is less definitely orientated from east to west than is that of the Skeena, adds to the obscurity of the topographical schema.

Thus we arrive at a fundamental property of mythical thought, other examples of which might well be sought elsewhere. When a mythical schema is transmitted from one population to another, and there exist differences of language, social organization, or way of life that make the myth difficult to communicate, it begins to become impoverished and confused. But one can find a limiting situation in which, instead of being finally obliterated by losing all its outlines, the myth is inverted and regains part of its precision.

Similar inversions occur in optics. An image can be seen in full detail when observed through any adequately large aperture. But as the aperture is narrowed, the image becomes blurred and difficult to see. When, however, the aperture is further reduced to a pinpoint, that is to say, when *communication* is about to vanish, the image is inverted and becomes clear again. This experiment is used in schools to demonstrate the propagation of light in straight lines—in other words, to prove that rays of light are not transmitted at random but within the limits of a structured field.

This study is in its own way an experiment, since it is limited to a single case, and the elements isolated by analysis appear in several series of concomitant variations. If the experiment has helped to demonstrate that the field of mythical thought, too, is structured, then it has achieved its object.

CHAPTER V

Four Winnebago Myths

Claude Lévi-Strauss

Among the many talents which make him one of the great anthropologists of our time, Paul Radin has one which gives a singular flavor to his work. He has the authentic aesthetic touch, rather uncommon in our profession. This is what we call in French flair: the gift of singling out those facts, observations, and documents which possess an especially rich meaning, sometimes undisclosed at first, but likely to become evident as one ponders the implications woven into the material. A crop harvested by Paul Radin—even if he should not choose to mill the grain himself—is always capable of providing lasting nourishment for many generations of students.

This is the reason why I intend to pay my tribute to the work of Paul Radin by giving some thought to four myths which he has published under the title *The Culture of the Winnebago: Described by Themselves* (1949). Radin himself pointed out in the Preface: "In publishing these texts I have only one object in view, to put at the disposal of students authentic material for the study of Winnebago culture." Despite this intention, and despite the fact that the four myths were each obtained from different informants, it seems that, on a structural level, there was good reason for making them the subject of a single publication. A deep unity underlies all four, notwithstanding the fact that one myth (as Radin has shown in his introduction and notes) appears to differ widely in content, style, and structure from the other three. My purpose will be to analyze the structural relationships among the four myths and to suggest that they can be grouped together, not only because they are part of a collection of ethnographic and linguistic data referring to one tribe (which Radin too modestly claims as his sole purpose), but also because they are of the same genre and their meanings logically complement each other.

The title of the first myth is "The Two Friends Who Became Reincarnated: The Origin of the Four Nights' Wake." This is the story of two friends, one of them a chief's son, who decide to sacrifice their lives for the welfare of the community. After their death, they undergo a series of ordeals in the underworld, and finally reach the lodge of Earthmaker, who permits them to become reincarnated and to resume their previous lives among their relatives and friends.

As explained by Radin in his commentary (p. 41, ¶32), there is a native theory underlying the myth. It is that every individual is entitled to a specific quota of years of life and experience on earth. If a person dies before his time, his relatives can ask the spirits to distribute among them the life span which he has failed to utilize.

There is more to this theory than meets the eye. The unspent life span given up by the hero, when he lets himself be killed by the enemies, will be added to the capital of life, set up in trust for the group. Nevertheless, his act of dedication is not entirely without personal profit. By becoming a hero an individual makes a choice, he exchanges a full life span for a shortened one. But while the full life span is unique, granted once and for all, the shortened one appears as the juridical cause of a kind of renewable lease taken on eternity. That is, by giving up one full life, an indefinite succession of half-lives is gained. But since all the years sacrificed by the hero will increase the life expectancy of the ordinary people, everybody gains in the process. This holds for both the ordinary people, whose average life expectancy will slowly but substantially increase generation after generation, and the warriors with shortened but indefinitely renewable lives, provided their minds remain set on self-dedication.

It is not clear, however, that Radin pays full justice to the narrator when he treats as a "secondary interpretation" the fact that the expedition is undertaken by the heroes to show their appreciation of the favors of their fellow villagers (p. 37, ¶2). My contention, based on the previous analysis, is that this motive of the heroes deserves primary emphasis, and it is supported by the fact that there are two war parties. The first is undertaken by the warriors while the heroes are still in their adolescent years, so that they are neither included in nor even informed of it. They hear about the party only as a rumor (¶11–14), and they decide to join it uninvited. We most conclude, then, that the heroes have no responsibility for the very venture wherein they distinguish themselves, since it has been instigated and led by others. Moreover, they are not responsible for the second war party, during which they are killed, since this latter foray has been initiated by the enemy in revenge for the first.

The basic idea is clear. The two friends have made good marriages and have developed into successful social beings (¶66–70). Accordingly, they feel indebted to their fellow tribesmen (¶72). As the story goes, they set out, intending to sacrifice themselves by accomplishing some useful action. They die in an ambush prepared by the enemy to revenge the former defeat. The obvious conclusion is that the heroes have willingly died for the sake of their people. They were innocent of those hostile acts that brought about their death and for which their compatriots bore the responsibility. Yet the latter will inherit the unspent portion of the heroes' lives, given up for their benefit. The heroes themselves will be permitted to return to earth and will probably behave in the same manner; thus the same process of life-transfers will be repeated all over again.

This interpretation is in agreement with information given elsewhere by Radin. In order to pass the test of the Old Woman who rids the soul of all the recollections belonging to its earthly life, each soul must be solicitous not of its own welfare, but of the welfare of the living members of the group.

Now at the root of this myth we find—as the linguists would say—a double opposition. First, there is the opposition between *ordinary life* and *heroic life,* the former realizing the full life span, not renewable, the latter gambling with life for the benefit of the group. The second opposition is between two kinds of death, one straight and final, although it provides a type of unearthly immortality in the villages of the dead; the other oscillating, and swinging between life and death.

Indeed, one is tempted to see the reflection of this double fate in the Winnebago symbol of the ladder of the afterworld as it is expressed in the Medicine Rite. One side is "like a frog's leg, twisted and dappled with light-and-life. The other [is] like a red cedar, blackened from frequent usage and very smooth and shiny" (p. 71,

¶91–93, cf. Radin 1945, especially the author's illuminating comments on pp. 63–65).

To sum up the meaning of the myth so far: If one wants a full life, one gets a full death; if one renounces life and seeks death, then one increases the full life of his fellow-tribesmen, and secures for oneself a state composed of an indefinite series of half-lives and half-deaths. Thus we have a triangular system, shown in Figure 14.

Reincarnation
(half-life, half-death)
Full life   ―――――――――   Full death

FIGURE 14

The second myth, entitled "The Man Who Brought His Wife Back from Spiritland," is a variation on the same theme, although there is a significant difference involved. Here too, we find a hero— the husband—ready to sacrifice his unspent life span; not, as in the first myth, for the benefit of the group, but rather for the benefit of only one individual, his beloved wife who has been taken away from him. Indeed, the hero is not aware at first that by seeking death he will secure a new lease on life for both his dead wife and himself. Had he been so aware—and this holds equally for the protagonists in the first myth—the essential element of sacrifice would have been missing. In both cases the result is similar: An altruistic loss of life means life regained, not only for the self- appointed victim, but also for the one or more persons to whom the sacrifice was consecrated.

The third myth, "The Journey of the Ghost to Spiritland, as Told in the Medicine Rite," belongs, as the title suggests, to a religious society. It explains how the members of the Medicine Rite, after death, undergo (as do the protagonists of the other myths) several tests in Spiritland, which they overcome, thus gaining the right to become reincarnated.

At first sight this situation seems to differ from the others, since nobody sacrificed his life. However, the members of the Medicine Rite actually spend their lives in symbolic sacrifice. As Radin has shown, in *The Road of Life and Death* and elsewhere, the Medicine Rite follows the pattern familiar in North America of letting oneself be "killed" and then "revived." Thus the only departure consists in the fact that, whereas in the first and second myths the heroes are willing to die once and (so they anticipate) permanently, the heroes of the third myth (the members of the Rite) repeatedly, though symbolically, have trained themselves to self-sacrifice. They have, so to speak, mithridatized themselves against real death by renouncing a full ordinary life which is replaced, in ritual practice, by a lifelong succession of half-lives and half-deaths. Hence we are entitled to assume that, in this case too, the myth is made up of the same elements, although the individual—and not another person, nor the group as a whole—is conceived as the primary beneficiary of his sacrifice.

Let us now consider the fourth myth, "How an Orphan Restored the Chief's Daughter to Life," a tale that has given Radin some concern. This myth, he says, is not only different from the other three: its plot appears unusual relative to the rest of Winnebago mythology. After recalling that in his book *Method and Theory of Ethnology* (1933, pp. 238–245), he suggested that this myth was a version, altered almost beyond recognition, of a type which he then called village-origin myths, he proceeds to explain in *The Culture of the Winnebago* (1949, pp. 74ff.) why he can no longer support this earlier interpretation.

It is worthwhile to follow closely Radin's new line of reasoning. He begins by recapitulating the plot—such a simple plot, he says, that there is practically no need for doing so: "The daughter of a tribal chief falls in love with an orphan, dies of a broken heart, and is then restored to life by the orphan who must submit to and overcome certain tests, not in spiritland but here, on earth, in the very lodge in which the young woman died" (p. 74).

If this plot is "simplicity itself," where do the moot points lie? Radin lists three which he says every modern Winnebago would question: (1) the plot seems to refer to a highly stratified society; (2) in order to understand the plot, one should assume that in that society women occupied a high position and that, possibly, descent was reckoned in the matrilineal line; and (3) the tests which in Winnebago mythology usually take place in the land of ghosts occur, in this instance, on earth.

After considering two possible explanations and dismissing them—that we are dealing here with a borrowed European tale or that the myth was invented by some Winnebago radical—Radin concludes that the myth must belong to "a very old stratum of

Winnebago history." He also suggests that two distinct types of literary tradition, divine tales and human tales, have merged with certain archaic elements and that all these disparate elements have then been reinterpreted to make them fit together.

I am certainly not going to challenge this elegant reconstruction backed by an incomparable knowledge of Winnebago culture, language, and history. The following analysis does not pretend to offer an alternative to Radin's own analysis, but to complement it. It lies on a different level, logical rather than historical, and it takes as its context the three myths already discussed—not Winnebago culture, old or recent. My purpose is to seek the structural relationship—if any—which prevails between the four myths, and to explicate it.

First, there is a theoretical problem which should be noted briefly. Since the publication of Boas' *Tsimshian Mythology*, anthropologists have often simply assumed that a full correlation exists between the myths of a given society and its culture. This, I feel, is going further than Boas intended. In the work just referred to, he did not suppose that myths automatically reflect the culture, as some of his followers always seemed to anticipate. More modestly, he tried to find out how much of the culture actually did pass into the myths, if any, and he convincingly showed that some of it does. It does not follow that whenever a social pattern is alluded to in a myth this pattern must correspond to something real and attributable to the past if, under direct scrutiny, the present fails to offer an equivalent.

There must be, and there is, a correspondence between the unconscious meaning of a myth—the problem it tries to solve—and the conscious content it makes use of to reach that end, i.e., the plot. However, this correspondence is not necessarily an exact reproduction; it can also appear as a logical transformation. If the problem is presented in straight terms—that is, in the way the social life of the group expresses and tries to solve it—the overt content of the myth, the plot, can borrow its elements from social life itself. But should the problem be formulated upside down, and its solution sought for *ad absurdo*, then the overt content can be expected to become modified accordingly to form an inverted image of the social pattern actually present in the consciousness of the natives.

If this hypothesis is true, it follows that Radin's assumption that the pattern of social life referred to in the fourth myth must belong to a past stage of Winnebago history is not inescapable. We may be confronted with the pattern of a nonexistent society, past or present—even one contrary to the Winnebago traditional pattern— only because the structure of that particular myth is itself inverted, in relation to those myths which use as overt content the traditional pattern. To put it simply, if a certain correspondence is assumed between A and B then if A is replaced by -A, B most be replaced by -B. without implying that, since B corresponds to an external object, there should exist another external object -B. which must exist somewhere: either in another society (borrowed element) or in a past stage of the same society (survival).

Obviously, the problem remains: Why do we have three myths of the A type and one of the -A type? This could be the case because -A is older than A. But it can also be so because -A is one of the transformations A_4 of A, which is already known to us under the three guises A_1, A_2, A_3 since we have seen that the three myths of the assumed A type are not identical.

We have already established that the group of myths under consideration is based upon a fundamental opposition between the lives of ordinary people unfolding toward a natural death, followed by the banal existence of their soul in one of the spirit villages, and the lives of heroes, whose unspent life span increases the life quota for the others and gives the hero a new lease on life. The first three myths do not envisage the first term of the alternative; they are exclusively concerned with the second. But there is a secondary difference which permits us to classify these myths according to the particular end assigned to the self-sacrifice in each In the first myth, the group is intended to be the immediate beneficiary; in the second it is another individual (the wife) and in the third it is the victim himself.

When we turn to the fourth myth, we will agree with Radin that it exhibits "unusual" features in relation to the other three. However, the difference seems to be of a logical, rather than of a sociological or historical nature. It consists in a new opposition introduced within the first pair of opposites (between "ordinary" life and "extraordinary" life). Now there are two ways in which an "extraordinary" phenomenon may be construed as such: by excess or by default, consisting in either a surplus or in a lack. While the heroes of the first three myths are all overgifted—with social dedication, conjugal love, or mystical fervor—the two heroes of the fourth myth are, if one may say so, "below standard" in at least one respect, which is not the same for each.

The chief's daughter occupies a high social position, so high, in face, that she is cut off from the rest of the group and is therefore paralyzed when it comes to expressing her feelings. Her exalted position makes her a defective human being, lacking an essential attribute of emotional life. The boy is also defective, but socially; he is an orphan and very poor. May we say, then, that the myth reflects a stratified society? This would compel us to overlook the remarkable symmetry which prevails between our two heroes, for it would be wrong simply to say that one is high and the other low. As a matter of fact, each of them is high in one respect and low in the other, and this pair of symmetrical and inverted structures belongs to the realm of ideological constructs rather than of sociological systems. We have just seen that the girl occupies a high social position, but that, as a living creature, thus from the natural point of view, she has a low position. The boy is undoubtedly very low in the social scale. However, he is a miraculous hunter, who entertains privileged relations with the natural world, the world of animals. This is emphasized over and over again in the myth (¶10–14, 17–18, 59–60, 77–90).

May we not therefore claim that the myth actually confronts us with a polar system bringing together—and at the same time opposing—two individuals, one male, the other female, and both exceptional insofar as each of them is overgifted one way (+) and undergifted in the other (-)? (See Figure 15.)

	Nature	Culture
Boy	+	−
Girl	−	+

FIGURE 15

The plot consists in carrying this disequilibrium to its logical extreme. The girl dies a *natural* death; the boy stays alone and goes through a *social* death. Whereas during their ordinary lives the girl was overtly above and the boy overtly below, now that they have become segregated (either from the living or from society), their positions are inverted: the girl is below (in her grave), the boy above (in his lodge). This, I think, is clearly implied in a detail stated by the narrator which seems to have puzzled Radin: "On top of the grave they then piled loose dirt, placing everything in such a way that nothing could seep through" (p. 87, (¶52). Radin comments: "I do not understand why piling the dirt loosely would prevent seepage. There must be something else involved that has not been mentioned" (p. 100, n. 40). I would like to suggest that this detail be correlated with a similar detail about the building of the young man's lodge: ". . . the bottom was piled high with dirt so that, in this fashion, they could keep the lodge warm" (p. 87, ¶74). There is implied here, I think, not a reference to recent or past custom but rather a clumsy attempt to emphasize that, relative to the earth's surface, the boy is now above and the girl below.

This new equilibrium, however, will be no more lasting than the first. *She who unable to live cannot die:* her ghost "lingers on earth." In that form, she finally induces the young man to fight the ghosts and take her back among the living. With a wonderful symmetry, the boy will meet, a few years later, with a similar, although inverted, fate: "Although I am not yet old," he says to the girl (now his wife), "I have been here [lasted] on earth as long as I can...." (p. 94, (¶341). *He who overcame death proves unable to live.* This recurring antithesis could develop indefinitely, and such a possibility is noted in the text (by giving the hero an only son, he too soon an orphan, he too a sharpshooter). But a different solution is finally reached. The heroes, equally unable to die or to live, will assume an intermediate identity, that of twilight creatures living under the earth but also able to come up on it. They will be neither men nor gods, but wolves; that is, ambivalent spirits combining good and evil features. So ends the myth.

If the above analysis is correct, two consequences follow. First, our myth makes up a consistent whole wherein the details balance and fit each other nicely. Secondly, the three problems raised by Radin can be analyzed in terms of the myth itself. No hypothetical past stage of Winnebago society, which could only be a conjecture, need be invoked.

Let us, then, try to solve these three problems, following the pattern of our analysis.

1. The society of the myth appears stratified, only because the two heroes are conceived as a pair of opposites, but their opposition is shown from the point of view of both nature and culture. Thus the so-called stratified society should be interpreted, not as a sociological vestige, but as a projection on some imaginary social order of a logical structure wherein all the elements are given both in opposition and in correlation.

2. The same answer can be given to the question of the assumed exalted position of the women. If I am right, our myths state three propositions, the first by implication, the second expressly stated in the myths 1, 2, and 3, the third expressly stated in myth 4.

These propositions are as follow:

a. Ordinary people live (their full lives) and die (their full deaths)
b. Extraordinary people with positive attributes die (earlier) and live (again).
c. Extraordinary people with negative attributes are able neither to live nor to die.

Obviously, proposition (c) offers an inverted demonstration of the truth of (a) and (b). Hence, it must use a plot starting with protagonists (here, man and woman) in inverted positions, so that each one may assume half of the demonstration, symmetrical to the other half incumbent to the other person. This leads us to state that a plot and its component parts should neither be interpreted by themselves nor relative to something outside the realm of the myth proper, but as substitutions given in and understandable only with reference to a group of myths.

3. We may now come to the last problem raised by Radin about the fourth myth: Why does the contest with the ghosts take place on earth instead of, as was usually the case, in Spiritland. To this query I shall suggest an answer along the same lines as the others. It is precisely because our two heroes are seen as *underliving* (one in respect to culture, the other to nature) that, in the narrative, the ghosts become a kind of *superdead.* It will be recalled that the whole myth develops and is resolved on an intermediary level, where human beings become underground animals and ghosts linger on earth. It tells about people who are, from the start, half-alive and half-dead; in the preceding myths, the opposition between life and

death is strongly emphasized at the beginning and overcome only at the end. Thus, the integral meaning of the four myths is that, in order to be overcome, the opposition between life and death should be first acknowledged, or else the ambiguous state will persist indefinitely.

I hope to have shown that the four myths under consideration all belong to the same transformational group and that Radin was even more right than he supposed in publishing them together. In the first place, the four myths deal with extraordinary (in opposition to ordinary) fate. The fact that ordinary fate is illustrated here and thus is reckoned as an "empty" category, does not imply, of course, that it cannot be illustrated elsewhere. In the second place, we find an opposition between two types of extraordinary fate, by excess or by lack. This new dichotomy which permits us to distinguish myth 4 from myths 1, 2, and 3 corresponds, on a logical level, to the discrimination that Radin makes on psychological, sociological, and historical grounds. Finally, myths 1, 2, and 3 have been classified according to the purpose of the sacrifice of the hero or heroes, which is the theme of each.

Thus the myths can be organized in a dichotomous system with several levels of correlations and oppositions. But we can go even further and try to order them on a common scale. This is suggested by the curious variations which can be observed in each myth with respect to the kind of test the hero is put to by the ghosts. In myth 3 there is no test at all, so far as the ghosts are concerned. The rests consist in overcoming material obstacles, while the ghosts themselves figure as indifferent fellow travelers. In myth they cease to be indifferent without yet becoming hostile; on the contrary, the hero most resist their overfriendliness by resisting inviting female spirits and the infectious good humor of male spirits who pose—to better fool him—as merrymakers. Thus, from *companions* in myth 3 they change to *seducers* in myth 1. In myth 2 they will behave as human beings, but they now act as *aggressors*, and permit themselves all kinds of rough play. This is even more evident in myth 4, but here their human appearance vanishes. It is only at the end that we know that ghosts, in the form of crawling insects, are responsible for the trials of the hero. We have thus, from one myth to the other, a twofold progression: from a peaceful attitude to an aggressive one, and from human to nonhuman behavior.

This progression can be also correlated with the kind of relationship which the hero (or heroes) of each myth entertains with the social group.

The hero of myth 3 belongs to a ritual brotherhood. He definitely assumes his privileged fate as member of a group, acting with and in his group. The two heroes of myth have resolved to part from the group, but the text states repeatedly that this is in order to find an opportunity to achieve some worthy deed that will benefit their fellow tribesmen. They act, therefore, for the group. But in myth 2 the hero is only inspired by his love for his wife. There is no reference to the group. The action is undertaken independently for the sake of another individual. Finally, in myth 4 the two heroes' negative attitude toward the group is clearly revealed; the girl dies of her inability to communicate; indeed, she prefers to die rather than speak, believing death to be her final exile. As for the boy, he refuses to follow the villagers when they decide to move away and abandon the grave. The segregation is thus willfully sought by both protagonists and their actions unroll against the group.

Figure 16 summarizes our discussion. I am quite aware that the argument, in order to be fully convincing, should not be limited to the four myths considered here, but should include more of the invaluable Winnebago mythology which Radin has given us. But I hope that by integrating more material, the basic structure outlined has, at least, become richer and more complex without being impaired. By singling out one small book which its author would perhaps consider a minor contribution, I have intended to emphasize, in an indirect way, the fecundity of the method followed by Radin, and the lasting value of the problems he posed.

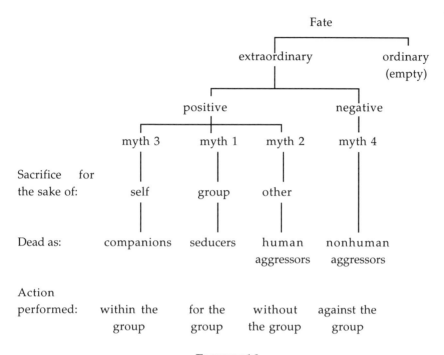

FIGURE 16

PART TWO:

ESSAYS ON LÉVI-STRAUSS

CHAPTER VI

Structuralism, Anthropology and Lévi-Strauss

Hans Penner

Let us start with Saussure once again. At the beginning of the *Course*, he had this to say about the place of linguistics in the human sciences (or at least this is what his students wrote in their notebooks):

"Language is a system of signs that expresses ideas and is therefore comparable to a system of writing, the alphabet of deaf-mutes, symbolic rites, polite formulas, military signals, etc. But it is the most important of these systems.
A science that studies the life of signs within society is conceivable; it would be a part of social psychology and consequently of general psychology; I shall call it *semiology* (from the Greek *semion* 'sign'). Semiology would show what constitutes signs, what laws govern them. Since the science does not yet exist, no one can say what it would be; but it has a right to existence, a place staked out in advance. Linguistics is only a part of the general science of semiology; the laws discovered by semiology will be applicable to linguistics, and the latter will circumscribe a well-defined area within the mass of anthropological facts" (*Course*; 16).

In his inaugural address for the chair of social anthropology at the Collège de France, Lévi-Strauss asked the following question: "What, then, is social anthropology?" He answered as follows:

Although he did not specifically name it, Ferdinand de Saussure came very close to defining it when he introduced linguistics as part of a science yet to be born, for which he reserved the name 'semiology'.... We conceive anthropology as the *bona fide* occupant of that domain of semiology which linguistics has not already claimed for its own. Four years earlier, he asserted that "From the standpoint with which we are concerned here, linguistics is in a very special position. It is classified as one of the sciences of man, but it is concerned with social phenomenon, for language not only implies life in a society but is indeed the very foundation of that life. What sort of society could there be without language? It is the most perfect and most complex of those communication systems in which all social life consists and with which all the social sciences, each in its special field, are concerned. Consequently, we may say that any revolution in linguistics is pertinent alike to the social sciences and the sciences of man. Between 1870 and 1920, two basic ideas were introduced into this sphere—first under the influence of the Russian, Beaudoin de Courtenay, and later under that of the Swiss, Saussure. The first was that language is made up of separate elements, or phonemes; the second, that it is possible, by linguistic analysis, to work out systems or in other words, combinations governed by some law of cohesion, in which, as a result, changes occurring in one part necessarily entail others, that can therefore be foreseen (*Structural Anthropology* Vol. II, 9–10, hereafter referred to as *S.A. II*).

And again, "Anthropology aims to be a *semiological* science and takes as a guiding principle that of 'meaning.' This is yet another reason. (in addition to others) why anthropology should maintain close contact with linguistics where, with regard to this social fact of speech, there is the same concern to avoid separating the objective basis of language (sound) from its signifying function (meaning)" (*Structural Anthropology*, Vol. I, 364–5, hereafter referred to as *S.A. I*). It is this inheritance from Saussure which permeates what Lévi-Strauss has written. The project is to investigate all levels and aspects of culture as a system of signs.

But this inheritance has a curious, if not important, ambiguity in it. In spite of all that has been written about Lévi-Strauss as a formalist unconcerned with history, it is precisely Saussure's radical opposition between the synchronic and diachronic that bothers him. Lévi-Strauss accepts the description of the synchronic as a relation between "simultaneous elements" and the diachronic as "the substitution of one element for another in time, an event." What he rejects from the *Course* is the notion that there is nothing in common between the synchronic and the diachronic, or, that they are in radical opposition to each other "This," says Lévi-Strauss, "is the very aspect of Saussurian doctrine from which modern structuralism, with Trubetzkoy and Jakobson, has most resolutely diverged, and about which modern documents show that the master's thought has at times been forced and schematized by the editors of the *Course*." He then goes on to assert that "For the editors *Course in General Linguistics,* an absolute opposition exists between the categories of fact: on the one hand, that of grammar, the synchronic, the conscious; on the other hand, that of phonetics, the diachronic, the unconscious" (*S.A. II*, 16).

Now unless the editors of the course got the lectures complete wrong, Lévi-Strauss, I think, must be mistaken in the above description of the Saussurian distinction between the synchronic and diachronic. (As we can see, when we disagree with Saussure we can always blame the editors.) Without entering into the debate about the author vs. his editors, I believe that Lévi-Strauss has distorted what Saussure had mind in using these important distinctions. We must assume that Saussure did use chess as an example at three different times in the lectures. The first is an excellent example of chess as an analogy of system and the synchronic. The origins of chess, whether we use ivory pieces, toothpicks, or no pieces at all, are irrelevant to chess as a synchronic system based on rules. The elements of the game (the pieces) are defined by the relations they enter into as defined by the rules.

In the second example, Saussure uses chess once again to illustrate the synchronic state in language. First, the respective value of the various pieces depends on their position on the board "just as each linguistic term derives its value from its opposition to all the other terms." Second, "the system is always momentary," and finally, to pass from one synchronic state to the next, only one piece has to be moved, which has an effect on the whole system, including those pieces which are not immediately involved. "In chess, each move is absolutely distinct from the preceding and the subsequent equilibrium. The change effected belongs to neither state: only states matter." Saussure then discovers a glaring weakness in this analogy. He realizes that it is the "chessplayer [who] *intends* to bring about a shift and thereby to exert an action on the system, whereas language premeditates nothing." He corrects this by asserting, "In order to make the game of chess seem at every point like the functioning of language, we would have to imagine an unconscious or unintelligent player." The context tells us that Saussure is describing synchronic states, which as the example demonstrates have nothing to do with "consciousness" or "intentions." In fact, by stressing the weakness of his analogy and correcting it, Saussure is satisfied that the correction, imagining an unconscious player, makes the analogy between chess and language fit at every point of comparison.

Thus, I think that Lévi-Strauss has made a mistake about the nature of the synchronic and diachronic in the *Course*. There seems to be no doubt that Saussure did mark them as in opposition to each other and that this opposition is absolute. It is this radical distinction between the two domains that Lévi-Strauss rejects and it is this revision of structural linguistics that has important consequences for what Lévi-Strauss has to say about history.

In his response to the criticisms of Haudricourt and Granai, Lévi-Strauss reduced their misunderstandings to two fundamental errors. The first is that the criticism overemphasized the arbitrary nature of language in contrast to the non-arbitrary nature of other cultural phenomena. The second error is based on an overemphasis on the contrast between the synchronic and the diachronic. Lévi-Strauss attempts to correct both of these errors by appealing to Jakobson who claimed that it was an illusion, both superficial and dangerous, to create a chasm between the synchronic and the diachronic. The first error was corrected by Benveniste who thought that the relation between the signifier and signified was in fact a necessary relation, and therefore, not at all arbitrary.

I think that anyone who has worked through the literature would agree that it is a mistake to make a radical distinction between the synchronic and the diachronic in an analysis of language. In fact, it might be best to view these terms as methodological devices which are useful in making important distinctions in our analysis of the object of linguistics rather than being inherent features of language. Be that as it may, I am not satisfied with Lévi-Strauss's solution to the criticism concerning the arbitrary nature of language. Here, briefly, is his solution to the problem:

> To simplify my argument, I will say that the linguistic sign is arbitrary *a priori*, but ceases to be arbitrary *a posteriori*. Nothing existing *a priori* in the nature of certain preparations made of fermented milk requires the sound-form *fromage* [cheese], or rather, *from* (since the ending is shared with other words). It is sufficient to compare the French *froment* [wheat], whose semantic content is entirely different, to the English word cheese, which means the same thing as *fromage*, though it utilizes different phonemic material. So far, the linguistic sign appears to be arbitrary.

On the other hand, it is in no way certain that these phonemic options, which are arbitrary in relation to the *designatum*, do not, once the choice has been made, imperceptibly affect, perhaps not the general meaning of words, but their position within a semantic environment. This *a posteriori* influence works on two levels, the phonemic and the lexical (*S.A.*, 91).

Lévi-Strauss sums up this complicated statement with "If we admit, therefore, in accordance with the Saussurian principle, that nothing compels, *a priori*, certain sound clusters to denote certain objects, it appears probable, nonetheless, that once they are adopted, these sound clusters transmit particular shadings to the semantic content with which they have become associated" (*S.A.*, 92).

This reply to his critics makes the same mistake that Benveniste points out that Saussure made when he claimed that language (signs) is arbitrary. Although we have referred to Benveniste's correction in the last chapter, it now becomes necessary to describe it more fully. Benveniste recognizes that Saussure is the source for the idea of the linguistic sign in works on general linguistics and he accepts it as an obvious truth that Saussure thought that the linguistic sign was arbitrary. He also recognizes that this notion has become obvious to everyone else who cites it in publications on linguistics. In his celebrated essay, Benveniste sets out to explain what Saussure meant by the term "arbitrary" and how he went about proving it.

Here are the central points made by Benveniste on Saussure's doctrine of the arbitrariness of the sign.

Saussure took the linguistic sign to be made up of a signifier and signified. Now—and this is essential—he meant by 'signifier' the *concept*. He declared in so many words that the 'linguistic sign unites, not a thing and a name, but as concept and a sound image.' But immediately afterward he stated that the nature of the sign is arbitrary because it 'actually has no natural connection with the signified.' It is clear that the argument is falsified by an unconscious and surreptitious recourse to a third term which was not included in the initial definition. This third term is the thing itself, the reality.... When he spoke of the difference between b-ö-f and o-k-s, he was referring in spite of himself to the fact that these two terms applied to the same reality. Here, then, is the *thing*, expressly excluded at first from the definition of the sign, now creeping into it by detour, and permanently installing a contradiction here." He goes on to assert that "One of the components of the sign, the sound image, makes up the signifier; the other, the concept, is the signified. Between the signifier and the signified, the connection is not arbitrary; on the contrary it is *necesS.A.ry*. The concept (the 'signified') *boeuf* is perforce identical in my consciousness with the sound sequence (the 'signifier') böf.... The mind does not contain empty forms, concepts without names.... The signifier is the phonic translation of a concept; the signified is the mental counterpart of the signifier. This consubstantiality of the signifier and the signified assures the structural unity of the linguistic sign' (*Problems in General Linguistics*, 43–45).

And then Benveniste appeals to Saussure: "Language can also be compared with a sheet of paper: thought is the front and the sound the back; one cannot cut the front without cutting the back at the same time; likewise in language, one can neither divide sound from thought nor thought from sound; the division could be accomplished only abstractedly, and the result would be either pure psychology or pure phonology." (*Problems in General Linguistics*, 43–45) Thus, what is arbitrary is the fact that one sign and no other is applied to a certain object, or thing, in the world. What Saussure demonstrated was that it is not the sign that is arbitrary but "signification," the designatum. If I understand this correctly, reference to an object, to something "in reality," is bracketed in structure linguistics.

The proper reply that Lévi-Strauss should have given his critics is that although the relation, the signification, between a sign and a thing in "reality" is indeed arbitrary this is irrelevant to an analysis of the nature of signs. He seems to assert this when he says that "The meaning of a word depends on the way in which each language breaks up the realm of meaning to which the word belongs; and it is a function of the presence or absence of other words denoting related meanings." (*S.A.*, 93) The problem of the relation of language to the world is, I believe, yet to be resolved. The early success of linguistics came about because it set aside the problem of semantics. Let us remember that linguistics, the study of signs, did not begin with "signification" as the fundamental object for analysis. This does not mean that "signification" is not a problem, it is as old as Plato's *Cratylus* and Cratylus has yet to return from the countryside with an answer. As we shall see, Lévi-Strauss remains for the most part consistent with the structuralist focus on the sign, and not signification, as the object of analysis.

He has also remained consistent in maintaining that the synchronic and diachronic are not to be viewed as in radical opposition. The criticism, therefore, that Lévi-Strauss operates purely on a synchronic level, or thinks that the diachronic is simply the synchronic in its transformations through time, misses the mark. To be sure, Lévi-Strauss can become his own worst enemy in creating dense stylistic paragraphs and mind-boggling examples on this subject. In most instances, however, I think that setting his remarks in their proper context helps make his position clear.

The common criticism on Lévi-Strauss' use of synchrony and diachrony is usually set in the context of the suspicion that he is an idealist, a formalist, if not an outright Hegelian. In most of such criticisms, these are labels which represent a characteristic unwillingness to take him seriously, defensive walls set up to protect positions he has threatened by his own criticism of historicism, naturalism, phenomenology, and essentialism.

An influential critic of Lévi-Strauss goes after him from a different perspective; Marxism. After describing the Hegelian notion of time and history, Althusser writes:

> I have insisted on the nature of historical time and its theoretical conditions to this extent because this [Hegelian] conception of history and of its relation to time is still alive amongst us, as can be seen from the currently widespread distinction between synchrony and diachrony.... The synchronic is contemporaneity itself, the co-presence of the essence with its determinations, the present being readable as a structure in an 'essential section' because the present is the very existence of the essential structure. The synchronic therefore presupposes the ideological conception of a continuous-homogeneous time. It follows that the diachronic is merely the development of this present in the sequence of a temporal continuity in which the 'events' to which 'history' in the strict sense can be reduced (cf. Lévi-Strauss) are merely successive contingent presents in the time continuum. (*Reading Capitol*; 95–96)

Nothing could be farther from the truth! Rather than simply stating this and then writing "cf. Lévi-Strauss" in parentheses, as is usually the practice, let us actually take a look at what Lévi-Strauss says. Let us also choose a text, *The S.A.vage Mind*, which was in print before Althusser published his own book.

In describing "The Logic of Totemic Classifications," in *The S.A.vage Mind*, Lévi-Strauss writes,

> Whenever social groups are named, the conceptual system formed by these names is, as it were, prey to the whims of demographic change which follows its own laws but is related to it only contingently. The system is given, synchronically, while demographic changes take place diachronically, in other words there are two determinations, each operating on its own account and independently of the other. This conflict between synchrony and diachrony is also found on the linguistic plane.... Nevertheless the connection between synchrony and diachrony is not rigid (*S.A.vage Mind*, 66–67, hereafter referred to as *SM*).

Here is a second example in the context of an analysis of an Osage legend,

> The legend suggests twin processes. One is purely structural, passing from a dual to a three-fold system and then returning to the earlier dualism; the other, both structural and historical at the same time, consists in undoing the effects of an overthrow of the primitive structure, resulting from historical events, or events thought of as such: migrations, war, alliance (*SM*, 69).

In the same context, Lévi-Strauss quotes M. Roger Priouret's concluding words at a conference (I shall paraphrase for the sake of brevity): "We are faced with two diametrically opposed theories. Raymond Aron thinks there are two basic political attitudes in France, Bonapartist and Orleanist. In moments of crisis France changes its attitude from one to the other. My view is that although actual change is not independent of these constants the change is connected with upheavals which industrialization brings into society." Lévi-Strauss then adds, "The Osage would probably have used these two types of opposition, one synchronic and the other diachronic, as a point of departure. Instead of expecting to be able to choose between them, they would have accepted both on the same footing and would have tried to work out a single scheme which allowed them to combine the standpoint of structure and event"(*SM*, 70). In reflecting on "Categories, Elements, Species, Numbers," he writes, "Even if consciously or unconsciously, they apply rules of marriage whose effect is to keep the social structure and rate of reproduction constant, these mechanisms never function perfectly; and they are also endangered by wars, epidemics, and famines. It is thus plain that history and demographic developments always upset the plans conceived by the wise. In such societies there is a constantly repeated battle between synchrony and diachrony from which it seems that diachrony must emerge victorious every time" (*SM*, 156).

The variations on the Althusserian misunderstanding are so widespread that I shall refer to one more statement from Lévi-Strauss. In "Time Regained" he has this to say about the synchronic and the diachronic in the context of myth and ritual:

> It can thus be said that the function of the system of ritual is to overcome and integrate three oppositions: that of diachrony and synchrony; that of the periodic or non-periodic features which either [i.e. historical or mourning rites] may exhibit; and finally, within diachrony, that of reversible and irreversible time, for, although the present and past are theoretically distinct, the historical rites bring the past into the present and the rites of mourning the present into the past, and the two processes are not equivalent (*SM*, 237).

We must also keep in mind the larger context which sets the framework for this analysis. There is indeed a polemic running through what Lévi-Strauss has to say. In "History and Dialectic" he makes clear what it is he opposes. He rejects those philosophies which attach a special privilege to historical knowledge and the temporal dimension as if "diachrony were to establish a kind of intelligibility not merely superior to that provided by synchrony, but above all more specifically human.... History seems to do more than describe beings to us from the outside, or at best give us intermittent flashes of insight into internalities, each of which are so on their own account while remaining external to each other: it appears to re-establish our connection, outside ourselves, with the very essence of change." He then says, "There could be plenty to say about this supposed totalizing continuity of the self which seems to me to be an illusion sustained by the demands of social life —and consequently a reflection of the external on the internal—rather: than the object of an apodictic experience." After an analysis of the claim that historical knowledge is somehow privileged, Lévi-Strauss concludes that historical facts are no more *given* than any others (*SM*, 256–7). This argument is similar to his rejection, throughout all of his publications, of claims such as those made by Levy-Bruhl that the mentality of "primitives" is different than ours or that, through some kind of historical evolution of stages, it is we who have reached the summit of rationality.

It would seem that Lévi-Strauss is closer to Althusser than he is to Hegel. Let us return to the last quotation in the above paragraph. What more could be said about the supposed totalizing continuity of the self which seems to Lévi-Strauss to be an illusion, "sustained by the demand of social life—and consequently a reflection of the external on the internal—rather than an object of an apodictic experience?" The first thing that can be said is that Lévi-Strauss in this passage is clearly rejecting the Cartesian *cogito* as well as all phenomenological notions c a transcendental subjectivity or ego. Secondly, he is also rejecting all forms of idealism. He was well aware of the fact that given what he wrote about society and culture he would be accused of idealism. He was right.

I do not wish to misunderstood. I am not mounting a defense of Lévi-Strauss against his critics. There is sufficient evidence to confirm that he is capable of defending himself. The task at present is to clarify structural analysis by an examination of its beginnings in the work of Lévi-Strauss. This is important simply because it is not an uncommon practice to read critiques or reviews instead of the actual text. A good example which should confirm or disconfirm the above accusation is the subject of ideology. What then has Lévi-Strauss actually said about ideology and its place in history and philosophy?

He has said that, "I do not at all mean to suggest that ideological transformations give rise to social ones. Only the reverse is true. Men's conception of the relations between nature and culture is a function of modifications of their own social relations" (*SM*, 117). And he repeats this claim several pages later:

> Here again I do not mean to suggest that social life, the relations between man and nature, are a projection or even result, of a conceptual game taking place in the mind.... Without questioning the undoubted primacy of infrastructures, I believe that there is always a mediator between *praxis* and practices, namely the conceptual scheme by the operation of which matter and form, neither with any independent existence, are realized as structures, that is as entities which are both empirical and intelligible. It is to this theory of superstructures, scarcely touched on by Marx, that I hope to make a contribution. The development of the study of infrastructures proper is a task which must be left to history—with the aid of demography, technology, historical geography and ethnography.... All that I claim to have shown so far is, therefore, that the dialectic of superstructures, like that of language, consists in setting up *constitutive units* (which,

for this purpose, have to be defined unequivocally, that is by contrasting them in pairs) so as to be able by means of them to elaborate a system which plays the part of a synthesizing operator between ideas and facts, thereby turning the latter into signs (*SM*, 130–1).

In a note to his analysis of "The Story of Asdiwal," he reminds us once again that, "From the very beginning the myth seems governed by one particular opposition which is more vital than the others... that between earth and water which is also the one most closely linked with methods of production and the objective relationships between men and the world. Formal though it be, analysis of a society's myths verifies the primacy of the infrastructures."

Ten years earlier he put it this way:

> All the models considered so far, however, are 'lived-in' orders: they correspond to mechanisms which can be studied as part of objective reality [i.e. infrastructures]. But no systematic studies of these orders can be undertaken without acknowledging the fact that social groups, to achieve their reciprocal ordering need to call on orders of different types, corresponding to a field external to objective reality and which we call the 'supernatural.' These 'thought-of' orders [i.e. superstructures] cannot be checked against the experience to which they refer, since they are one and the same as this experience. Therefore, we are in the position of studying them only in their relationships with the other types of 'lived-in' orders (*S.A.*, 312-3).

It is within this context, I think, that Lévi-Strauss' famous definition of myth can be fully understood. "The purpose of myth," says Lévi-Strauss, "is to provide a logical model capable of overcoming a contradiction (an impossible achievement if, as it happens, the contradiction is real), a theoretically infinite number of slates will be generated, each one slightly different from the others." Overcoming a contradiction will be an impossible achievement if, as it happens, the contradiction is "real," that is to say, if the contradiction is inherent in the infrastructure, the objective conditions of existence, the "lived-in" order of human existence. In brief, "existence is not determined by consciousness, but consciousness by existence."

These passages should confirm that Lévi-Strauss's brand of structuralism is not a philosophically transformed extension of Hegelian or Kantian idealism. But, it must also be noted that it is not an extension of "vulgar" Marxism either! From a personal point of view, I think that when a new approach appears in the history of the human sciences that is attacked by both phenomenological idealism and Marxian materialism, as well as from the side of British and American empiricist/functionalism, then it might just be the case that this new approach deserves careful attention. Lévi-Strauss must be doing something right!

Personal opinion aside, Lévi-Strauss is vulnerable precisely because of the position he takes. Scholars from different disciplines who are sympathetic with what he has accomplished have pointed out in one way or the other that what has not been resolved is the precise relations between the infrastructure and the superstructure, between the "lived-in" and "thought-of' orders of life. Lévi-Strauss cannot evade this issue by stating that the one belongs to ethnography and the other to ethnology, or that one belongs to history, the other to psychology. But, Lévi-Strauss is also aware of the fact that an analysis of the relation between the material conditions (infrastructure) of existence and ideology (superstructure) cannot simply be solved by a return to functionalism, even though at times he does seem to slip back into this type of explanation. He is also aware of the fact that the history of social infrastructures and superstructures does not explain anything; it is the history that needs to be explained. Although I shall not make an attempt to solve this crucial problem, I think that specialists in the study of religion could provide competence and knowledge which would be an important contribution towards resolving it. I am not optimistic that this contribution will be forthcoming. If my critique of the history and phenomenology of religion is accurate, then it should become apparent that these disciplines are moving in the opposite direction in the attempt, as yet unsuccessful, to establish their own autonomy.

The remainder of this chapter will demonstrate how structural method has been applied by Lévi-Strauss to explain three well-known subjects of study in anthropology; kinship, totemism, and myth. Before turning to this, however, it is important to set straight a final, but important, misunderstanding involving the meaning of the terms "structure" and "structural system" as these terms are used by Lévi-Strauss.

When we read through the corpus of Lévi-Strauss' publications it becomes obvious that he is conscious of this misunderstanding;

from "Social Structure" (1952) to "Structure and Form" (1960) and *The Raw And The Cooked* (1964), Lévi-Strauss has repeatedly returned to a clarification of these terms.

One use of "structure" is consistently rejected by Lévi-Strauss: the widespread British-American assumption that structure is the order which explains the observable relations between individuals or units of a social system. Structures from this point of view are relations that can be observed directly and empirically. Once we have described the principles or the arrangement by which individuals enter into institutional relations, we have also established the structure of these relations. In brief, structures are visible relations, and the construction of models of these relations represents the actual behavior of individuals within institutionalized relations.

Lévi-Strauss has made it clear that structural analysis is not an empirical description. Here is what he says:

> Passing now to the task of defining 'social structure', there is a point which should be cleared up immediately. The term 'social structure' has nothing to do with empirical reality but with models that are built up after it. This should help one to clarify the difference between two concepts which are so close to each other that they are often confused, namely, those of social structure and of social relations. It will be enough to state at this time that social relations consist of the raw materials out of which the models making up the social structure are built, while social structure can, by no means, be reduced to the ensemble of the social relations to be described in a given society (*S.A.*, 279).

Although it might have been enough to state it this way at the time, it did not prevent misunderstandings. Eight years later and with apparent frustration, Lévi-Strauss once again tried to clarify his point in a reply to Maybury-Lewis:

> To sum up, may I point out to what extent my critic remains the prisoner of the naturalistic misconceptions that have so longed pervaded the British school. He claims to be a structuralist.... But he is still a structuralist in Radcliffe-Brown's terms in that he believes the structure to lie at the level of empirical reality and to be a part of it. When therefore, he is presented a structural model which departs from empirical reality, he feels cheated in some devious way. To him, social structure is like a kind of jigsaw puzzle, and everything is achieved when one has discovered how the pieces fit together. But, if the pieces

have been arbitrarily cut, there is no structure at all. On the other hand, if—as is sometimes done—the pieces were automatically cut in different shapes by a mechanical saw, the movements of which are regulated by a camshaft, the structure of the puzzle exists, though not at the empirical level (since there are many ways of recognizing the pieces which fit together). Its key lies in the mathematical formula expressing the shape of the cams and their speed of rotation. This information does not correspond in any perceptible manner to the puzzle as it appears to the player, but it alone can explain the puzzle and provide a logical method to solve it (*S.A. II*, 79–80).

Lévi-Strauss closes his reply with the following example:

The ultimate proof of the molecular structure of matter is provided by the electronic [sic.] microscope, which enables us to see actual molecules. This achievement does not alter the fact that henceforth the molecule will not become any more visible to the naked eye. Similarly, it is hopeless to expect a structural analysis to change our way of perceiving concrete social relations. *It will only explain them better*. If the structure can be seen, it will not be at the earlier, empirical level, but at a deeper one, previously neglected; that of those unconscious categories which we may hope to reach by bringing together domains which, at first sight, appear disconnected (*S.A. II*, 80).

The above quotation is reasonably clear but open to serious misunderstanding. We can for example stop after reading that social structures have nothing to do with empirical reality since they have to do with models. That is to say, models we construct, that are in our heads, that explain, in some sense of explain, the empirical reality we have observed. I think that this interpretation of Lévi-Strauss is mistaken since it would place him squarely within the empiricist/positivist tradition he has rejected. Part of the problem is due to Lévi-Strauss himself. First of all, it does not help the reader to discover that Lévi-Strauss refers approvingly to Leach in the passage quoted above. Secondly, the passage is ambiguous in that "structure" and "model" seem to be the same. What is clear is that Lévi-Strauss makes a distinction between "social relations" and "social structures." Social relations are the raw material from which models are built that make manifest the social structure itself.

Structuralism is not a form of behaviorism or empiricism. The object for study is not to be confused with the observations, as rigorous as we can make them, of actual human behavior wherever we find it. The distinction between language and speech, social structure and social relations implies that we must not confuse the evidence with the object of our study. What I think Lévi-Strauss is saying in the above statement is that we use "the raw material" of social relations as evidence for the rules which constitute the social structure. To suppose that the rules are rules of empirical social relations is to think that the evidence is the object of study. I believe this interpretation of Lévi-Strauss can be demonstrated by turning to what he actually does in his analysis of kinship, totemism and myth. In turning to these three examples I do not intend to describe the details Lévi-Strauss uses in his analysis. What I am interested in is how he goes about establishing the analysis and the results.

Kinship, let us recall, was at one time the central object of study in anthropology. It had also become a central problem. For it seemed to be the case that there was an inverse relation between the increase in data and the established definition of "kinship" as a cultural universal. Put in other terms, there seemed to be a breakdown in the relation between the established definitions of kinship and the increasing number of accounts of "kinship" in various societies. Lévi-Strauss examined this problem in a significant article entitled "Structural Analysis in Linguistics and Anthropology" published in 1945. I believe this is the earliest essay in which structural linguistics is explicitly used as a theory for explaining anthropological data.

He cites structural linguistics as a revolution and describes its methodology by referring to Troubetzkoy: "First, structural linguistics shifts from the study of *conscious* linguistic phenomena to study their *unconscious* infrastructure; second, it does not treat *terms* as independent entities, taking instead as its basis of analysis the *relations* between terms; third, it introduces the concept of *system*... finally, structural linguistics aims at discovering *general laws*, either by induction 'or... by logical deduction, which would give them an absolute character'" (*S.A.*, 33). He notes that the final aim is nothing less than the capacity to formulate necessary relations by means of the first three rules. It is important to focus on this final aim simply because functionalists, as we have seen, reached for it without success. We must also notice that although Troubetzkoy's methodology involves hypothetico/deductive operations it is not causal in its mode of explanation.

Lévi-Strauss, I believe, is the first scholar in the human sciences to appropriate this set of methodological procedures for resolving an important problem. He is also careful to point out that we cannot simply move from a structural analysis of phonemes to an analysis of kinship systems. There are important differences, yet, the four rules are applicable: "Although they belong to *another order of reality*, kinship phenomena are *of the S.A.me type* as linguistic phenomena." Thus, contrary to many interpretations of Lévi-Strauss, he has never asserted that kinship or myth, are synonymous with language. All he wishes to point out is that there are significant relations and analogies between them.

Lévi-Strauss found at least two fundamental errors in his review of various attempts to resolve the problem mentioned above. The first is an attempt to resolve the problem historically; kinship terminology and rules are based on specific customs. If this is true, then how do we explain the regularity of kinship? How do discrete, historical customs explain an apparent universal institution across cultures? One way to do it is to assert that a specific element of a kinship system is the survival or residue of a previous custom now lost. Thus, the importance of the mother's brother in many kinship systems is "explained" as a survival of matrilineal descent or the consequence of several distinct customs now lost. This, of course, is sheer speculation which generates more problems than it attempts to solve.

The second error was to attempt to explain kinship by an analysis of the biological family; father, mother, children. Once we begin by focusing on this unit of kinship the avunculate remains external to the system and cannot be explained. Although Radcliffe-Brown made a great step forward in proposing that the problem of the avunculate could be solved by demonstrating that it involves two antithetical systems of attitudes (authority/familiarity) determined by either patrilineal or matrilineal descent, the problem remained unresolved. The avunculate, for example, does not occur in all patrilineal or matrilineal societies and is present in some societies that are neither matrilineal nor patrilineal. The problem with Radcliffe-Brown's solution is that it remained on the surface of social relations, arbitrarily restricting the "structure" to two sets of terms, father/son, maternal uncle/nephew.

As we know, Lévi-Strauss proposed what he called the "atom of kinship" as composed of the following set of relations; brother/sister, husband/wife, father/son, maternal uncle/nephew.

And it is this set of relations which also accounts for the three constituent kinship relations; affinity, consanguinity, and filiation. Furthermore, this set of relations is the result of "the universal presence of the incest taboo." Lévi-Strauss concludes by asserting that "This is really saying that in human society a man must obtain a woman from another man who gives him a daughter or a sister. Thus we do not need to explain how the maternal uncle emerged in kinship structure: He does not emerge—he is present initially. Indeed, the presence of the maternal uncle is a necessary precondition for the structure to exist. The error of traditional anthropology, like that of traditional linguistics, was to consider the terms, and not the relation between the terms" (*S.A.*, 46).

This is indeed a striking illustration of a procedure which first constructs a model consisting of a set of relations and then makes manifest the structure as it actually exists in societies. It is a deductive operation, not observable on the empirical level and surely not in the consciousness of an informant. The explanation is also not causal, but rather a set of necessary relations in which the relations function as definitions of the terms. It is also theoretically possible to construct such a symmetrical structure in which the sexes would be reversed.

And what about the problem Lévi-Strauss laid at the foot of Radcliffe-Brown, the fact that we have the avunculate in systems which are neither patrilineal nor matrilineal and so on? First, not all societies are regulated by kinship. But, second, we may construct more complex systems in which the avunculate relation may be present but submerged. For example, "we can conceive of a system whose point of departure lies in the elementary structure but which adds, at the right of the maternal uncle, his wife, and at the left of the father, first the father's sister and then her husband" (*S.A.*, 48). In brief, what Lévi-Strauss is asserting is that this construction is based on a set of relations which are syntagmatic.

The structure of kinship is not founded on the biological family, it is, to use a term from structural linguistics "unmotivated." It would seem to be the case, therefore, that the elements of kinship have no intrinsic value, their value is established by the relationships into which they enter.

Let us now turn to Lévi-Strauss's analysis of totemism. It is important to first point out that totemism, like kinship, had been the focus of study for many scholars. Totemism was identified as the origin of culture and religion, totemism was the primitive institution. We need only recall the importance of totemism in the works of such scholars as Durkheim, Freud and Radcliffe-Brown as a reminder that this subject was thought by many to be the key that would unlock the mystery of the origins of culture and religion. For many years the journal *Anthropos* reserved a special section in each of its volumes for continued work on the subject.

The history of this intellectual enterprise is fascinating in itself when we remember the attention given to the subject for almost one hundred years. The subject, as we now know, was primarily created in the minds of scholars who then went in search of it among societies. The history of the study of this intellectual creation called "totemism" did not suddenly collapse but endured for many years in spite of the internal problems which were fully recognized by various scholars. Why it endured for as long as it did is an interesting topic in itself.

I shall resist the temptation to answer this question. Let me just point out that by 1910 Alexander Goldenweiser, inspired by Boas, had proved convincingly that there was no such thing as universal totemism resulting from a single historical or psychological origin. And yet, once having shown the diversity and heterogeneity of the features identified as totemism, Goldenweiser continued to insist on a "totemic complex" which included exogamy, a mystical relation between man and nature, and a set of social units which are equivalent, as universal features. The task, then, was to find a general formula which would explain these three features as constituting totemism.

By 1954 we are no longer reading about totemism, but totemisms. For A. P. Elkin the issue was no longer a quest for an institution known as totemism, but placing totemism back into the cultures where it was originally found. Once we place totemism back into its particular social context, he believed, we can solve the problems by making a distinction between social totemism and cult totemism. The first is associated with kinship, the regulation of marriage, and the differentiation of social groups. The second, cult totemism, is associated with explaining group origins, the maintenance of custom, and certain rituals related to the maintenance of the social group.

Four years earlier Piddington after studying what had been written about totemism wrote, "It will seem that the term 'totemism' has been applied to a bewildering variety of relationships between human beings and natural species or phenomena. For this reason it is impossible to reach any satisfactory definition of totemism, though many attempts have been made to do so.... All definitions of totemism are either so specific as to exclude a number of systems which are commonly referred to as 'totemic' or so general as to include many phenomena which cannot be referred to by this term" (*Totemism*, see Chapter II, this volume). The study of totemism was in disarray. No one had taken Lowie seriously when about forty years earlier he raised the question whether it might not be best to pause and "first inquire whether... we are comparing cultural realities or merely figments of our logical modes of classification."

Given this most remarkable chapter in the history of the human sciences, Lévi-Strauss did heed the call of Lowie and turned to an investigation of this peculiar problem and its history. The problem is made very clear by Lévi-Strauss. "If totemism is defined," he writes, "as the joint presence of animal and plant names, prohibitions apply[ing] to the corresponding species and the forbidding of marriage between people of the same name and subject to the same prohibition, then clearly a problem arises about the connection of these customs. It has however long been known that any one of these features can be found without the others and any two of them without the third" (*SM*, 97).

Lévi-Strauss proceeds to resolve the problems by means of a method that is strikingly similar to the one used in explaining what he called the atom of kinship. Here is how he begins:

Let us try to define objectively and in its most general aspects the semantic field within which are found the phenomena commonly grouped under the name of totemism. The method we adopt, in this case as in others, consists in the following operations:

(1) define the phenomenon under study as a relation between two or more terms, real or supposed;

(2) construct a table of possible permutations between these terms;

(3) take this table as the general object of analysis which, at this level only, can yield the necessary connections, the empirical phenomenon considered at the beginning being only one possible

combination among others, the complete system of which must be reconstructed beforehand (*Totemism*, see Chapter II, this volume).

Lévi-Strauss arbitrarily chooses the terms "natural" and "cultural" to cover relations which are posited ideologically between two series. He then chooses "categories" and "particulars" as terms which comprise the natural series, and "groups" and "persons" as terms which comprise the cultural series.

Thus, we have the following set of relations between two or more terms, real or supposed:

NATURE:	Category	Particular
CULTURE:	Group	Person

By constructing a table of possible permutations between these terms, we get the following set of relations which exists between the two series:

	1	2	3	4
NATURE:	Category	Category	Particular	Particular
CULTURE:	Group	Person	Person	Group

Lévi-Strauss then moves on to demonstrate that the four combinations correspond to observable data among various societies. It will be best to quote his correlations. Australian totemism fits the first combination, since,

> under 'social' end 'sexual' modalities, [it] postulates a relation between a natural category (animal or vegetable species, or class of objects or phenomena) and a cultural group (moiety, section, sub-section, cult-group, or the collectivity of members of the same sex). The second combination corresponds to the 'individual' totemism of the North American Indians, among whom an individual seeks by means of physical traits to reconcile himself with a natural category. As an example of the third combination we may take Mota, in the Banks Islands, where a child is thought to be the incarnation of an animal or plant found or eaten by the mother when she first became aware that she was pregnant.... The group-particular combination is attested from Polynesia and Africa, where certain animals (guardian lizards in New Zealand, sacred crocodiles and lion or leopard in Africa) are objects of social protection and veneration (*Totemism*, see Chapter II, this volume).

The "totemic illusion" is the result of distorting the semantic field by focusing on the first two combinations, abstracting them from a system of logical relations which are, in fact, equivalent transformations of the same set. And once this abstraction takes place, we cannot account for either the remaining combinations, or the presence or absence of certain "totemic features" in the societies we examine.

But, there is more to this analysis than the creation of a set of relations which constitute a structure in which, among other things, totemic features can be placed and explained. The principles of this method show why it was a fatal error to seek certain properties of a totem as the key for its selection and use. It remains a popular notion that totems are symbols. Thus, a society may have the lion as totem because it symbolizes courage. Or, the bear becomes a totem for a clan because of its strength, the eagle because of its swiftness, and so on. Apart from the difficulty of demonstrating the semantic relations between lion/courage or bear/strength (why not lion/lazy, bear/stink), there is another difficulty that has not been solved. What does the fly, the mosquito, vomit, or the wind "symbolize" as a totem in certain societies? We have now entered the realm of creative imagination rather than explanation.

What we must clearly grasp is that totems as elements in a system have no intrinsic significance as such. They are to be analyzed as "signs" in a system. "There is no such thing as the real totem," writes Lévi-Strauss, "the individual animal plays the part of the signifying, and the sacredness attaches neither to it nor to its icon but to the signified, which either can stand for" (*SM*, 239).

Once this is fully understood, it becomes obvious that when we think about the enormous amount of raw material that could be selected from the world about us it is possible that an indefinite number of systems could be created that would be just as coherent as the structures we actually find in different societies. Thus, there is no particular system that is necessary, or originally given, as the structure for all societies. As Lévi-Strauss puts it,

> The operative value of the systems of naming and classifying commonly called totemic derives from their formal character; they are codes suitable for conveying messages which can be transposed into other codes, and for expressing messages received by means of different codes in terms of their own system. The mistake of classical

ethnologists was to try to reify this form and tie it to a determinate content when in fact what it provides is a method for assimilating any kind of content. Far from being an autonomous institution definable by its intrinsic characteristic totemism, or what is referred to as such, corresponds to certain modalities arbitrarily isolated from a formal system, the function of which is to guarantee the convertibility of ideas between different levels of social reality (*SM*, 75–6).

The axiomatic principle, as Lévi-Strauss calls it, of the totemic concept can be described as follows: it is "an homology not between social groups and natural species, but between differences existing, on the one hand within the social system, and on the other within the natural system. Two systems of differences are conceived as isomorphic, although one is situated in nature, and the other in culture." The structure can be schematized as follows, with vertical lines indicating relations of homology:

NATURE:	species 1 +	species 2 +	species 3 +	species n
	|	|	|	|
CULTURE:	group 1 +	group 2 +	group 3 +	group n

(SM, 115)

The schema is to be read as follows; group 1: group 2 :: species 1: species 2, or clan 1 differs from clan 2 as eagle differs from bear. The point is that we must refuse to look on the so-called totemic features in a society as first of all animals who resemble each other because of their overall behavior and then social groups which resemble each other. As Lévi-Strauss says, "The resemblance presupposed by so-called totemic representations is *between these two systems of differences*" (*Totemism*, see Chapter II, this volume).

Before turning to the example of myth, I think it best to pause here in order to illustrate how structural analysis differs from functionalism. As we have seen, structuralism does not explain social relations by using a type of causal explanation. On the contrary, it rejects this attempt by moving to an explanation which although deductive in nature is primarily interested in the function of terms as a logical set of relations. And Lévi-Strauss, rather than using a type of Hempelian criticism of functionalism comes up with another argument against it. In closing his critique of functionalist theories of totemism which is based on need and emotion, he says,

As affectivity is the most obscure side of man, there is the constant temptation to resort to it, forgetting that what is refractory to explanation is *ipso facto* unsuitable for use in explanation. A datum is not primary because it is incomprehensible: this characteristic indicates solely that an explanation, if it exists, must be sought on another level. Otherwise, we shall be satisfied to attach another label to the problem, thus believing it to have been solved.... Actually, impulses and emotions explain nothing: they are always results, either of the power of the body or of the impotence of the mind. In both cases they are consequences, never causes. The latter can be sought only in the organism, which is the exclusive concern of biology, or in the intellect, which is the sole way offered to psychology, and to anthropology as well (*Totemism*, see Chapter II, this volume).

He therefore, concludes with the well-known phrase, "totems are not good to eat, they are first of all good to think." We have first of all to know our world before it becomes useful to us. In brief, totemism is not a matter of utilitarian satisfactions of need, but of epistemology!

Let us now turn briefly to a description of Lévi-Strauss's structural analysis of myth. Lévi-Strauss once again begins with a problem; the chaotic situation in the study of mythology. This is how he described the situation in 1955: "Precisely because the interest of professional anthropology has withdrawn from primitive religion, all kinds of amateurs who claim to belong to other disciplines have seized this opportunity to move in, thereby turning into their private playground what we have left as a wasteland" (*S.A.*, 206). The cause of this wasteland is attributed to an early attempt at explaining myth from a psychological approach, which when discredited, was turned into an attempt to explain myths as a function of affectivity, "inarticulate emotional drives." We may note that this is precisely his criticism of the attempts to explain "totemism."

As a result, the situation remains chaotic. "Myths are still widely interpreted in conflicting ways: as collective dreams, as the outcome of a kind of esthetic play, or as the basis of ritual. Mythological figures are considered as personified abstractions, divinized heroes, or fallen gods. Whatever the hypothesis, the choice amounts to reducing mythology either to idle play or to a crude kind of philosophic speculation" (*S.A.*, 207). Or, we might add, myths become an ontological quest for being, with Plato as the first philosopher to decipher the symbolic meaning of myth.

Given this situation, what does Lévi-Strauss think is the fundamental problem, and how does he attempt to solve it? The problem seems to be an inherent contradiction; myths themselves seem to be chaotic. In myth anything goes, everything becomes possible. Yet, anyone who has studied mythology also knows that there is a striking similarity between myths from diverse regions of the world. Lévi-Strauss resolves this apparent "antinomy" by moving directly to Saussure and structural linguistics.

The misconception in the study of mythology is based on the notion that myth like language links a particular sound to a particular meaning. Thus, there are "sun", "lunar", "water," "earth" and "sky' myths and patterns or archetypes which possess a certain meaning The error is comparable to thinking that similar or identical sounds across languages entail similar or identical meanings. But this is contradicted by our knowledge that although there may be identical sounds across languages, the meanings related to the sounds may be entirely different. The contradiction is resolved by an analysis which demonstrates that it is not sounds, but the combination of sounds which is significant, and that linguistic signs are arbitrary as vehicles of signification.

Lévi-Strauss applies this development in structural linguistics in the following way:

> (1) If there is a meaning to be found in mythology, it cannot reside in the isolated elements which enter into the composition of a myth, but only in the way those elements are combined. (2) Although myth belongs to the same category as language, being, as a matter of fact, only part of it, language in myth exhibits specific properties. (3) These properties are only to be found above the ordinary linguistic level, that is, they exhibit more complex features than those which are to be found in any other kind of linguistic expression (S.A., 210).

Myths, then, like language are made up of "constituent units" which Lévi-Strauss calls "mythemes." Lévi-Strauss is quite aware of the hypothetical nature of this construction, but the guidelines are clear.

> How shall we proceed," he writes, "in order to identify and isolate these gross constituent units or mythemes? We know that they cannot be found among phonemes, morphemes, or sememes, but only on a higher level; otherwise myth would become confused with any other

kind of speech. Therefore, we should look for them on the sentence level. The only method we can suggest at this stage is to proceed tentatively, by trial and error, using as a check the principles which serve as a basis for any kind of structural analysis: economy of explanation; unity of solution, and ability to reconstruct the whole from a fragment, as well as later stages from previous ones" (*S.A.*, 211).

This hypothesis together with the methodological guidelines has been consistently followed by Lévi-Strauss throughout his work on myth. It is this approach that has produced a radical change in the study of mythology. Let us briefly review some of the important features of this change.

First of all, it is important to notice that a structural analysis of myth puts an end to the quest for the "original" myth. It is simply useless to speculate about which myth is the more "genuine." A myth consists of all its versions, there simply is no preferred myth which discloses the meaning of myth. "Properly speaking, there is never any original: every myth is by its very nature a translation [or, transformation of other myths] and derives from another myth belonging to a neighboring, but foreign, community, or from a previous myth belonging to the same community or from a contemporaneous one belonging to a different social sub-division" (*The Naked Man*, 644, hereafter referred to as *NM*). Second, remaining true to the development of structural linguistics with regard to the nature of the "sign," we must view the "constituent" elements of a myth as essentially without content, without signification. Following Jakobson, Lévi-Strauss asserts that a mytheme "is a purely differential and contentless sign." It may well be the case that in ordinary language, the sun is the star of the day, but,

> in and of itself, the mytheme "sun" is meaningless. Depending on the myths that one chooses to consider, "sun" can cover the most diverse ideal contents. Indeed, no one who finds "sun" in a myth can make any assumptions about its individuality, its nature, or its function there. Its meaning can emerge only from its correlative and oppositive relations with other mythemes within the myth. This meaning does not really belong to any of the mythemes; it results from their combination (*The View From Afar*, 145).

What follows from the above hypothesis is that myths have no obvious practical function. And as Lévi-Strauss has convincingly shown, it is very dangerous if not erroneous to view myths as symbolic representations of actual social realities or of some cultural psyche, whatever that may mean. Furthermore, it is also a mistake to study myths as concealing some hidden "mystical" meaning. The meaning of a myth is given in its concrete relations with other versions. Thus, it is clearly a misunderstanding to call this type of analysis reductionistic. Lévi-Strauss has consistently claimed that the meaning of myth must be sought on its own level. Thus, myths disclose their own meaning, and we must "resign ourselves to the fact that the myths tell us nothing instructive about the world order, the nature of reality or the origin and destiny of mankind. We cannot expect them to flatter any metaphysical thirst, [sic.] or to breathe new life into exhausted ideologies." And yet, the structural analysis of myth does teach us a great deal about the societies from which they originate, and most important of all, "they make it possible to discover certain operational modes of the human mind, which have remained so constant over the centuries, and are so widespread over immense geographical distances, that we can assume them to be fundamental..." (NM, 639).

At this point, I think it best to allow Lévi-Strauss to summarize what he is doing. The lengthy quotation from an interview given below serves four purposes. First, it allows Lévi-Strauss to speak for himself, since he has often complained that he has been misunderstood. Second, it demonstrates that no description of his structural analysis of myth can be given without some ethnographic detail. Third, it also highlights how structural analysis of myth is not an explanation of the function of myth as providing social cohesion or maintenance, but an analysis which explains the meaning of myth as a translation or transformation of relations that are to be found at different levels from within the myth. Finally, it might help put an end to popular assertions that the analysis is the result of Lévi-Strauss' creative imagination; thus, structural analysis, like myth itself, is dramatic, expressive, an art, not a science which can be disconfirmed.

Lévi-Strauss points out in the interview that the initial situation which confronts us as we study myth is one of total arbitrariness, and confusion. He then states that myth instead of formulating abstract relationships, sets one element against another, sky and earth, earth and water, man and woman, light and darkness, raw and cooked, fresh and rotten. He is then asked to give an example and here is his reply.

> The Salish-speaking peoples who inhabited North America between the Rocky Mountains and the Pacific Ocean near the fiftieth parallel often speak in their myths of a deceitful genie who, whenever a problem puzzles him, excretes his two sisters imprisoned in his bowels, whereon he demands their advice by threatening them with a torrential downpour; they, being excrement, would disintegrate. The tale seems like a clownish farce without any basis, defying all interpretation except, some would argue, through psychoanalysis. But this wouldn't get you very far for the simple reason that the storytellers' individual psychic constitutions are not a causal factor. Rather, an anonymous tradition has thrust these stories on them.
>
> As in the previous instance, one may well ask himself if the apparent absurdity of the motif is not a result of our having arbitrarily isolated it from a much larger ensemble in which it would represent one possible combination among others produced as well, so that there would be no meaning to each one taken alone, but only in its relation to the others. Now, in Salish myths, the same genie creates for himself two adaptive daughters, out of raw salmon roe. When they are fully grown, he desires them. Testing his position, he pretends to call them by mistake 'my wives' instead of 'my daughters.' They promptly take offense and leave.
>
> Finally, the Salish tell of a third pair of supernatural women. These women are married and are incapable of expressing themselves in articulate speech. They live at the bottom of natural wells and, on request, send up dishes of hot, well-cooked food to the surface.
>
> These three motifs cannot be understood apart from one another. On the other hand, once you compare them, you notice their common origin. All the women are related to water: either, as in the case of the well-women, to stagnant water, or to running water for the two other pairs.
>
> The latter are distinct from one another in that the salmon-roe daughters come from a positive, earthly source of water—salmon streams—and the excrement-sisters are threatened with destruction by a negative, heavenly source of water—the disintegrating rain. That's not all: the salmon-roe daughters and excrement-sisters are the products of either raw (in the first case) or cooked (in the other) food, while the well-women are themselves producers of cooked food. Further, the well-women, if you permit me, are 'marrying-types' as wives and good cooks. The other two pairs are 'non-marrying types' whether because they are labeled as sisters or because they avoid incestuous marriage with their foster father. Finally, two pairs of women are endowed linguistically: one for their wise counsel, the other because they catch on to a half-spoken, improper hint. In this way they contrast with the third pair, the well-women, who cannot speak.

Thus from three meaningless anecdotes you extract a system of pertinent oppositions: water, stagnant or moving, from the earth or sky; women created from food or producing it themselves, raw or cooked food; women accessible or opposed to marriage depending on linguistic or non-linguistic behavior. You arrive at what I'd call a 'semantic field' which can be applied like a grill to all the myths of these populations, enabling us to disclose their meaning.

And what is this meaning? "You realize that the Salish myths compose a vast sociological, economical and cosmological system establishing numerous correspondences between the distribution of fish in the water network, the various markets where goods are exchanged, their periodicity in time and during the fishing season, and finally exogamy; for, between groups, women are exchanged like foodstuffs (*Diacritics* 1971, 48–49).

This long quotation is the best summary I have come across which describes what Lévi-Strauss is doing in the monumental four volume work on mythology. The analysis attempts to show that there is a differential, oppositional logic which is inherent in myths. The analysis begins by demonstrating the structure, the grill, of this logic in a particular myth, and then proceeds to establish the meaning of myth as this structure is translated or transformed into other myths. This logic shows that it is the *differences*, not the resemblances, which are significant. I might add that this is precisely the opposite of most historians' and phenomenologists' interpretations of myths.

Lévi-Strauss has consistently described this inherent logic in mythology by the following formula, A : B :: C : D. He has also described it by the following algebraic formula:

$$f_x(a): f_y(b) :: f_x (b): f^{(a-1)}(y)$$

The formula, once again, is explained as follows: "Here, with two terms, *a* and *b*, being given as well as two functions, *x* and *y*, of these terms, it is assumed that a relation of equivalence exists between two situations defined respectively by an inversion of *terms* and *relations*, under two conditions: (1) that one term be replaced by its opposite (in the above formula, *a* and *a-1*); (2) that an inversion by made between the *function value* and the *term value* of two elements (above *y* and *a*)."

This formula has been used by Lévi-Strauss in his study of myth and is clearly at work in his analysis of "The Story of Asdiwal" which, as we will recall, begins with a mother and daughter in a valley and ends with a father and son on a mountain, as well as the various oppositions of the various sociological, geographical, economic and cosmological levels. The formula can also be seen at work in the four volumes on mythology in South and North America.

The major problem I have with this analysis is not that it is speculative, that there is no way we can falsify what he is doing, or that only Lévi-Strauss can perform this kind of magic. None of this kind of criticism is true. The major problem is to be found in Lévi-Strauss' notion that it is the transformations of the myths into different sets of oppositions that is the meaning of the myths. It simply is not clear to me how such transformations can generate meaning. Nor am I satisfied with his notion that such meanings are hidden; it is the structural grill which "discloses" the meaning of the myths. There is not doubt about the fact that myths pick up aspects of culture and nature as elements to be woven into the myths. Thus, we usually find social, economic, and political relations as well as geographical and cosmological elements in the stories. "Case III," in the following chapter will provide a good example of this. We have learned, thanks in part to Lévi-Strauss, however, that it is very dangerous to interpret the myths as symbolic representations of social or natural structures. Often we find that it is just the opposite which is the case; the myth represents a matrilocal system, the society is partrilocal. Forced into the corner we are then tempted to look for the hidden meaning of myth. I agree with Sperber that we should try this response as an answer of last resort. One of the difficulties with the notion of hidden meanings is the answer we must give to, "why all these hidden meanings?" Why do so many societies insist upon speaking in a cryptic language which we must decode? The usual response to these questions leads us straight into the mine-field of functionalism (See Sperber, Ch. XI, this volume).

It is precisely this synchronic structure of oppositions, of differences, which has caused the most criticism of his analysis of myth. What his critics want is precisely what he refuses to give them; an empirical and causal explanation of myth based on need or an interpretation of myth as symbolic of a metaphysical reality. Since, as we have seen, both of these approaches have led to a theoretical impasse, Lévi-Strauss is quite correct in his refusal to move down these pathways. He has offered his hypotheses and methodological principles as tentative, open to falsification. His procedures have been by trial and error. His theory may well turn out to be wrong, but I know of no more adequate place to begin than from the place Lévi-Strauss started from, i.e., linguistics.

CHAPTER VII

Science or Bricolage?

David Maybury-Lewis

Du miel aux cendres is precisely the sort of sequel one would have expected to *Le Cru et le cuit* (1964). It is in its way a total Lévi-Straussian experience, which the *aficionados* are certain to enthuse over. From its dust jacket, taken from a 1554 copy of a book on hunting in the library of Fountainebleau castle, to the woodcuts that illustrate it, the book is an aesthetic treat. Sections of it are introduced by excerpts in Latin from Roman authors calculated to establish an atmosphere of erudite eclogue. But the maze of diagrams, couched in Lévi-Strauss's own parody of logical notation, warns the reader that there is hard work ahead. After a brief résumé of *Le Cru et le cuit*, we are plunged into the analysis of a further 166 myths, largely in order to elucidate the symbolic significance of honey and tobacco in the thought of the South American Indians.

Allusions to honey and tobacco abound in myth, literature, and popular sayings, and they are by no means confined to South America. Lévi-Strauss considers them in the special context of South American myth and draws from them a cosmic significance that only his most devoted followers are likely to find convincing. Nevertheless, the book will give great pleasure to anyone who enjoys intellectual acrostics and delights in fearless scholarship. It is essential reading for those who take a serious interest in South American Indians or in the study of myth. I found, however, that reading it for review was the most exasperatingly onerous task I can remember assuming. A reviewer must, after all, try to evaluate the argument of a work under review, and a major difficulty, though not the only one, with *Du miel aux cendres* is to find out precisely what the argument is. The style of the work does not help. It is a sort of Chinese puzzle, full of diversions, false trails, metaphoric asides, and inconclusive perorations. The serious reader, who either cannot or will not allow himself to be borne along unresisting on the waves of verbiage, will spend much of his time trying to remember what the point of a given section is supposed to be. By the end, he may still be trying to unravel the argument.

After the appearance of *Le Cru et le cuit*, it was claimed that anthropologists would no longer be able to consider "the content of myths to be unimportant or unworthy of attention *per se*" (N. Yalman, in *The Structural Study of Myth and Totemism*. E. Leach, ed. 1967:72). I doubt that they ever did. In the past they often ignored myths because their attention was focused elsewhere, which is not the same thing at all. Alternatively, they did not quite know what to do with myths once they had them. Well, Lévi-Strauss has now shown what he thinks ought to be done with them. He is convinced that myths are statements in some sort of metalanguage that his approach enables him to decode. Even those who do not accept his renderings of their meaning are unlikely, after those books, to doubt that such decoding is possible. There is no doubt that *Le Cru et le cuit* charted a new course in the study of myth. The trouble with *Du miel aux cendres* derives from that fact. It is no longer a pioneering work and cannot claim any critical forebearance on that score. Technically, it is a continuation of *Le Cru et le cuit* and cannot properly be appreciated without constant reference to the latter. Moreover, it ends abruptly, leaving the reader up in the air with the promise of yet another volume to come. The old virtues are still in striking evidence and have already earned respectful accolades in the intellectual weeklies. But what was pardonably experimental in *Le Cru et le cuit* becomes frankly irritating in its sequel. There is no reason why anthropological readers should any longer grant the author a willing suspension of their disbelief. The time has come, however provisionally, to take stock.

Lévi-Strauss points out that honey is ambiguous: now toxic, now delicious, now maleficent, now associated with all the good things of this world. There is, he suggests, a similar polarity in the role of tobacco, and honey and tobacco form a pair of mythic opposites. It should be noted that honey and tobacco are treated throughout like algebraic symbols, so that myths that make no mention of either are said to be dealing with honey/tobacco issues, to be related to such issues, or to be transformations of such issues. Since honey is seductive, myths dealing with seduction or any uncontrollable passion may be treated as honey myths. Similarly, tobacco requires burning, so that its role in myth is treated as part of the study of those myths where there is reference to burning, smoke, cooking, and the origin of fire. In *Le Cru et le cuit* an entire system of myths relating to the origin of fire was discussed. It was also argued that myths about the origin of wild pig systematically invoked the action of smoke/tobacco. But wild pigs are held to be prototypical of meat, and meat is the item par excellence requiring the action of fire. Tobacco thus enters meat myths, which are a prerequisite for fire myths. Surely, then, there must be a system of tobacco myths, explaining the origin of tobacco. Similarly, honey is symmetrical with tobacco. Honey enters myths that explain the origin of feather necklaces (and feathers are often burned to make smoke). Surely there is, therefore, a system of myths explaining the origin of honey, and surely all these systems form a group of systems.

Du miel aux cendres is about the isolation and analysis of those systems. Lévi-Strauss points out the associations of the honey/tobacco notions with the wet/dry opposition, and this leads to a discussion of the mythic significance of climate and constellations, of periods of fasting and periods of abundance. The final section of the book, piquantly entitled "The instruments of darkness," seeks to establish the symbolic significance of sounds, and even of smells and physical states. By the interpretation, some would say the manipulation, of associations of ideas in myths, Lévi-Strauss argues that the relationships between certain types of sound are analogous to and thus represent the relationships between notions that the myth seeks to express. The rationale for this analogy is not, however, made clear in his lengthy treatment of the topic. In any case, the nub of the argument is that in South American myth the honey idea is seen as such a potently seductive force that it severs the link between man and the supernatural, whereas the function of the tobacco idea is to recreate, or at any rate to maintain, this link.

The conclusions drawn from all this are characteristically sweeping. We are told, and this is a direct outcome of the argument of *Le Cru et le cuit*, that cooking "seen in its pure state" (i.e., the cooking of meat) and alliance similarly looked at (i.e., exclusively as a

wife-giving and wife-taking relationship between brothers-in-law)
express in Indian thought "the essential articulation of nature and
culture" (p. 259). The myths tell us furthermore that with the
appearance of a neolithic economy and the consequent multiplication
of peoples and diversification of languages, social life encountered its
first difficulties, which resulted from population growth and a
chancier composition of family groups than the models allowed for.
Thus, motifs relating to famine, fasting, and the absence of fire are
interpreted as the abolition of cooking, or as a sort of return to nature.
Nature itself is ambiguous, offering either unbearable privations
leading to famine or a natural (as opposed to cultural) abundance,
and the polarity of honey ideas symbolizes these contradictory
aspects (p. 356). South American myths, and by implication myth in
general since evidence is also adduced on occasion from the Old
World, are all variations on a grand theme of the relationship
between nature and culture. At one stage, Lévi-Strauss suggests that
the myths he is discussing describe the fall from a golden age, when
nature was prodigal, through a bronze age when man had clear ideas
and distinct oppositions at his disposal that enabled him to dominate
his environment, to a state of misty indistinction where nothing can
be properly possessed or preserved since everything is confused (p.
221).

What is one to make of all this? Above all, what is the evidence
behind such hyperbole? Lévi-Strauss discusses his procedures at the
beginning of *Le Cru et le cuit*. Lest I be accused of yet another of those
obtuse failures of comprehension with which his critics are
commonly charged these days, I shall quote the passage in French. In
speaking of his undertaking (*entreprise*) and the objections to it, which
he anticipates from mythographers and specialists in tropical
America, he explains:

> Quelle que soit la façon dont on l'envisage, elle se développe comme une
> nébuleuse, sans jamais rassembler de manière durable ou systématique la
> somme totale des éléments d'où elle tire aveuglément sa substance,
> confiante que le réel lui servira de guide et lui montrera une route plus
> sûre que celle qu'elle aurait pu inventor [1964:10].

The image of a nebulous method, blindly sucking its substance
from the myths but nevertheless confident that the Real (or the True?)
will keep it on the right track, is hardly one to inspire confidence or

even to be taken seriously. Unfortunately, a great deal of what Lévi-Strauss writes cannot be taken seriously. His style is packed with similar conceits. The total effect is notoriously unclear—there are passages in both books that are unintelligible even to Frenchmen—and it systematically obscures important issues, dismissing them elegantly and epigrammatically just as a conjurer's patter distracts attention from what is really happening. In this instance he is smoothly skirting an issue left unresolved in both books, namely, the precise status of his interpretations of myth. What is this reality that he feels confidently will guide his enquiry? Is it to be found in his conclusions? If so, what sort of a reality do they represent? Again we are fobbed off with an epigram that has been much quoted. Lévi-Strauss proposes to show not so much how men think in myths but *"comment les mythes se pensent dans les hommes, et à leur insu"* (1964:20). But what does this mean, if anything? As for the crucial question of whether his interpretations of myths may be no more than something he chooses to read into his own manipulations of them, a sort of intellectual haruspication, Lévi-Strauss replies serenely that it does not matter:

> For, if the final goal of anthropology is to contribute to a better knowledge of objective thought and its mechanisms, it comes to the same thing in the end if, in this book, the thought of South American Indians takes shape under the action of mine, or mine under the action of theirs [1964:21].

In this way, he sidesteps the real difficulty, which is how to get at the thought of South American Indians at all.

The way he sets about it is certainly unorthodox. He is dealing, he tells us, with mythology but sees no reason therefore to ignore the evidence of tales, legends, pseudohistorical traditions, ceremonies, and ritual (1964:12). His refusal to be bound by traditional distinctions or to be drawn into sterile definitional discussions is surely laudable. But some distinctions, nevertheless, have to be made and some working definitions provided. Lévi-Strauss never tells us how he knows whether a story is a myth or not or why he selects the "myths" that he does for consideration. He anticipates the objection that he may have selected his myths in order to prove his points, ignoring those that might serve as contrary evidence, and replies with two separate arguments. First, by *reductio ad absurdum*, he suggests that such an objection is utopian, for it requires an analysis of all myths before a comparative analysis of any myths can be undertaken. But this argument is in itself absurd.

Nobody expects a scholar to examine all the evidence in such a field. He is expected merely to state clearly how he selects the evidence he does examine and to show that he has made a serious attempt to ensure that there is not contrary evidence available and ignored. Alternatively, Lévi-Strauss argues that it is possible to write the grammar of a language without knowing all the words that have ever been uttered in it. He proposes therefore to provide at least the outline of a syntax of South American mythology (1964:16), without feeling bound to consider every myth ever recorded from that continent. This linguistic analogy, which has been the leitmotiv of all his work, will be discussed briefly below. For the moment it is enough to note that Lévi-Strauss ignores some of the conventional precautions of mythography. He presents some myths in paraphrase, some only in partial versions. He does not as a rule consider how the myth was collected, by whom, from whom, and what sort of a story it was supposed to be. This might not be of much significance for some purposes. But Lévi-Strauss on occasion goes into a microscopic *explication de texte*, where the style of a myth, its precise words and their associations are all considered as evidence for highly abstract theorizing. Under the circumstances it is reasonable to expect that he should take more care to establish his texts and their contexts.

For example, a crucial point in the complex pastiche developed in both books is Lévi-Strauss's contention that the jaguar of the Central Brazilian fire myths is married to a human wife. His evidence for this is a parenthesis in one of the Kayapó versions of the myth. None of the other Gê versions mentions that she is human. They do not mention that she is not human either, but if she were a female jaguar, this would hardly be necessary. Inquiries carried out among the present-day Kayapó, Apinaye, Sherente, and Shavante, all of whom know the story well, have provoked categorical assertions that the jaguar's wife was indeed a jaguar. One must therefore consider the Kayapó variant on which Lévi-Strauss bases his argument to be a curious anomaly rather than a typical text. Lévi-Strauss may of course argue that these Indians really think of the jaguar's wife as a human and of the jaguar as a brother-in-law, in spite of what they say. I find the argument unconvincing, but in any case this is quite different from his statement that the Gê are explicit on the point (1964:91).

This brings us to the central difficulty. How does one attempt to validate the analysis of a myth? One might turn to the other aspects of the culture of the people who tell it. Yet in these books there is surprisingly little evidence adduced from ritual, a domain to which one might expect a scholar to turn for clues to mythical symbolism. There is much mention of sociological evidence, but this "evidence" turns out on inspection to have a curious status in the argument. When it is elaborately detailed, as for the Bororo (1964:45–52), it transpires that it has only the most tenuous connection with the subsequent analyses of myth. On the other hand, the *"armatures sociologiques"* to which Lévi-Strauss does link the myths are extremely general and abstract, consisting mostly of combinations built out of oppositions such as conjunction/disjunction, male/female, kinship/alliance (p. 37). Most myths could be expressed in these terms, especially if the oppositions are assigned as arbitrarily or even as metaphorically as Lévi-Strauss assigns them. Thus, the elaborate superstructure of interpretation rests on weak sociological foundations. But this does not appear to matter, for the relationship between social arrangements and mythical structure is postulated at such an abstract level as to be quite nondiscriminatory. Virtually any society could be shown to be appropriate for any myth, provided that the tellers lived in the proper environment. This is convenient, for it enables Lévi-Strauss to use and closely analyze myths from societies about which very little is known. At the same time it renders his analyses comparatively impervious to the progress of ethnography, for, if an earlier report is proved incorrect, it is unlikely to affect the myth analysis. In sum, these interpretations of myth do not require us to establish the ethnography.

The crucial evidence, it is soon clear, comes from ecology and from the myths themselves. Lévi-Strauss argues that myths are not told in order to explain natural phenomena. Rather they use the elements of the environment as symbols in a discourse that deals with the vital problems affecting man, or at least affecting the tellers of the myths. So he combs the literature for information about terrain, climate, flora, fauna, constellations, and anything else which might help him to elucidate the language of myth in given societies. The most helpful sources for his purpose are therefore ethnoscientific treatises, but there are few of these for South America, or indeed for anywhere else in the world. Nevertheless, he sets out with extraordinary industry and ingenuity to determine the salient characteristics of natural phenomena in order to speculate on how such features are likely to be perceived. From such speculations he derives a sort of dictionary of potential symbols. Such potentialities only acquire meaning, however, from their position in the constituent elements of myth and the relationship among such elements. Lévi-Strauss usually elucidates this in terms of a dialectic of bipolar oppositions. His insistence in a footnote (p. 74) that he does not always use binary models is accurate but misleading. The fact is that his interpretations of myth, the theoretical assumptions behind them, and the very style in which they are couched all rely heavily and monotonously on binary oppositions. So too did his programmatic paper, "The Structural Study of Myth," and the canonical formula it contained (*Anthropologie structurale*, 1958:252), which was expressly suggested as holding for all myths and which has, on Lévi-Strauss's own admission, guided his work ever since (pp. 211–212). But how does one arrive at these myth structures, or rather, how does one evaluate such postulated formulas once they are arrived at?

Mary Douglas wrote of one of Lévi-Strauss's earlier myth analyses (*La Geste d'Asdiwal*): "Although I have suggested that the symmetry has here and there been pushed too hard, the structure is indisputably there, in the material and not merely in the eye of the beholder" (in Leach 1967:56). But this is a faulty perception of the difficulty. If I read a myth, select certain elements from it, and arrange them in a pattern, that "structure" is bound to be in the material unless I have misread the text or demonstrably misrendered it. The fact of its being there does not, however, indicate that my arrangement is anything more than my personal whim. As a matter of fact, in the case of *La Geste d'Asdiwal*, it is quite possible to emphasize other arrangements that are equally inherent in the myth, especially if one uses the full text and not the abridged version presented by Lévi-Strauss. A myth is therefore bound to have a number of possible "structures" that are both in the material and in the eye of the beholder. The problem is to decide between them and to determine the significance of any of them.

Lévi-Strauss arrives at his structures by determining the referents of mythical symbols from a study of popular sayings, ethnography, and ecology, and then postulating the relationship of these symbols to one another. In order to do this, he frequently deals with groups of myths, selected by him as relating to a single theme. The structure or message (for Lévi-Strauss it amounts to the same thing) that emerges from them is the message of them all, although it may be a set of permutations on a mythic statement. Once such a group has been assembled, Lévi-Strauss feels justified in building the structure out of one feature from one myth and another from another myth, where neither feature appears in the myth containing the other. Having done so, he argues that the groups can be transformed into other groups by the systematic application of certain procedures. The validity of these groups, depending as they do on considerable interpretative abstraction, is open to question. Yet Lévi-Strauss treats them from start as firmly established. This confusion of his method with its results is exemplified by the way in which he deals with a group of "equations" that generate the six variations of a group he calls "The Frog's Feast." In a series of lengthy and ingenious analyses of myths taken from the Guianas, the Chaco, the Tupi, and the Gê, he argues that it is possible to trace a series of transformations. An Arawak myth describes how a woman marries a man and introduces him and his people to honey. When he inadvertently utters her name in public, she turns into a bee and flies away. Bee is here a woman. In a Warrau myth a man marries a girl, shows himself a miraculous and prodigious hunter, but finally turns into a bee and dissolves into honey. This gives the transformation of bee-woman into bee-man. Subsequent transformations deduced occasionally cryptically, from this corpus are bee-man into frog; frog into frog-woman; frog-woman into jaguar-woman; jaguar-woman into jaguar-man; jaguar-man into jaguar-woman. The two final transformations double back on themselves. In Lévi-Strauss's words:

> Just as a seamstress finishing her work folds back the border of her material and sews it on the reverse side where it cannot be seen so that the whole thing does not unravel, [so] the group is completed by turning back the sixth transformation over the fifth one like a hem [p. 220].

On the next page we are told that, because the sixth transformation takes us back to the theme preceding the first one, this shows that there is no need to look further; the group, thus bounded at one of its extremities, is a closed one. But this is to mistake his procedure for his discovery. The sequence and the group are both postulates that depend on each other. One cannot be confirmed by reference to the other.

This type of "confirmation" abounds in the *Mythologiques*. There are references to similar "verifications." There is even talk of "proof." Lévi-Strauss speaks of his rules of method, of his predictions, of their confirmation. He shows his working in a series of diagrams, equations, and graphs, using a notation that imparts an air of science or, at the very least, of rigorous logic to the enterprise, so that it has duly been accepted in some circles as a "science of myth." The kindest thing to be said about such pretensions is that they should be taken as more Lévi-Straussian metaphor. They need not, indeed they cannot, be taken seriously. The rules that are so eloquently discussed are nevertheless imprecisely formulated and intuitively applied. The "verifications" depend on a tissue of assumptions that the reader is supposed to take on trust. Even the pseudological notation, which is undoubtedly convenient, does not mask the fact that Lévi-Strauss is quite causal about relationships that are crucial to his arguments, such as distinction, opposition, and contradiction. For those who find the interpretations implausible, there is little supporting evidence in the "verifications."

This problem of validation is the central difficulty, not only in Lévi-Strauss's analyses of myth, but in all of his structuralism. Unfortunately, he does not recognize it. Again and again he proposes his own theory as the only logically satisfactory solution, when this means it is the only solution that follows from his assumptions. At the beginning of this sustained investigation of myth he could write: "In spite of the formal perspective which it adopts, structural analysis thus validates ethnographic and historical interpretations which we proposed over twenty years ago and which [though] considered overbold at the time, have constantly gained ground [ever since] [1964: 17]." Yet this passage refers to certain papers on the social structures of Brazil that are notorious for their unverifiable speculations, unwarranted inferences, and untenable conclusions. (I am at present preparing a work that sets out the evidence for these categorical assertions.) This is not to say there is nothing in these papers that a specialist in the area would find acceptable or useful. But significantly the useful ideas they contain are not the interpretations Lévi-Strauss erroneously believes to have been validated, but certain general theoretical suggestions. The *Mythologiques* are similarly full of provocative suggestions. Some of them are tossed out as hypotheses about topics on which the author says he is no specialist and into which he does not wish to venture. Certainly it is this imaginative boldness that makes Lévi-Strauss exciting to read, but he can indulge in it at little risk. Since his ideas are infrequently stated as testable propositions, they are not normally refuted. If any of them, however unspecific, are taken up, however tenuously, by area specialists, then he may claim they have been "validated." At the very worst, they are simply left as exciting hypotheses. But when the excitement has died down, it still remains to be seen whether they lead anywhere and which, if any of his suggestions are "right."

Yet even if these theses are unprovable or unproven, this does not necessarily mean that they are inconsiderable or even implausible. This is why *Du miel aux cendres* is so tantalizing. There is so much of it that feels right. Nobody could doubt after reading it that Lévi-Strauss has correctly perceived the paradoxical aspects of the power of honey and tobacco symbolism in South America. He has demonstrated that there are recurrent themes in myth, not merely in the traditional folkloristic sense of textual motifs, but structural messages that may be expressed by varying symbols. His brilliant suggestions concerning the nature of mythic structure have certainly opened new perspectives in the anthropological study of symbolism. Meanwhile, the details of his investigations fascinate even where they fail to convince. Sights, sounds, smells, textures, tastes, their ramifications throughout the environment, their intellectual associations, all are investigated and codified, so that his is a cultural anthropology in its widest sense, peering into those recesses of human activity that anthropologists so often ignore or find inexplicable. But it is all pushed too far. In detail it often achieves self-parody, as when bull-roarers are said to have the function of chasing away women because they expel all the feminine terms from the periodic chain of marriage alliances, which offers a sociological equivalent of the cosmological chain formed by the alternation of night and day, thus:

$$\overset{\urcorner}{\Delta} = \overset{\ulcorner\urcorner}{O\Delta} = \overset{\ulcorner\urcorner}{O\Delta} = \overset{\ulcorner\urcorner}{O\Delta} = \overset{\ulcorner}{O} \equiv$$

= (day-night, day-night, day-night, day-night, etc.) (p.363)

In general, Lévi-Strauss throws out ideas that he does not investigate satisfactorily. Instead, he simply piles on more ideas, till his whole enterprise looks less like a science than a piece of his own *bricolage*.

Finally, one is led to wonder, as others have wondered before (e.g., Douglas 1967), whether peoples all over the world, or even the peoples of South America, really construct such elaborate myth systems in order to transmit coded messages about nature and culture, wife-givers and wife-takers. And should these myths then be treated as hymns or as five-finger exercises? Lévi-Strauss does not discriminate. But an analysis of his own work is illuminating for it reveals an obsession with the nature/culture opposition and the notion of alliance. The patterns of Lévi-Strauss's thought emerge clearly, but what of the Indians, the tellers of the myths? It is not enough to say that structural analysis will reveal what they are trying to say in them simply because myth is a language and structuralism was successful in linguistics. Myth is not language, it is like language. The analogy is useful, but it has its limitations. In language the message is consciously communicated and consciously received by native or fluent speakers. It is not found at the level of syntax. Yet by compiling a syntax of myth, Lévi-Strauss claims to be decoding its unconscious message. Nor do linguists expect to find language universals at the level of syntax, yet Lévi-Strauss implies that there may be a universal language of myth, and he speaks of *"la pensée mythique"* as he sets about writing a grammar for it. There may be indeed, but if so it differs radically from ordinary languages and the same rules cannot be held automatically to apply to them both. So it will not do to suggest, as Leach does (1967:xviii), that those who are sceptical about Lévi-Strauss's revealed syntax of a pan-South American myth language are like the diehards who refused to believe in the deciphering of linear B. The analogy is a false one. After all of Lévi-Strauss's dialectical ingenuity we still do not know who is supposed to be saying what and in what language to whom.

CHAPTER VIII

Lévi-Strauss and Myth

K.O.L. Burridge

I.

The subject of myth is, and has been, anybody's plaything. And because Claude Lévi-Strauss is 'one of the few', a truly great anthropologist who is at once fecund and seminal, as original as he is ingenious, the subject, Lévi-Strauss himself, and Lévi-Strauss's mode of dealing with myth must first be given some general placement.

Most students of culture would agree that their central concern is an understanding of developmental processes. And for anthropologists in particular the central problem remains tied to a still unresolved opposition between History on the one hand and Evolution on the other. Whether the question is how and by what means some hominid crossed 'the threshold' to become *Homo sapiens*, or the movement from one kind of economic or political or symbolic system to another, the same dilemma emerges: how, given a positivist approach and so debarred from a useful if often treacherous transcendentalism, may one reconcile the implications of History with those of Evolution? Given an Aristotelian respect for the so-called 'facts' of ethnography, how, other-than by admitting a Platonic primacy for thought and idea, may such 'facts' be given an appropriate relevance?

Ever since the diffusionist criticism made the dilemma apparent, anthropologists have sought to escape from or reconcile the implications of man as a plaything of nature and evolutionary forces, on the one hand, and man as the arbiter of his fate, stamping the environment with his thought, on the other. Ever since the establishing of the fieldwork tradition—roughly coinciding with the diffusionist criticism—anthropologists have been aware that the inescapable moral relationship between observer and observed precludes anything but a highly coloured and multivalent relevance to an observation. Unable to measure accurately everything they observe, unable to repeat and so re-examine a situation, often disinclined to note what may be repugnant to themselves as moral observers anthropologists have been forced to seek their common departures or 'objectivity' within the schemes or 'languages' of their more illustrious predecessors. And these 'languages' coincide with those devices—such as description and analysis modelled on the natural sciences or 'Marxism' or 'functionalism' or 'structure' or 'topology' or 'statistics', 'numeration', 'communications systems', and the like—which seek either to evade or to approach a reconciliation of the primary terms of the dilemma.

Within such a context the study of myth or myths is of crucial importance. Myths are reservoirs of articulate thought on the level of the collective. But they are not simply 'articulate thought' in a vacuum. They represent the thought of people about themselves and their condition. Moreover, the words of a myth, especially when set down in writing, appear to have an 'objective' existence irrespective of the attitudes and approaches of narrator, listeners, or observer. The question is whether Lévi-Strauss has provided us with a 'language' capable of resolving the dilemma as between History and Evolution, capable of dealing with myth as a social representation as opposed to dealing with myth as a linguistic phenomenon simply.

II.

Three features of the work of Claude Levi-Strauss seem to be relevant here. First, that he is interested in thought, in logic, in modes of articulate thought. Again and again he comes round to saying in one way or another, 'The same logical processes are put to work... man has always been thinking equally well... the improvement in thinking lies not in any alleged progress in man's conscience, but in the discovery of new things to which it may apply its unchangeable abilities' (1963a, p. 230). Second, in his address to this problem of articulate thought, Lévi-Strauss appears to lean heavily on Hegel who, it will be remembered, sought to reconcile the events contained in the progress of history with God and human mental activities or mind; and this largely through the formula 'thesis-antithesis-synthesis', the method of the dialectic. Third, while eschewing Hegel's transcendentalism, Lévi-Strauss's handling of ethnographic materials seems coloured by a Darwinian evolutionism on the one hand and Marxian thought on the other.

Regarding 'Hegel', 'Marx', and 'Darwin' as shorthand characterizations, and recognizing in them the ingredients of the very dilemma which we have already identified, we may say, very briefly and in summary terms, that for Hegel truth or reality consisted in the unification of contradictory elements: and these elements, representing partial aspects of truth, were to be related not only as contradictory but also as logical contraries. An idea or object which seemed to the mind to possess a unity could be broken down into contrary and contradictory elements, and these elements could themselves be further broken down into successive contraries and contradictions. In attempting a synthesis, the building-up of a unitary idea or object from a variety of elements, the same process was involved. This, the method of the dialectic, represented for Hegel a 'negative' reason: it was sceptical, dislocating, even temporarily destructive. Where 'thesis' stood for unity or a unitary formulation, 'antithesis' stood for a breaking-down of this unity into contraries which were also contradictions, and 'synthesis' stood for a rebuilding of the unitary.

In Hegelian terms experience exists within the limits of the categories of language. And even if Hegel had had the benefit of the formulations of Freud or Jung, one cannot see him allowing validity to an experience that could not be reduced to language, the vehicle of the collective. Not simply a question of linguistics, of grammar, phonemes and syntax, the categories of language—the categories of articulate thought—formed, for Hegel, a system with their own laws and relations which appeared in a less obvious form in the theories of nature and the mind. That is, the workings of the mind and the vehicle through which it expresses itself determine not only the ways in which we interpret the workings of nature and ourselves, but the ways in which we view the workings of the mind itself—a theoretically infinite interplay between the mind and its object which is exemplified in the use of, and the thought about, computing machines and communications engineering as well as in the way Lévi-Strauss handles totemism (1962a)—and, indeed, most topics apart from kinship (1949).

Assuming, as one most, a general familiarity with Lévi-Strauss's work, the summary passages above may show something of his reliance upon Hegel. The encounter with Marx is no less interesting. Marx, one might say, seized upon the 'contradictory' rather than the 'contrary' in Hegelian thought, and on the 'material' rather than the 'idealistic' elements in Hegel's dialectic. If, for Hegel, the dialectical process was logical, ontological, and chronological, the dynamic of history lying in the 'Idea', divinely inspired, Marx seems to have taken from Hegel process, progress, the method of the dialectic, the impersonality of history, and the priority of the collective. But he rejected the metaphysical, the theological, and, to a certain extent, the ethical content of Hegel's system. Eschewing, too, the Hegelian gloss of the 'hero' as an embodiment of the collective will, Marx seems to have thought of the 'collective' as necessarily implying a 'group' or 'class', and certainly concentrated upon that dialectical process which is defined and expressed by the struggle for power as between different economic classes or groups within a given environment. But in spite of this narrower and more satisfying definition of the problem in contrast to the much wider and larger Hegelian view, the dilemma is not simply one between a 'larger' and 'narrower' view. Rather does it reside in a logic and an ontology which assume the existence of God, on the one hand, and an empiricism and a materialism which negate the existence of a transcendent deity, on the other. Or, to put it more sharply, 'In the beginning was the word', the primacy of articulate thought as definitive of man, and from which culture flows, as against an economic determinism which, if initially based upon cultural features, has become muddled with environmental determinism and ideas borrowed from biology and evolutionary theory.

Between these two standpoints, there can be no real compromise. If the first acknowledges and admits the force of the second, realizing through the use of the active voice that there must also be a passive, the second can hardly accommodate the first—even though, in fact, the habitual use of the passive tends to invest the active 'natural' or 'evolutionary', or 'social' forces with some vague but always convenient transcendentalism. And though most anthropologists, as it seems to me, tend to try to avoid the implications of these contrary positions by the use of private eclecticisms, by the use of active or passive as occasion seems to demand, in doing so they fall into a trap which seems also to have claimed Lévi-Strauss. For, while Lévi-Strauss accepts the primacy and priority of thought, in his handling of ethnographic data he feels constrained to take a materialist standpoint. Unable to accept a transcendental ontology in relation to the problem of thought, he assumes an evolutionist position by taking 'nature' as his widest context of relevance. His 'nature', indeed, corresponds on the whole to Hegel's 'God'. Never clear about the difference between 'contrary' and a 'contradiction', to whom particular features appear as either one or the other, whether what appears as logically 'contrary' is necessarily ontologically 'contradictory', when a 'contrary' is not a complementarity, or in what circumstances a 'contradiction' is not a complementary opposition, Lévi-Strauss seems to me to be continually attempting to reconcile and resolve three very recalcitrant terms: Hegel, Marx, and that eclecticism which, while reluctant to admit the real animality of man and so the implications of that animality, still insists upon using the more pleasing and flattering aspects of biological evolution while seeking to pin the cultures of man to particular environmental bases.

We may carry these points a little further. In the last chapter of *La Pensée sauvage*, where he engages with Satre on whether or not 'analysis' is compatible with 'dialectic', Lévi-Strauss clearly favours Hegel as against Marx. For, apart from following Hegel in arguing that 'analysis' is contained in, and indeed is, the dialectic, he goes on to say that logical contraries in themselves contain a dynamism of process. Which is a restatement of Hegel—providing that the contraries are also contradictions. Then again, in the last few sentences of *Tristes Tropiques*, there is a quite remarkable reference to exchanging a wink 'with a cat' (1955a, p. 449; 1961, p. 398). And it is not an aside, it is a final fling. What on earth does he mean, if he means anything? What kind of communicative experience is he trying to instance? If one thinks for a moment of the refractions of meaning involved in *La Pensée sauvage*, the terminable dialogue between the mind and its object is inevitably evoked and the whimsical reference to the cat looks like either the shy admission of an ontology based on a mutual participation in 'nature', or, since cats are notoriously disdainful, the admission that the cat cannot relevantly exist outside perceptions of what it might be.

Still, if only because life is relatively short, there must come a point at which the dialogue between the mind and its object may be taken to be concluded. And, it seems to me, Lévi-Strauss finds this terminal within the positivist and materialist limits set by Marx coupled, however, with a regard for 'man in nature'. That is, where Marx is concerned with 'man in society', Lévi-Strauss would seem to want to transcend the empirical facts of observation in a particular view of 'nature': which is an escape from Marx into Hegel, even if it is a Hegel on Lévi-Strauss's own terms.

In a discourse based upon the empirical observation of different cultures a pertinent question, in moving towards the general statement, is at what point and with reference to what kind of vocabulary may a generalization subsume the mass of empirical observations. Lévi-Strauss's answer is in some contrast to most of those to be found in the history of the development of anthropology in Britain and the United States—though the dilemma is the same. On the one hand, there are resorts to eclectic pragmatisms and biological, introspective, technological, and statistical models, a marked reluctance to become 'either history or nothing', a determination to pursue a comfortable middle way, while, on the other hand, there is the realization that the new knowledge may not be as new as all that, and that the central opposition of History and Evolution is best evaded by tapping the springs of thought of the great systematists. Lévi-Strauss was a pupil of Mauss. And if all the members of that community of scholars which one thinks of as the 'French School' owe much to each other, for Lévi-Strauss the debt is greatest to Hegel and Marx rather than to Durkheim or Comte or Montesquieu.

All this is simply to emphasize that if Lévi-Strauss succeeds in representing himself to some of us as alternately windy, or deft, or overgiven to confusing metaphors or ironies, or stimulat ing, or as clever as the boatswain of yore, it is not only because he belongs to a not wholly familiar tradition, but because he is absolutely his contrary self. Not a Marxist, through Marx the bare bones of an ethnographic record are given coherence. Not wholly a Hegelian, at the level of total social fact, and in relation to articulate thought, a Hegelian treatment is demanded. Not a Darwinian, man in nature is his base.

III.

Though Lévi-Strauss's main concern is with the subject of articulate thought, is with the relations between 'the word', 'being', and 'process', myths—which might have pushed him further along the path of his main problem—become for him, on the whole, simply data by means of which an attempted resolution of the Hegelian and Marxian dialectics may be demonstrated. In attempting to reconcile the positive and the transcendental, however, Lévi-Strauss is himself contrary. If he criticizes what he calls the 'functionalist position', making it clear that he thinks that myths ought to be understood as 'things in themselves' without reference to the culture which produced them, his own 'La Geste d'Asdiwal', when compared with his analysis of the Oedipus story in 'The Structural Study of Myth', shows how much more satisfying his method can be when it is related to the culture concerned. Again, the rather laboured passages in 'The Structural Study of Myth' in which he opposes *langue* to *parole*, *traduttore*, and *tradittore*, and goes on to say that the language of myth is the opposite of poetic because it does not suffer from translation (1963a, p. 210), are contradicted by his own acute use of the meanings of words in both 'La Geste d'Asdiwal' and 'Four Winnebago Myths' (1960a). And vagary comes into full flower with the suggestion that American foundations might well lay aside thousands dollars for the structural analysis of myth!

Behind the whimsy and irony, however, as often hidden in as revealed by the clutter of analogies and asides, an obviously powerful and exciting mind is at work. So, quite briefly, Lévi-Strauss's basic approach may be summarized as follows:

1. The whole of culture may be regarded as a communications system. Myth is but a particular form of communication.
Just as one may use the dialectic to analyse culture as a whole, so with myth. To find out what a myth is communicating, the elements must be broken down into pairs of contraries and their resolutions. This breakdown is the structure. What are these elements? Stemming from the dilemma as between Marx and Hegel, Lévi-Strauss is verbose but nothing if not ambiguous On the whole, however, since myths are to be understood as things in themselves, and though his previous best work would deny just this, by 'elements' he means translated words.

2. Lévi-Strauss does not oppose sociology to psychology: instead he contraposes psychology and structure.
This is an important point. In the first place, since the word 'sociology' hardly appears in Lévi-Strauss's work it seems futile to assume that he means by 'structure' any one arbitrarily chosen reference of the many attached to 'sociology', or that

his 'structure' coincides with any one particular usage in English. In the second place, since psychology—*pace* those social anthropologists who still like to think that psychology is concerned only with the single individual and weaning—attempts to systematize human relationships and interrelationships, the distinction which Lévi-Strauss is making seems to be one between form and content, category and behaviour. What interests Lévi-Strauss is not so much what people do, or why they might do what they do, but what they should be called when they do it. Form and category are determined by language rather than by other kinds of behaviour.

3. Lévi-Strauss refuses to be pinned down by the implications of the differences between 'contrary' and 'contradiction'. This is consistent with his overt refusal to consider content, as well as with the model he draws from structural linguistics.

Is this model taken from structural linguistics a sufficient or complete picture of what Lévi-Strauss means by the 'structure of a myth'? One may speak of the structure of a short story being contained in the formula *situation-complication-resolution-rider or twist*, where the last term provides a new situation itself capable of being complicated if necessary, resolved, and followed by a further rider. And at this level the formula could be said to represent the 'structure' of all or most short stories: By applying the formula to successively smaller parts of the whole story one would eventually have the 'structure' of a particular short story. Moreover, if the formula corresponds to the dialectic cycle, since it refers at any level to contradiction and conflict in terms of content, it is Marxian rather than Hegelian—in the sense that Marx would neglect contraries of verbal form, emphasizing contradictions of situational content or organizational incompatibilities, whereas Hegel would not admit such a contradiction unless he could find it to imply a logical contrary and *vice versa*. As I understand him in what he does as opposed to what he says one ought to do, Lévi-Strauss's notion of 'structure' in relation to myth is an attempt to marry the kind of formulation instanced above with that part of the Hegelian system which refers to logical contraries.

Consistently applied this, I think, would be good. But Lévi-Strauss is not consistent. Where Hegel insisted that 'contrary' and 'contradiction'—the statement about the behaviour and the behaviour itself—should coincide or correspond to each other, and

Marx emphasized the element of 'contradiction', leaving the 'contraries' or statements about the behaviour to look after themselves, Lévi-Strauss employs an *ad hoc* and arbitrary mixture of systems, overtly inclining tot emphasize the 'contrary' only. Given this mixture of dialectics, and given the common experience of the fieldworker writing up his data that apparent contradictions on one level appear as harmonies or consistencies on another, the methodology itself will predicate what a particular myth 'is about'; and what a myth 'is about' is likely to be arbitrary in one sense or another. Lévi-Strauss wants it both ways, and he attempts to reconcile the opposed positions of Hegel and Marx in the formula, '...the purpose of myth is to provide a logical model capable of overcoming a (real) contradiction' (1963a, p. 229). That is, a myth informs its bearers of contradictions in life, and then it attempts—as I would prefer to put it here—to explain them away.

Is this really what myths do or 'are about'? Let us be clear. If Lévi-Strauss, often gives the impression that he is almost contemptuous of the futilities of men, he is always concerned with the uniqueness and primacy of Man—particularly with his definitive attribute, articulate thought. Really what a myth 'is about' or is 'telling' us or its bearers is, for Lévi-Strauss, a secondary consideration, a by-product of the main point at issue: the structure of articulate thought. Further, what Lévi-Strauss wants to demonstrate—as against, for example, such writers as Lévy-Bruhl—is the universality of the processes of articulate thought. Symbols, things, and particular relations may differ from culture to culture, but the address of the human mind towards them is the same—'unchangeable' Moreover, it is just this 'sameness' that constitutes the 'structure'. Whether the context involves one or more cultures, structure' is to be found at that level of abstraction which resolves apparently different relations into corresponding relations or 'sameness'. In his approach to myth, that is, Lévi-Strauss attempts to demonstrate the assumption that used to be known as the 'psychic unity of mankind'; and his notion of 'structure' is predicated by the point—which must vary according to context—at which differences are merged in sameness or correspondence. Which is excellent if correspondences refer to relations or sets of relations in their content, not so happy perhaps where form and category are not necessarily derived from content.

Having made these points about Lévi-Strauss's usage of the term 'structure', his opposition to 'psychological explanations'—though he never makes it clear except by implication what kinds of explanation these are or can be—as well as his reluctance to talk about 'sociology' or 'sociological' become clearer. By 'psychological explanation', Lévi-Strauss cannot mean simply explanations which lean on, or are borrowed from, psychology or psychologists. These are part and parcel of our general ambience of ideas. He means, presumably, that kind of explanation in which the investigator assumes that the cultural experiences and reactions of the people under survey are, or are almost, identical with his own at their own levels—or that kind of explanation which depends upon a shifting and ethnocentric concept of 'normality' and is not referred to an objective and persistent formal collective. And for Lévi-Strauss this objective collective is to be discovered in language, in the categories of articulate thought. If it can be shown that all peoples everywhere think articulately in the same way, have the same logic, then this logic will provide the common framework within terms of which any culture may be described and analysed. Hence, perhaps, the reluctance to use the term 'sociology'; 'sociologies' tend to come in different and not wholly compatible varieties.

'Structure', for Lévi-Strauss, is concerned with logical categories and the form of the relations between them. He explicitly eschews, though in fact in this he is as guilty as most of us, those verbose circumlocutions which so often conceal explanations referable not to a collective form but rather to an author's private emotional state or psychology, or are at bottom a 'herd instinct' or 'natural proclivity' kind of explanation. Further, such interest as Lévi-Strauss has in social relations, in the ways in which offices, groups, statuses, roles, and the rest are related, is simply a preliminary towards elucidating 'total social fact'—normally linguistically and adjectivally determined—and then the logical structure which appears to contain these relations.

Lévi-Strauss's priorities may, therefore, be summed up as follows:

1.   Structure, in which are entailed—
      (a) the primacy of the collective,
      (b) extrication from involvement in concrete behavior

(c) a frame of reference which has objective value, if it can be shown that the processes of thought follow a universal logic.
2.   The 'structure' of thought.
3.   The use of myth to demonstrate (1) and (2) above.
4.   Almost incidentally, as it were, to elucidate what the myth 'is about' in terms of content and communicative meaning.

Given these priorities, and coming closer to the specific problems, the purpose of myth, says Lévi-Strauss, is to provide a logical model capable of overcoming a real contradiction Elements of the myth (thesis) are to be broken down into pairs of contraries (antithesis), resolved through mediators (synthesis and thesis), and further broken down into contraries (antithesis again) which are to be resolved again in mediators (synthesis and thesis) only to be broken down yet again into contraries. These elements—which I have suggested tend in fact to be words—tend to be restricted in number in any particular myth, and are themselves composed of further elements whose different combinations—of the kind b-a-t, r-a-t, t-a-r, t-a-b—provide the inner contradictions and mediations which, in turn point to the main contradiction which it is felt that the myth is trying to 'explain away', or provide a logical model capable of overcoming or reconciling.

IV.

How does all this work out?

Both critique and appreciation are provided by examining a very short myth collected in New Guinea:

> Once upon a time the leading man of the village was fishing by the light of his bamboo torch in Cipenderp stream when it came on to rain. The leading man and all the other men and women of the village took shelter under the lee of a large stone. The last to come were a boy and his sister, orphans. They were dirty, unwashed, and smelly.
>
> 'Hey! You two can't come in here!' exclaimed the leading man. 'You smell too much!"
>
> The storm increased in intensity, the rain poured down, the two orphans sought shelter in a hollow tree.
>
> Seeing what had happened, the Great One on High sympathized with the orphans. He caused the stone to envelope the villagers.
>
> The orphans returned to the village, mourning their fellows. Later they tried to crack open the stone. It was no use. They killed all

the pigs in the village, collected piles of foodstuffs and, with the help of neighbours, put all the meat and tubers by the stone.
It was no good. The villagers died of hunger inside the stone.

Some preliminary points. I cannot honestly say that I wholly follow Lévi-Strauss's treatment of the Oedipus story in 'The Structural Study of Myth'. In what follows I am not attempting to be, or be like, Lévi-Strauss. I am simply going to try to follow his instructions. If I end up by demonstrating an inability to follow him, well, perhaps a critique is implied. Farther, since we have been asked to deal with Lévi-Strauss in relation to our own fieldwork, it becomes virtually impossible to detach oneself from a host of 'prejudices' as to what the myth is 'really about'. And, finally, if the purpose of myth is to overcome a real contradiction, and one has particular kinds of contradiction in mind, then it will no doubt be possible to find those contradictions. There are few purposes a myth will not adequately serve.

Putting the story onto cards, then (1963a, p. 211), resulted in not just one pack but three slightly different packs. So, by slipping round some facets of meaning which I thought I knew were there, I reduced the three packs to one. Four results are worth setting out, the first on Lévi-Strauss's Zuñi model, the others on the Oedipus model.

The initial situation may be broken down into the 'contraries' 'light' and 'darkness', which may be said to be mediated by 'stream'. For, since a stream flows on in the same way whether it is light or dark, it is unaffected by the contraries and so resolves them. But a stream is water, water is rain, and rain is the source of the stream: we get the contraries 'in the rain' and 'out of the rain'. This pair is resolved in the notion of 'shelter' which is itself broken down into 'good' people in one kind of shelter and 'smelly'—or, as is the case if we take note of the cultural content of the vernacular terms—'bad' people, the orphans, in another kind of shelter: stone, which makes cultural tools, as opposed to hollow tree, a wild or non-cultural place. If these contraries are mediated by more rain, the latter introduces the Great One who, in two contexts, further separates the orphans from the 'good' people. We are left with the shadow presence of the Great One, and the orphans who, one may presume, restart community life through an incestuous union. As between 'good' people and 'bad' people, or the Great One and community, or the Great One and the orphans, or incest and non-incest, or perhaps dual origin and single origin (orphans, Great One), which is the main contradiction that the myth attempting to overcome by the positing of a logical model?

Turn now to the Oedipus example. A first result may be obtained by picking out relationships which are characterized by aid or reciprocity and opposing them to relationships in which non-reciprocity appears as definitive. Thus the leading man and the villagers, the Great One sympathizing with the orphans, and the orphans putting food against the stone may be opposed to the villagers and leading man excluding the orphans, the Great One enveloping the villagers, the Great One not acceding to the wishes of the orphans. What is left to go into the other two columns? 'Rain' and 'shelter', 'in the rain' as opposed to 'out of the rain'. Perhaps we may resolve this in the formulae, *Reciprocity: Shelter :: Non-reciprocity : Rain; or Reciprocity : Non-reciprocity :: Shelter: Rain;* or, by a rearrangement of the terms above, and ignoring things or phenomena, *Brother-and-sister incest : Reciprocity :: Self-will of the Great One : Good people in community.*

So far as I am concerned, knowing the culture, all the formulae obtained are good. But, again, I leave it to the reader to assess whether they are the kind of formulae Lévi-Strauss would like, and to state the real contradiction that is being overcome.

Take another result. Forget reciprocities and substitute relations of 'exclusion' and 'inclusion'. This yields the following: *Inclusion: Incest :: Bamboo torch and shelter: Exclusion; or Inclusion: Exclusion :: Bamboo torch and shelter: Rain and hollow tree; or, Exclusion: Community :: Brother-and-sister incest: Inclusion; or, Hollow tree: Shelter :: Incest: Community; or, Exclusion: Inclusion :: Incest: Community.* One could in fact go on. The last is probably the best from Lévi-Strauss's point of view because it does not bring in concrete things. Still, I have brought in these concrete things in order to go back to them presently. Let us say, though, that by combining all the results so far obtained, the 'real contradiction' between reciprocity and non-reciprocity, or between inclusion in community and exclusion from community, is logically resolved or explained away by the notion that incest is non-human or non-social. And then let us impose upon the myth Lévi-Strauss's favourite contraries Life and Death, which he also seems to assume imply a contradiction.

Here pause for a moment.... For in his usage of Life and Death Lévi-Strauss seems persistently to assume the standpoint not only of an individual but of a very particular individual—what life and death may mean to him, how these contraries may be resolved on the level of the myth for an individual. Is this not precisely that worst kind of psychologism against which Lévi-Strauss so inveighs! For most peoples death is but a passage from one kind of being to another, and as a passage death usually corresponds to birth and the movement from child to adult—the kind of movement in which Hegel would have delighted. But if Life and Death are to be taken as relevant 'contraries' and 'contradictions' then they should be referred to the collective, to the culture or community concerned: the survival or death of the community. And if we do take Life and Death in this way, and not as Lévi-Strauss would appear to regard them, we arrive at the formula, *Life: Death :: Community : Incest (between brother and sister)*. Which is good. Yet we could go even further. For, granting that death is but a passage from one kind of being to another, the same formula could be used in the case where a traditional community is dying and a new one is emerging. Which is precisely the burden of the Hegelian dialectic, but not what Lévi-Strauss seems to have in mind.

However, given the results above, what, in particular, is the myth 'about'?

The first point that emerges is that if the method works the answer is predicated by the initial address. Given the dialectics, and given that the purpose of myth is to provide a logical model capable of overcoming a real contradiction, if it is not clear—at least to me— in what sense real contradictions are overcome, it is demonstrable that contraries appear to be resolved, and that the structure of thought might be the same as elsewhere. But, and it needs to be repeated, the results seem to sprig from the imposition of a particular mode of thought rather than from the material. Someone who was resolved to show that the structure of articulate thought as demonstrated by to myth was different might be able to do so. And the riposte would be, I suppose, that since differences have been elicited the investigator has not been working at the level of structure

The second point that emerges is that, given Lévi-Strauss' technique, or 'language', or mode of address, much more might be done.

V.

To see how much more might be done, and for the purposes of a more constructive critique, turn now to an approach that climbs blatantly upon Lévi-Strauss's broad back and goes to content rather than the form. Given that culture is the primary and prior reality to be examined, allow primacy of place to articulate thought which may express itself in words, in a carving, or in other ways. Instead of attempting to peg the parts of culture to contingent facets of nature, physical environment, biology, instincts, or proclivities, let us be content with clusters of mutually defining relations—to start with at any rate. Suppose that a myth is a mode of cognition, not simply communication, which informs its bearers of the possibilities of awareness in the culture concerned. Suppose we say that the resonances of words do matter, and that in this sense mythical language, *contra* Lévi-Strauss, is poetic. Suppose we use an old literary technique and, quite coincidentally, try to demonstrate Lévi-Strauss's own dictum in relation to totemism... not 'good to eat, but... good to think' with (1964a, p. 89). Then further suppose that, for heuristic purposes, we separate myth (Myth) from the rest of culture (Culture) and attempt a dialogue between the relevant parts contained in the two main terms—what do we get?

It is neither practicable nor, indeed, necessary to proceed to a full and exhaustive demonstration of what is involved in the approach summarized above. It is sufficient to show the potential. Take first, 'bamboo torch'. In the culture, bamboo is used in a variety of ways as a container, primarily for water and for cooking strips of pig-meat. More dramatically, however, bamboo slivers were used as razors for circumcising boys, and the circumciser was a mother-brother. In the corpus of myths available in the culture, bamboo frequently occurs in association with mother-brother and circumcision, but only rarely explicitly as a razor. Yet within the dialogue Myth-Culture—and it should be remembered that the myth is not there on a piece of paper, but is being presented to an audience each of whom knows the myth, knows what has happened and what is going to happen next—we may speak of bamboo as evoking circumcision, the meaning of circumcision, and particular relevances of the mother-brother. Indeed, if one goes through the whole corpus of the mythology to which the story of the orphans belongs, substituting 'circumcision' for 'bamboo', the correspondences turn out to be very precise. That is, in Myth the word 'bamboo' means, signals or stands for, or evokes 'circumcision'. Since, however, the contextual references of 'bamboo' in Myth vary in certain particulars, and those latter provide additional resonances of meaning, we can in the end obtain reasonably accurate and objective indications of the thought about the relations between father, mother, son, mother-brother, and circumcision. Further, these indications of themselves cannot but throw 'water', 'pig-meat', and 'light' into a more meaningful perspective. All of which is at the least very useful when, as happens to be the case, circumcision is no longer practiced.

Second, consider the word 'shelter'. Both in Myth and in Culture a 'shelter' is primarily shelter from the storm; and the word 'shelter' in fact connotes community and culture as distinct from the forest and natural world, the controlled and ordered as distinct from the uncontrolled or uncontrollable and unordered or wild. After a close scrutiny of the mythology, and after a process of testing and retesting, we find that 'roof thatch' is a synonym for 'shelter', and that both terms stand for, indicate, or evoke a clubhouse and associated organization, now defunct, known as the *garamb*.

The *garamb* was a men's house. Boys spent a period of apprenticeship there, and the climax to this was circumcision, a rite which took place in or near the *garamb,*, and which is said to have 'made a boy into a man'. Indeed, circumcision qualified a youth for marriage, set him on the road to full manhood, gave him full membership of the clubhouse where responsible men foregathered. So that the word 'shelter' in its varying contexts both in Myth and in Culture indicates something of the thought about the relations between the clubhouse and the rite of circumcision.

Yet we may go even further. Men, but not boys, it is represented in the Culture, were originally made from the flesh of a pig; and when a youth was circumcised father had to provide him with a 'pig of the circumcision'. So that it is not just 'men in the beginning' who were made from pig-flesh, but all men as they become men and are circumcised. 'Light', we would come to know, is associated with whiteness, with an appropriate passage of the *garamb* through circumcision, with responsibility in the moral community, with the ability to see and so be aware of what is entailed in moral responsibility; 'Darkness', on the other hand, is associated with the wild, with the colour black with blindness, and so with the inability to see and be aware, with sorcerers who, excluded from the moral community, paint their faces black when engaged in their nefarious and amoral activities. In the corpus of myths water is always the stuff from which the seminal male element emerges; maidens who are about to become wives go down to the stream to fish, rain is associated with semen, and the storm—thunder, lightning, and earthquake (which latter is represented in the stone enveloping the villagers)—generally figure male attributes, particularly those qualities which a father ought to pass on to his son, and which are thought of as having been passed to the son when, upon the son being circumcised in or near the *garamb*, father presented the pig of the circumcision....

Certainly, the myth may be said to be providing a 'logical model capable of overcoming the 'real contradiction' between reciprocity and non-reciprocity, or between inclusion in community and exclusion from community. And certainly, paraphrasing Lévi-Strauss and his Oedipus model, one could say that the myth provided a logical model capable of overcoming the 'contradiction' between the decisive and singular seminal power of the male (the Great One), on the one hand, and the necessity to maintain the incest taboo and marry a woman who is not a sister, on the other. Certainly, too, most of the formulae we have obtained from a use of Lévi-Strauss's method are good, informative, so far as they go. But do they go far enough? Somehow one wishes that the formulae obtained by Lévi-Strauss's method could have told us that the myth not only was about incest but also indicated what was involved—or what was involved in thinking about—the qualities of maleness, fatherhood, the particular features of the father-son, the role of the *garamb* and the mother-brother, the value of circumcision, how a youth grows into responsible manhood, the nature of moral responsibility, and why dirty and smelly people should not have access to the *garamb*....

For the purposes of the rather slight demonstration above, we have but taken two words, words referring to things, 'bamboo torch' and 'shelter'. Even so, the beginnings of a symbolic system, of clusters of interrelated features, have become evident. Yet a complete examination would involve extending the scrutiny to include the referents of the categories of characters and relationships as well as of things in themselves. Thus the evocations of stream, rain, bamboo torch, shelter, stone, hollow tree, pig, and foodstuffs may be related to leading man, orphans, Great One, neighbours, and further related to leading man and community, orphans and leading man and community, Great One and orphans, Great One and community, orphans and neighbours, brother and sister.... Only after one has examined a myth on its own terms within the context of a corpus of myths, and discovered the idiom of myth, does it become possible to enter into a meaningful dialogue between Culture and Myth.

One result of the engagement between the two forms of collective is, of course, an incomparably richer understanding of the culture concerned. And for most anthropologists this ought to be reward enough. Another result is that one can obtain at least an outline of the symbolic system within which the members of a culture have their being, and this in terms of interrelated clusters of ideas which are themselves quite clearly tied to, or more closely associated with, particular sets of activities. Further, since the engagement is on the level of the collective, since two forms of collective are being engaged a thesis-antithesis to yield a synthesis, one may obtain a reasonably precise evaluation of the possibilities of awareness which a particular culture holds out to its members, and different kind of awareness may be seen as attaching to particular processes in the life cycle as well as to particular relationships. Finally, since in any culture people relate their myths to each other and discuss them, so subtly changing their content, whether one is examining 'Coronation Street', sacred stories, or the story of the two orphans, the encounter between living people and their myths precisely corresponds to the dialogue between Myth and Culture, and is, indeed, the living dialectic of history.

VI.

Claude Lévi-Strauss's pioneering contribution to the study of myth will take its place beside Rivers's 'Genealogical Method' as one of those essential techniques upon which anthropological studies depend. Even so, it seems to be a limited technique, a technique which is self-explanatory and self-justifying. Which is why it has been found necessary to offer an alternative approach: internally, on his own ground, Lévi-Strauss's method is unassailable simply because it is self-justifying and self-explanatory. And so far as the suggested alternative approach seems to promise more than Lévi-Strauss's mode of address thus far may one be justified in feeling that the alternative is more useful. Given that the alternative has not been, and within the scope of this paper cannot be, fully demonstrated, and given that its promise must be in the nature of assertions which cannot possibly be fulfilled entirely, still there seem to be good reasons, beyond mere usefulness, for choosing to use it rather than follow Lévi-Strauss. So, assuming for the moment that we are not dealing with a mere personal difference of concern or interest, with a division of labour within a particular field, it is worth while concluding by summing up what is involved in the two approaches.

1. Either the term 'culture' connotes a field of study which exists within its own right, something *sui generis* which flows from and expresses and articulates thought, to be examined on its own terms as a complex of interior and mutually defining, relations whatever the kinds of abstraction that may be made from it; or culture must ever be subject to those exterior anchorages which are, most usually, reductionisms of a biological or physical environmental kind.

The approach suggested here plumps for the first alternative: culture is irreducible, depends upon words and articulate thought, and should be studied in terms of itself. Maybe there is a relation between culture and environmental conditions, just as there may be a relation between madness and phases of the moon. But medical science would scarcely have advanced as far as it has if it insisted on anchoring all illnesses to the movements and phases of heavenly bodies. Lévi-Strauss is unclear and ambiguous on the matter. He seems to want Hegel and Marx and Darwin where he can only have Hegel or Marx or Darwin.

2. Lévi-Strauss's whole argument in 'The Structural Study of Myth' rests on the direct translatability of myth, on the assumption that the language of myth is non-poetic, that a myth may be translated without any concern for the resonances of words on either hand. If I have not actually demonstrated that the meanings and resonances of words can be decisive, then Lévi-Strauss's own 'La Geste d'Asdiwal' does. Not only is Lévi-Strauss, in fact if not in explicit statement, ambiguous about biological and environmental reductionisms, but he wants to anchor the terms of one culture in the terms of another The alternative approach suggested rests on giving the resonances of words their full values. Only in this way, it seems to me, may we arrive at correspondences in relations rather than correspondences dependent on adventitious translations. Witchcraft among the Azande does not correspond to witchcraft in England; but there are sets of relations in England which do correspond to witchcraft relations among the Azande. The exotic vocabulary of

anthropology has been a screen, not a door—as Lévi-Strauss himself has illustrated in relation to totemism.

3. Though he is nothing if not consistently ambiguous, on the whole Lévi-Strauss goes to form rather than content. The approach suggested emphasizes content, regarding form as simply a convenient if revealing mode of ordering the content in a particular cultural context.

4. Lévi-Strauss ignores Hegel's insistence that a contrary should also be a contradiction, and he leaves out of account whether what is contrary, or a contradiction, in one culture necessarily so in another. To be sure, there is no reason why he should stick to Hegel if he does not wish to do so. Nor is under any compulsion to be rigorously Marxian. But explicitly expounding a methodology dependent on the meanings of 'contrary' and 'contradiction' there is a need for precision. 'Life' and 'Death' are certainly 'contraries'. But in what sense are they necessarily 'contradictions'? By 'contradictions' we normally refer, surely, to goal-directed activities, or on-going processes, which effectively and simultaneously negate each other. 'Life' and 'Death' are alternatives: either 'alive' or 'dead'. A 'real contradiction' would involve, at any level, the experience of 'life' and the experience of 'death' at one and the same time. Which is unusual without shading in the meanings of 'life' and 'death'.

Despite his formal strictures against 'psychologisms', Lévi-Strauss frequently falls into just this trap. In his use of 'life' and 'death', for example, those favourite contraries of his, Lévi-Strauss evidently has in mind the meaning of 'life' and death' for himself or for an imaginary individual. The alternative approach suggested would, on the other hand, relate such a contrary to the collective. Thus incestuous relations of themselves do not necessarily predicate the deaths of particular people; but they would, for example, predicate the death of a culture built on exchange relationships dependent on the incest categories.

6. The history of anthropology is studded with formulations as to the purpose of myth. If we must keep to Lévi-Strauss's terms—that the purpose of myth is to provide a logical model capable of overcoming a contradiction—then, since all myths in fact present an audience with quasi-concrete situations, it is just as adequate to say that myths provide concrete situations capable of overcoming logical contradictions. Which is to reveal Lévi-Strauss's assertion as of the

kind which asks whether the purpose of the skull is to keep the ears apart, or whether the ears are separated in order to allow for the skull. Myths serve many purposes, almost any purpose. The problem, surely, is not to discover a particular purpose but, since myths are a part of total culture, to systematize their value as modes of cognition, as parts of that on-going process which Hegel thought of as the dialectic of history, and which the engagement between Culture and Myths seems to offer.

7. Finally, an initial hesitation in offering an alternative procedure as critique rather than making piecemeal criticisms of Lévi-Strauss on his own ground has been overcome by several considerations. One can only criticize or evaluate in the light of alternatives. Lévi-Strauss is extremely persuasive. Like the children who followed the pied piper, once caught by the jigging beat of binary oppositions, enthusiasts may jump for joy, not caring whether the next meal is raw or cooked. Like Freud, Marx, or Jung, Lévi-Strauss offers us a sweet-scented haven with many floral bowers in which to dally—or so it might seem. Yet perhaps it is an Erehwon. For Lévi-Strauss's method seems to impose a spurious uniformity on the material, spurious because order springs not from the encounter between investigator and data but from the categories of a closed system which cannot admit further possibilities. It negates the whole task of discovering the different kinds of forms within which the same sets of relations are organized or given coherence. All myths become much the same, dealing with the same things in the same ways. Yet it is evident—at least to the present writer—that this is just what myths do not do. Methodologically, Lévi-Strauss's procedure seems to represent much the same kind of imposture as was made by those of our predecessors who, by defining religion, law, economies, and political system in particular ways, could conclude that such and such had no law or religion, or political system, or economies. What of the singular and unbifurcated? Obsessed as he is with binary oppositions, with pairs and contraries, Lévi-Strauss seems scarcely to notice that contemplation and accommodation of the idea of the singular which could be said to lie at the roots of civilized life.

In conclusion, lest it be thought that these last paragraphs undervalue Lévi-Strauss, let it be stressed that the formulae obtained by Lévi-Strauss's method in relation to the story of the two orphans are all good. I know they are good, and, having access both to the culture and its mythology, more than anyone else I can appreciate how good they are. The issues are whether the empirical exercise, fieldwork, can invalidate Lévi-Strauss's method—I do not see how it can—and whether such formulae as may be produced are self-explanatory or refer to something other than themselves. If fieldwork cannot invalidate a method—should the method be followed? If formulae are self-explanatory—can they pose any further problems?

CHAPTER IX

The Meaning of Myth
with special reference to 'La Geste d'Asdiwal'

Mary Douglas

Social anthropology, as we know it, was born of a professedly empirical approach. And it was first developed in Britain. These two marks, of being British and empirical, are not accidentally linked. This is the home of philosophical scepticism, an attitude of thought which has insulated us more effectively than the North Sea and the Channel from Continental movements of ideas. Our intellectual climate is plodding and anti-metaphysical. Yet, in spite of these traditions, we cannot read much of Lévi-Strauss without feeling some excitement. To social studies he holds out a promise of the sudden lift that new methods of science could give. He has developed his vision so elaborately and documented it so massively from so many fields of our subject that he commands our attention.

He has developed most explicitly in connection with myth his ideas of the place of sociology within a single grand discipline of Communication. This part of his teaching draws very broadly on fine structural analysis of linguistics, and on cybernetics and communication theory in general, and to some extent on the related theory of games. Briefly, its starting-point is that it is the nature of the mind to work through form. Any experience is received in a structured form, and these forms or structures, which are a condition of knowing, are generally unconscious (as, for an example, unconscious categories of language). Furthermore, they vary little in modern or in ancient times. They always consist in the creation of pairs of opposites, which are balanced against one another and built up in various (algebraically representable) ways,. All the different kinds of patterned activity can be analyzed according to the different structures they produce. For example, social life is a matter of interaction between persons. There are three different types of social communication. First, there is kinship, the structure underlying the rules for transferring women; second, there is the economy, that is the structure underlying transfer of goods and services; third, there is the underlying structure of language. The promise is that if we can get at these structures, display and compare them, the way is open for a true science of society, so far a will-o'-the-wisp for sociologists.

So far myth has not been mentioned. Lévi-Strauss recognizes that its structures belong to a different level of mental activity from those of language, and the technique correspondingly different. The technique is described in 'Structural Study of Myth' (1955) and is also made very clear Edmund Leach's two articles (1961, 1962) in which he applies the technique to the Book of Genesis. It assumes that the analysis of myth should proceed like the analysis of language. In both language and myth the separate units have no meaning by themselves, they acquire it only because of the way which they are combined. The best comparison is with musical notation: there is no musical meaning in a single isolated note. Describing the new science of mythologies which is to parallel linguistics, Lévi-Strauss unguardedly says that the units mythological structure are sentences. If he took this statement seriously it would be an absurd limitation on analysis. But fact, quite rightly, he abandons it at once, making great ply with the structure underlying the meaning of a set of names. What are sentences, anyway? Linguists would be at a loss identify these units of language structure which Lévi-Strauss claims to be able to put on punched cards and into a computing machine as surely and simply as if they were phonemes and morphemes. For me and for most of us, computer talk is a mysterious language very apt for prestidigitation. Does he really mean that he can chop a myth into semantic units, put them through a machine, and get out at the other end an underlying pattern which is not precisely the one he used for selecting his units? The quickness of the hand deceives the eye. Does he further believe that this underlying structure is to real meaning or sense of the myth? He says that it is the deepest kind of sense, more important than the uninitiated reader would suspect. However, I do not think it is fair to such an ebullient writer to take him literally. In other contests it is plain that Lévi-Strauss realizes that any myth has multiple meanings and that no one of them can be labelled the deepest or the truest. More of this later.

From the point of view of anthropology, one of his novel departures is to treat all versions of a myth as equally authentic or relevant. This is right, of course. Linguistic analysis can be applied to any literary unit, and the longer the better, so long as there is real unity underlying the stretches of language that are analysed together. Why stop short at one of Shakespeare's historical plays? Why not include the whole of Shakespeare? Or the whole of Elizabethan drama? Here Lévi-Strauss gives one of his disturbing twists of thought that make the plodding reader uneasily suspect that he is being duped. For by 'version' we find that Lévi-Strauss means both version and interpretation He insists that Freud's treatment of the Oedipus myth must be put through the machine together with other earlier versions This challenging idea is not merely for the fun of shocking the bourgeois mythologist out of his search for original versions. Freud used the Oedipus myth to stand for his own discovery that humans are each individually concerned with precisely the problem of 'birth from one' or 'birth from two' parents. On Lévi-Strauss's analysis of its structure, this problem is revealed as underlying the Oedipus cycle. So there is no inconsistency between Freud and Sophocles. But the reference to Freud interestingly vindicates Lévi-Strauss on a separate charge. Some must feel that the themes which his technique reveals are too trivial and childish either to have been worth the ovation, or to have been worth the erecting of an elaborate myth series in the first place. But after Freud no one can sure that an individual's speculation about his own genesis is a trivial puzzle without emotional force.

I admit that the use of all interpretations of a great myth might not always so triumphantly vindicate this method. Meyer Fortes (1959) treated Oedipus rather differently in *Oedipus and Job in West Africa*. Compare St Augustine, Simone Weil (1950), and Edmund Leach (1962) on the Biblical story of Noah drunk in the vineyard: for one the drunken, naked Noah is Christ humiliated; for the other he is the dionysian mysteries too austerely rejected by the Jewish priesthood, and for the last the tale is a trite lesson about Hebrew sexual morality. I will say more below of how those 'versions' would look coming out of the mythologic computer. At this stage of the discussion we should treat the computer as a red herring and forget for the moment the quest for the real meaning. We can then begin seriously to evaluate Lévi-Strauss's approach to mythology.

First, we should recognize his debt to the dialectical method of Hegelian-Marxist philosophy. The dialectic was Hegel's speculation about the nature of reality and about the logical technique by which it could be grasped. When Lévi-Strauss says that mythic thought follows a strict logic of its own, he means a Hegelian logic of thesis, antithesis, and synthesis, moving in ever more complex cycles to comprehend all the oppositions and limitations inherent in thought. According to Lévi-Strauss, the structure of myth is a dialectic structure in which opposed logical positions are stated, the oppositions mediated by a restatement, which again, when its internal structure becomes clear, gives rise to another kind of opposition, which in its turn is mediated or resolved, and so on.

On the assumption that it is the nature of myth to mediate contradictions, the method of analysis must proceed by distinguishing the oppositions and the mediating elements. And it follows, too, that the function of myth is to portray the contradictions in the basic premises of the culture. The same goes for the relation of myth to social reality. The myth is a contemplation of the unsatisfactory compromises which, after all, compose social life. In the devious statements of the myth, people can recognize indirectly what it would be difficult to admit openly and yet what is patently clear to all and sundry, that the ideal is not attainable.

Lévi-Strauss does not stick his neck out so far as to say that people are reconciled better or worse to their makeshift arrangements and contradictory formulae—but merely that myth makes explicit their experience of the contradictoriness of reality.

A summary of 'La Geste d'Asdiwal' best demonstrates how this is to be understood. It is a cycle of myths told by the Tsimshian tribes. These are a sparse population of migratory hunters and fishers who live on the Pacific coast, south of Alaska. They are culturally in the same group with Haida and Tlingit, northernmost representatives of Northwest Coast culture. Topographically their territory is dominated by the two parallel rivers, Nass and Skeena, which flow southwest to the sea. In the summer they live on vegetable products collected by women, and in winter on marine and land animals and fish killed by the men. The movements of fish and game dictate their seasonal movements between sea and mountains, and the northern and southern rivers. The Tsimshian were organized in dispersed matrilineal clans and lived in typical Northwest Coast composite dwellings which housed several families. They tended to live with their close maternal kin, generally practicing avunculocal residence at marriage and the ideal was to marry a mother's brother's daughter.

> The myth begins during the winter famine in the Skeena valley. A mother and daughter, separated hitherto by their marriages but now both widowed by the famine, set out from East and West, one from upstream and one from downstream of the frozen Skeena, to meet each other half-way. The daughter becomes the wife of a mysterious bird who feeds them both and when she gives birth to a miraculous child, Asdiwal, its bird father gives him a magic bow and arrow, lance, snow-shoes, cloak, and hat which make him invisible at will, invincible, and able to produce an inexhaustible supply of food. The old mother dies and the bird father disappears. Asdiwal and his mother walk West to her natal village. From there he follows a white bear into the sky where it is revealed as Evening-Star, the daughter of the Sun. When Asdiwal has succeeded, thanks to his magic equipment, in a series of impossible tasks, the Sun allows him to marry Evening-Star, and, because he is homesick, to take his wife back to the earth generously supplied with magic food. On earth, because Asdiwal is unfaithful to her, his sky wife leaves him. He follows her half-way to the sky, where she kills him with a thunderbolt. Via father-in-law, the Sun, brings him to life and they live together in the sky until Asdiwal feels homesick again. Once home, Asdiwal finds his mother is dead and, since nothing keeps him in her village, he continues walking to the West. This time he makes a Tsimshian marriage, which starts well, Asdiwal using his magic hunting-weapons to good effect. In the spring he, his wife, and her four brothers move along the coast northward towards the River Nass, but Asdiwal challenges his brothers-in-law to prove that their sea-hunting is better than his land-hunting. Asdiwal wins the contest by bringing home four dead bears from his mountain hunt, one for each of the four brothers, who return empty handed from their sea expedition. Furious at their defeat, they carry off their sister and abandon Asdiwal, who then joins some strangers also going North towards the Nass for the candlefish season. Once again, there are four brothers, and a sister whom Asdiwal marries. After a good fishing season, Asdiwal returns with his in-laws and wife to their village, where his wife bears them a son. One day, however, he boasts that he is better than his brothers-in-aw at walrus-hunting. Put to the test, he succeeds brilliantly, again infuriating his wife's brothers, who abandon him without food or fire to die on a rocky reef. His bird father preserves him through a raging storm. Finally, he is taken by a mouse to the underground home of the walruses whom he has wounded. Asdiwal cures them and asks in exchange a safe return. The King of the Walruses lends Asdiwal his stomach as a boat, on which he sails home.

There he finds his faithful wife, who helps him to kill her own brothers. But again Asdiwal, assailed by homesickness, leaves his wife and returns to the Skeena valley, where his son joins him. When winter comes, Asdiwal goes hunting in the mountains, but forgetting his snow-shoes, can go neither up nor down and is changed into stone.

This is the end of the story. In the analysis which follows, Lévi-Strauss draws out the remarkably complex symmetry of different levels of structure. Asdiwal's journeys take him from East to West, then North to the Nass, then Southwest to the sea fishing of walrus, and finally Southeast back to the Skeena River. So the points of the compass and the salient points of order of Tsimshian migration are laid out. This is the geographical sequence. There is another sequence concerned with residence at marriage, as follows.

The two women who open the tale have been separated by the daughter's virilocal residence at marriage. Living together, they set up what Lévi-Strauss calls a 'matrilocal residence of the simplest kind, mother and daughter'. Lévi-Strauss counts the first marriage of the bird father of Asdiwal as matrilocal. Then the sky marriage of Asdiwal himself with Evening-Star is counted as matrilocal, and matrilocal again the two human marriages of Asdiwal, until after he has come back from the walrus kingdom, when his wife betrays her brothers. So, Lévi-Strauss remarks that all the marriages of Asdiwal are matrilocal until the end. Then the regular pattern is inverted and 'patrilocalism triumphs' because Asdiwal abandons his wife and goes home, accompanied by his son. The story starts with the reunion of a mother and daughter, liberated from their spouses (and paternal kin in the case of the daughter), and ends with the reunion of a father and son, liberated from their spouses (and maternal kin in the case of the son). To the English anthropologist some of this symmetry and inversion seems rather far-fetched. The evidence for counting the bird marriage as matrilocal is dubious and the sky marriage is plain groom service. The rejection of the third wife is hardly 'patrilocalism'. But more about inversion below. I want to go into details of another sociological sequence which produces two more pairs of oppositions which are also inverted at the end.

The same symmetry is traced in the cosmological sequence. First, the hero sojourns in the sky where he is wounded and cured by the sky people; then he makes an underground sojourn where he finds underground people whom *he* has wounded, and whom *he* cures. There is a similar elaboration of recurring themes of famine and plenty. They correspond faithfully enough to the economic reality of Tsimshian life. Using his knowledge of another myth of the region, Lévi- Strauss explains their implication. The Northwest Coast Indians attribute the present condition of the world to the disturbances made by a great Crow, whose voracious appetite initiated all the processes of creation. So hunger is the condition for movement, glut is a static condition. The first phase of the Asdiwal tale opposes Sky and Earth, the Sun and the earthly human. These appositions the hero overcomes, thanks to his bird father. But Asdiwal breaks the harmony established between these elements: first he feels homesick, then, once at home, he betrays his sky wife for terrestrial girl, and then, in the sky, he feels homesick again. Thus the whole sky episode ends on a negative position. In to second phase, when Asdiwal makes his first human marriage a new set of oppositions are released: mountain-hunting and sea-hunting; land and sea.

Asdiwal wins the contest as a land-hunter, and in consequence is abandoned by his wife's brothers. Next time Asdiwal marriage allies him with island-dwellers, and the same conflicts between land and sea takes place, this time on the sea in a boat, which Asdiwal has to leave in the final stage of the hunt in order to climb onto the reef of rock. Taken together, these two phase. can be broken down into a series of unsuccessful mediation. between opposites arranged on an ever-diminishing scale: above and below, water and earth, maritime hunting and mountain hunting. In the sea hunt the gap is almost closed between sea- and mountain-hunting, since Asdiwal succeeds where his brothers-in-law fail because he clambers onto the rock. The technique by which the oppositions are reduced is by paradox and reversal: the great mountain-hunter nearly dies on a little half-submerged rock; the great killer of bears is rescued by a little mouse; the slayer of animals now cures them; and, most paradoxical of all, the great provider of food himself has provender become—since he goes home in the stomach of a walrus. In the final dénouement, Asdiwal, once more a hunter in the mountains, is immobilized when he is neither up nor down, and is changed to stone, the most extreme possible expression of his earthly nature.

Some may have doubted that myths can have an elaborate symmetrical structure. If so, they should be convinced of their error.

Lévi-Strauss's analysis slowly and intricately reveals the internal structure of this myth. Although I have suggested that the symmetry has here and there been pushed too hard, the structure is indisputably there, in the material and not merely in the eye of the beholder. I am not sure who would have argued to the contrary, but myths must henceforth be conceded to have a structure as recognizable as that of a poem or a tune.

But Lévi-Strauss is not content with revealing structure for its own sake. Structural analysis has long been a respectable tool of literary criticism and Lévi-Strauss is not interested in a mere literary exercise. He wants to use myth to demonstrate that structural analysis sociological value. So instead of going on to analyse and compare formal myth structures, he asks what is the relation if myth to life. His answer in a word is 'dialectical'. Not only is the nature of reality dialectical, and the structure of myth dialectical, but the relation of the first to the second is dialectical too.

This could mean that there is a feedback between the worlds mythical and social discourse—a statement in the myth sets off a response which modifies the social universe, which itself then touches off a new response in the realm of myth, and so on. Elsewhere, Lévi-Strauss (1962b, pp. 283–284) has shown that this complex interaction is indeed how he sees the relation between symbolic thought and social reality. And he even attempts to demonstrate with a single example how this interaction takes place (1963b; cf. 1962b, Ch. IV). But in his analysis of myth itself he leaves out this meaning of dialectic. This is a pity, but perhaps inevitable because there is so little historical formation about the tribes in question, and still less about the dating of different versions of the myth.

Rather, he develops the idea that myth expresses a social dialectic. It states the salient social contradictions, restates them in more and more modified fashion, until in the final statement the contradictions are resolved, or so modified and masked as to be minimized. According to Lévi-Strauss, the real burden of the whole Asdiwal myth and the one burning issue which all the antinomies of sky and earth, land and sea, etc., are assimilated, is the contradiction implicit in patrilocal, matrilateral cross-cousin marriage. This comes as a surprise, since there has never been any mention whatever of matrilateral cross-cousin marriage in the myth of Asdiwal. But the Asdiwal story has a sequel. His son, Waux, grows up with his maternal kin, and his mother arranges for him to marry a cousin. He inherits his father's magic weapons and becomes, like him, a great hunter. One day he goes out hunting, having forgotten his magic spear which enables him to split rocks and open a path through the mountains. There is an earthquake. Waux sees his wife in the valley and shouts to her to make a sacrifice of fat to appease the supernatural powers. But his wife gets it wrong and thinks he is telling her to eat the fat, on which she proceeds to stuff herself until, gorged, she bursts and turns into a rock. Waux, now without either his father's spear or his wife's help, also turns into stone. With this story the Asdiwal cycle is completed. Waux's wife dies of glut, thus reversing the opening gambit in which Asdiwal's mother is started on her journey by a famine. So the movement set going by famine ends in the immobility of fullness. Asdiwal's marriages were all with strangers. Waux makes the approved Tsimshian marriage with his maternal cousin, but she ends by ruining him; the myth makes thus the comment that matrilateral cross-cousin marriage is nothing but a feeble palliative for the social ills it seeks to cure.

Lévi-Strauss points out that the Tsimshian, along with other Northwest Coast cultures, do not benefit from the equilibrium which cross-cousin marriage could produce for them in the form of a fixed hierarchy of wife-givers and wife-receivers. They have chosen instead to be free to revise their whole system of ranking at each marriage and potlatch. So they are committed to deep-seated disequilibrium. Following Rodney Needham (1962), one suspects that this far-fetched reference to Lévi-Strauss's theory of elementary structures of kinship is misplaced. There is no reason to suppose that matrilateral cross-cousin marriage among the Tsimshian is prescribed. However, in reaching these basic antagonisms of social structure, Lévi-Strauss feels he has got to the rock bottom of the myth's meaning.

> 'All the paradoxes... geographic, economic, sociological, and even cosmological, are, when all is said and done, assimilated to that less obvious yet so real pardox which marriage with the matrilateral cousin attempts but fails to resolve...' (*supra*, pp. 27, 28).

A great deal of this myth certainly centres on marriage, though very little on the cross-cousin marriage which is preferred. Lévi-Strauss says that the whole myth's burden is as negative comment on social reality. By examining all the possibilities in marriage and showing every extreme position to be untenable, it has as its core message to reconcile the Tsimshian to their usual compromises by showing that any other solution they attempt is equally beset with difficulty. But as I have said, we cannot allow Lévi-Strauss to claim the real meaning of such a complex and rich myth. His analysis is far from exhaustive. Furthermore, there are other themes which are positive, not negative, as regards social reality.

In the first place, this area of Northwest Coast culture combines a very elaborate and strict division of labour between the sexes with a strong expression of male dominance. The myth could well be interpreted as playing on the paradox of male dominance and male dependence on female help. The first hero, Asdiwal, shows his independence of womankind by betraying his first wife. He is betrayed by his second wife, abandons his third wife, but in the sequel his son, Waux, dies because of his wife's stupidity and greed—so the general effect is that women are necessary but inferior beings, and men are superior. Surely this is a positive comment?

In the second place, the potlatch too is built on a paradox that the receiver of gifts is an enemy. One-up-manship, in potlatch terms, brings success, rank, and followers, but two-upmanship inflicts defeat on the opponent and creates hostility. Asdiwal went too far when he brought four huge bears down from the mountain to confront his empty-handed brothers-in-law. Here again, the myth is positive and true to life, so no wonder they abandoned him. The ambivalent attitude in Northwest Coast culture to the successful shaman is a third theme that can plausibly be detected in the myth. Great shamans are always victims of jealousy. Asdiwal, the great shaman, is abandoned. So the myth is plain and simply true to life.

I feel that we are being asked to suspend our critical faculties if we are to believe that this myth mirrors the reverse of reality. I shall return again to give a closer look at the social realities of Tsimshian life.

The ideas of reversal and of inversion figure prominently is Lévi-Strauss's argument. First, he suggests that the myth is the reverse of reality in the country of its origin. Then he has formulated a curious law according to which a myth turn' upside down (in relation to its normal position) at a certain distance from its place of origin. These are both developed is the Asdiwal analysis. Third, a myth which appears to have no counterpart in the ritual of the tribe in which it is told is found to be an inversion of the rites of another tribe (cf. Lévi-Strauss, 1956). On this subject the stolid English suspicion of cleverness begins to crystallize.

If ever one could suspect a scholar of trailing his coat with his tongue in his cheek, one would suspect this law of myth-inversion. The metaphor is borrowed from optics, without any explanation of why the same process should be observed in the unrelated science of mythics:

> 'When a mythical schema is transmitted from one population to another, and there exist differences of language, social organization or way of life which make the myth difficult to communicate, it begins to become impoverished or confused. But one can find a limiting situation in which, instead of being finally obliterated by losing all its outlines, the myth is inverted and regains part of its precision' (*supra*, p. 42).

So we must expect that exported myths will give a negative or upside-down picture of what the original myth portrayed. Is the scholar being ingenuous, or disingenuous? He must recognize that opposition is a pliable concept in the interpreter's hands. The whole notion of dialectic rests on the assumption that opposition can be unequivocally recognized. But this is an unwarranted assumption, as appears from a critical reading of his treatment of a Pawnee myth (Lévi-Strauss, 1966).

To demonstrate the relation of myth to rite he takes the Pawnee myth of the pregnant boy. An ignorant young boy suddenly finds he has magical powers of healing and the makings of a great shaman. An old-established shaman, always accompanied by his wife, tries to winkle his secret from him. He fails, since there is no secret learning to transmit, and then ensorcells the boy. As a result of the sorcery the boy becomes pregnant, and goes in shame and confusion to die among wild boasts. But the beasts cure him and he returns with even greater power, and kills his enemy. The analysis distinguishes at least three sets of oppositions.

Shamanistic powers through initiation:	without initiation
child:	old man
confusion of sex:	distinction of sex

Lévi-Strauss then invites us to consider what rite this Pawnee myth corresponds to. His problem, which seems very artificial, is that there is at first sight no correlated rite. The myth underlines the opposition of the generations, and yet the Pawnee do not oppose their generations: they do not base their cult associations on age-classes, and entry to their cult societies is not by ordeals or by fee; a teacher trains his pupil to succeed him on his death. But, as he puts it, all the elements of the myth fall into place confronted with the symmetrical and opposite ritual of the neighbouring Plains Indian tribes. Here the shamanistic societies are the inverse of those of the Pawnee, since entry is by payment and organization is by age. The sponsor and his sponsored candidate for entry are treated as if in a father-son relation, the candidate is accompanied by his wife, whom he offers for ritual intercourse to his sponsor. 'Here we find again all the oppositions which have been analyzed on the plane of the myth, with inversion of all the values attributed to each couple.' The initiated and uninitiated are as father to son, instead of as enemies; the uninitiated knows less than the initiated, whereas in the myth he is the better shaman; in the ritual of the Plains Societies it is the youth who is accompanied by his wife, while in the myth it is the old man. 'The semantic values are the same but changed in relation to the symbols which sustain them. The Pawnee myth exposes a ritual system which is the inverse, not of that prevailing in this tribe, but of a system which does not apply here, and which belongs to related tribes whose ritual organization is the exact opposite.'

Mere difference is made to qualify as opposition. Some of the oppositions which Lévi-Strauss detects in myth are undeniably part of the artistic structure. But opposition can be imposed on any material by the interpreter. Here we have an unguarded example of the latter process. To me it seems highly implausible that we can affirm any opposition worthy of the name between cult organization with age-grading and entrance fees, and cult organization by apprenticeship without age-grading. Old male with wife versus young man without wife, and with contusion of sex, these seem equally contrived as oppositions. If to alleged oppositions are not above challenge, the whole demonstration of inversion falls to the ground.

Here we should turn to the relation of myth to literature in general. Lévi-Strauss recognizes that a myth is 'a work of art arousing deep aesthetic emotion' (Jakobson & Lévi-Strauss 1962, p. 5). But he strenuously rejects the idea that myth is a kind of primitive poetry (Lévi-Strauss, 1963a, p. 210). 'Myth,' he says, 'should be placed in the gamut of linguistic expression at the end opposite to that of poetry.... Poetry is a kind of speech which cannot be translated except at the cost of serious distortions; whereas the mythical value of the myth is preserved even through the worst translation.' He goes on in terms more emotional than scientific to declare that anyone can recognize the mythic quality of myth. Why does he want so vigorously to detach myth criticism from literary criticism? It is on the literary plane that we have his best contribution to the subject of mythology. He himself wrote a splendid vindication of his own technique of literary analysis by working it out with Jakobson on a sonnet of Baudelaire (Jakobson & Lévi-Strauss, 1962). This essay is an exercise in what T. S. Eliot calls 'the lemon-squeezer school of criticism, in which the critics take a poem to pieces, stanza by stanza, line by line, and extract, squeeze, tease, press every drop of meaning out of it' (Eliot, 1957, p. 112). After reading the analysis, we perceive the poem's unity, economy, and completeness, and its tremendous range of implication.

When the lemon-squeezer technique is applied to poetry it has a high rate of extraction and the meaning flows out in rich cupfuls. Furthermore, what is extracted is not a surprise—we can see that it was there all the time. Unfortunately, something goes wrong when the technique is applied to myth: the machine seems to spring a leak. Instead of more and richer depths of understanding, we get a surprise, a totally new theme, and often a paltry one at that. All the majestic themes which we had previously thought the Oedipus myth was about—destiny, duty, and self-knowledge, have been strained off, and we are left with a worry about how the species began. When Edmund Leach applies the same technique to the Book of Genesis, the rich metaphysical themes of salvation and cosmic oneness are replaced by practical rules for the regulation of sex. When Lévi-Strauss has finished with the Tsimshian myth it is reduced to anxieties about problems of matrilateral cross-cousin marriage (which anyway only apply to the heirs of chiefs and headmen). It seems that whenever anthropologists apply structural analysis to myth they extract not only a different but a lesser meaning. The reasons for this reductionism are important. First, there is the computer analogy, for the sake of which Lévi-Strauss commits himself to treating the structural units of myth as if they were unambiguous. This takes us back to the basic difference between words and phonemes. The best words are ambiguous, and the more richly ambiguous the more suitable for the poet's or the myth-maker's job. Hence there is no end to the number of meanings which can be read into a good myth. When dealing with poetry, Lévi-Strauss gives full value to the rich ambiguity of the words. When dealing with myth he suggests that their meaning is clear cut, lending itself to being chopped into objectively recognizable, precisely defined units. It is partly in this process of semantic chopping that so much of the meaning of myth gets lost.

But there is another reason, more central to the whole programme. There are two possible objectives in analyzing a piece of discourse. One is to analyse the particular discourse itself; to analyse what has been said. The other is to analyse the language, seen as the instrument of what is said. No reason has so far been given to suppose that the structure of discourse is necessarily similar to that of language. But there is reason to point out that if the language analogy is adopted, research will look for a similar structure, a logic of correlations, oppositions, and differences (Ricoeur, 1963). We can say that the first kind of analysis, of what has been said in a discourse, aims at discovering a particular structure. This is what the literary critics do and what Jakobson and Lévi-Strauss did in 'Les Chats', and what Lévi-Strauss in practice does most of the time. This kind of analysis is not intended to yield a compressed statement of the theme. It is not reductionist in any sense. The other kind of analysis discovers a formal or general structure which not particular to any given stretch of language. For instance, the alexandrine or the sonnet form is not particular to a given poem, and to know that a particular poem has been written in sonnet form tells you nothing about what that poem is about. In the same way, a grammatical structure is formal. A book of grammar gives the conditions under which communication of a certain kind can take place. It does not give a communication.

Lévi-Strauss claims to be revealing the formal structures of myths. But he can never put aside his interest in what the myth discourse is about. He seems to think that if he had the formal structure it would look not so much like a grammar book as like a summary of the themes which analyzing the particular structure of a myth cycle has produced. Hence the reductionist tendency is built in to his type of myth analysis. He falls into the trap of claiming to discover the real underlying meanings of myths because he never separates the particular artistic structure of a particular set of myths from their general or purely formal structure. Just as knowing that the rhyme structure is a, b, b, a, does not tell us anything about the content of a sonnet, so the formal structure of a myth would not help very much in interpreting it. Lévi-Strauss comes very near this when he says (Lévi-Strauss, 1957) that the structural analysis of a Pawnee myth consists of a dialectical balancing of the themes of life and death. It might have been better to have said that it was a balanced structure of pluses and minuses, or of positives and negatives. If he had actually used algebra to present the pattern he discerned, then Edmund Leach might have been less tempted to speculate on the similarity of mythic themes all over the world. He himself had found a structure of pluses and minuses in the Garden of Eden myth (1961) and remarked that the recurrence of these themes of death versus life, procreation versus vegetable reproduction, have the greatest psychological and sociological significance. But I think that their significance is that of verb/noun relations in language.

Their presence signifies the possibility of finding in them formal structures. But they are not the formal myth structure that we have been promised. These can hardly be knowable in ordinary language. If they are to be discovered special terms will have to be invented for recording them, comparable to the highly specialized terminology of grammar. To say simply that myth structures are built of oppositions and mediations is not to say what the structures are. It is simply to say that there are structures.

I will return later to the question of whether these formal myth structures are likely to be important for sociology. At this stage of publication (though three new volumes are in the press), Lévi-Strauss has not succeeded in revealing them. I should therefore do better to concentrate on the particular artistic structures he has revealed.

The meaning of a myth is partly the sense that the author intended it to convey, and the sense intended by each of its recounters. But every listener can find in it references to his own experience, so the myth can be enlightening, consoling, depressing, irrespective of the intentions of the tellers. Part of the anthropologist's task is to understand enough of the background of the myth to be able to construct its range of reference for its native hearers. To this Lévi-Strauss applies himself energetically, as for example when he finds that the myth of the creative Great Crow illuminates the themes of hunger and plenty in Tsimshian life.

From a study of any work of art we can infer to same extent the conditions under which it was made. The maidservant who said of St Peter, 'His speech betrays him as a Galilean' was inferring from his dialect; similarly the critic who used computer analysis to show that the same author did not write all the epistles attributed to St Paul. This kind of information is like that to be obtained from analyzing the track of an animal or the finger-prints of a thief The anthropologist studying tribal myths can do a job of criticism very like that of art critics who decide what 'attribution' to give to a painting or to figures in a painting. Lévi-Strauss, after minute analysis of the Asdiwal myth, could come forward and, like a good antiquarian, affirm that it is a real, genuine Tsimshian article. He can guarantee that it is an authentic piece of Northwest Coast mythology. His analysis of the structure of the myth can show that it draws fully on the promises of Tsimshian culture.

Inferences, of course, can also be made within the culture the native listener can infer a moral, and indeed myths are one of the ways in which cultural values are transmitted. Structural analysis can reveal unsuspected depths of reference and inference meaning for any particular series of myths. In order to squeeze this significance out, the anthropologist most apply his prior knowledge of the culture to his analysis. He uses inference the other way round, from the known culture to the interpretation of the obscure myth. This is how he discerns the elements of structure. All would agree that this is a worthwhile task. But in order to analyse particular structures, he has to know his culture well first.

At this stage we should like to be able to judge how well Lévi-Strauss knows the social reality of the Tsimshian. Alas, very little is known about this tribe. He has to make do with very poor ethnographic materials. There are several minor doubts one can entertain about his interpretation of the facts, but the information here is altogether very thin. A critic of Lévi-Strauss (Ricoeur) has been struck by the fact that all his examples of mythic thought have been taken from the geographical areas of totemism and never from Semitic, pre-Hellenic, or Indo-European areas, whence our own culture arose. Lévi-Strauss would have it that his examples are typical of a certain kind of thought, a type in which the arrangement of items of culture is more important and more stable than the content. Ricoeur asks whether the totemic cultures are not so much typical as selected, extreme types? This is a very central question which every anthropologist has to face. Is *La Pensée sauvage* as revealed by myth and rite analysis typical, or peculiar, or is it an illusion produced by the method? Here we are bound mention Lévi-Strauss's idea of mythic thinking as *bricolage*. The *bricoleur*, for whom we have no word, is a craftsman who works with material that has not been produced for the task he has in hand. I am tempted to see him as an Emmett engineer whose products always look alike whether they are bridges, stoves, or trains, because they are always composed of odd pieces of drainpipe and string, with the bells and chains and bits of Gothic railing arranged in a similar crazy way. In practice this would be a wrong illustration of *bricolage*. Lévi-Strauss himself is the real Emmett engineer because he changes his rules as he goes along. For mythic thought a card-player would be a better analogy, because Emmett can use his bits how he likes, whereas the *bricolage* type of culture is limited by pattern-restricting rules. Its units are like a pack of cards continually shuffled for the same game. The rules of the game would correspond to the general structure underlying the myths. If all that the myths and rites do is to arrange and rearrange the elements of the culture, then structural analysis would b exhaustive, and for that reason very important.

At the outset of any scientific enterprise, a worker must know the limitations of his method. Linguistics and any analysis modelled on linguistics can only be synchronic sciences. They analyse systems. In so far as they can be diachronic it is in analysing the before-and-after evolution of systems. Their techniques can be applied to any behaviour that is systematic. But if the behaviour is not very systematic, they will extract whatever amount of regularity there is, and leave a residue. Edmund Leach has shown that the techniques of Lévi-Strauss can be applied to early Greek myths, to Buddhist, and to Israelite myths. But I suppose he would never claim that the analysis is exhaustive. In the case of his analysis of Genesis, I have already mentioned above that the residue is the greater part.

Lévi-Strauss in his publications so far seems blithely unconscious that his instrument can produce only one kind of tune. More aware of the limitations of his analysis, he would have to restrict what he says about the attitude of mythic thought to time, past and future. Structural analysis cannot but reveal myths as timeless, as synchronic structures outside time. From this bias built into the method there are two consequences. First, we cannot deduce anything whatever from it about the attitudes to time prevailing in the cultures in question. Our method reduces all to synchrony. Everything which Lévi-Strauss writes in *La Pensée sauvage* about time in certain cultures or at a certain level of thinking, should be to apply only to the method he uses. Second, if myths have got an irreversible order and if this is significant, this part of their meaning will escape the analysis. This, as Ricoeur points out, is why the culture of the Old Testament does not fit into the *bricolage* category.

We know a lot about the Israelites and about the Jews and Christians who tell and retell these stories. We know little about the Australian aborigines and about the no longer surviving American Indian tribes. Would this be the anthropologist's frankest answer to Ricoeur? We cannot say whether the *bricolage* level of thought is an extreme type or what it is typical of, for lack of sufficient supporting data about the examples But we must say that the *bricolage* effect is produced by the method of analysis. For a final judgement, then, we can only wait for a perfect experiment. For this, richly abundant mythical material should be analysed against a known background of equally rich ethnographic records. We can then see how exhaustive the structural analysis can be and also how relevant its formulas are to the understanding of the culture.

CHAPTER X

Structure, Sign, and Play in the Discourse of the Human Sciences

Jacques Derrida

Perhaps something has occurred in the history of the concept of structure that could be called an "event," if this loaded word did not entail a meaning which it is precisely the function of structural—or structuralist—thought to reduce or to suspect. But let me use the term "event" anyway, employing it with caution and as if in quotation marks. In this sense, this event will have the exterior form of a *rupture* and a *redoubling.*

It would be easy enough to show that the concept of structure and even the word "structure" itself are as old as the *epistémé* —that is to say, as old as western science and western philosophy—and that their roots thrust deep into the soil of ordinary language, into whose deepest recesses the *epistémé* plunges to gather them together once more, making them part of itself in a metaphorical displacement. Nevertheless, up until the event which I wish to mark out and define, structure—or rather the structurality of structure—although it has always been involved, has always been neutralized or reduced, and this by a process of giving it a center or referring it to a point of presence, a fixed origin. The function of this center was not only to orient, balance, and organize the structure—one cannot in fact conceive of an unorganized structure—but above all to make sure that the organizing principle of the structure would limit what we might call the *freeplay* of the structure. No doubt that by orienting and organizing the coherence of the system, the center of a structure permits the freeplay of its elements inside the total form.

And even today the notion of a structure lacking any center represents the unthinkable itself.

Nevertheless, the center also closes off the freeplay it opens up and makes possible. *Qua* center, it is the point at which the substitution of contents, elements, or terms is no longer possible. At the center, the permutation or the transformation of elements (which may of course be structures enclosed within a structure) is forbidden. At least this permutation has always remained *interdicted*(I use this word deliberately). Thus it has always been thought that the center, which is by definition unique, constituted that very thing within a structure which governs the structure, while escaping structurality. This is why classical thought concerning structure could say that the center is, paradoxically, *within* the structure and *outside* it. The center is at the center of the totality, and yet, since the center does not belong to the totality (is not part of the totality), the totality *has its center elsewhere.* The center is not the center. The concept of centered structure—although it represents coherence itself, the condition of the *epistémé* as philosophy or science—is contradictorily coherent. And, as always, coherence in contradiction expresses the force of a desire The concept of centered structure is in fact the concept of a freeplay based on a fundamental ground, a freeplay which is constituted upon a fundamental immobility and a reassuring certitude, which is itself beyond the reach of the freeplay. With this certitude anxiety can be mastered, for anxiety is invariably the result of a certain mode of being implicated in the game, of being caught by the game, of being as it were from the very beginning at stake in the game. From the basis of what we therefore call the center (and which, because it can be either inside or outside, is as readily called the origin as the end, as readily *archè* as *telos),* the repetitions, the substitutions, the transformations, and the permutations are always *taken* from a history of meaning *[sens]*—that is, a history, period— whose origin may always be revealed or whose end may always be anticipated in the form of presence. This is why one could perhaps say that the movement of any archeology, like that of any eschatology, is an accomplice of this reduction of the structurality of structure and always attempts to conceive of structure from the basis of a full presence which is out of play.

If this is so, the whole history of the concept of structure, before the rupture I spoke of, must be thought of as a series of substitutions of center for center, as a linked chain of determinations of the center. Successively, and in a regulated fashion, the center receives different forms or names. The history of metaphysics, like the history of the West, is the history of these metaphors and metonymies. Its matrix— if you will pardon me for demonstrating so little and for being so elliptical in order to bring me more quickly to my principal theme—is the determination of being as *presence* in all the senses of this word. It would be possible to show that all the names related to fundamentals, to principles, or to the center have always designated the constant of a presence—*eidos, archè, telos, energeia, ousia* (essence, existence, substance, subject) *aletheia,* transcendentality, consciousness, or conscience, God, man, and so forth.

The event I called a rupture, the disruption I alluded to at the beginning of this paper, would presumably have come about when the structurality of structure had to begin to be thought, that is to say, repeated, and this is why I said that this disruption was repetition in all of the senses of this word. From then on it became necessary to think the law which governed, as it were, the desire for the center in the constitution of structure and the process of signification prescribing its displacements and its substitutions for this law of the central presence—but a central presence which was never itself, which has always already been transported outside itself in its surrogate. The surrogate does not substitute itself for anything which has somehow pre-existed it. From then on it was probably necessary to begin to think that there was no center, that the center could not be thought in the form of a being-present, that the center had no natural locus, that it was not a fixed locus but a function, a sort of non-locus in which an infinite number of sign-substitutions came into play. This moment was that in which language invaded the universal problematic; that in which, in the absence of a center or origin, everything became discourse—provided we can agree on this word—that is to say, when everything became a system where the central signified, the original or transcendental signified, is never absolutely present outside a system of differences. The absence of the transcendental signified extends the domain and the interplay of signification *ad infinitum.*

Where and how does this decentering, this notion of the structurality of structure, occur? It would be somewhat naïve to refer to an event, a doctrine, or an author in order to designate this occurrence. It is no doubt part of the totality of an era, our own, but still it has already begun proclaim itself and begun to *work*. Nevertheless, if I wished to give some sort of indication by choosing one or two "names," and by recalling those authors in whose discourses this occurrence has most nearly maintained its most radical formulation, I would probably cite the Nietzschean critique of metaphysics, the critique of the concepts of being and truth, for which were substituted the concepts of play, interpretation, and sign (sign without truth present) the Freudian critique or self-presence, that is, the critique of consciousness, of the subject, of self-identity and of self-proximity or self-possession; and, more radically, the Heideggerean destruction of metaphysics, of onto-theology, of the determination of being as presence. But all these destructive discourses and all their analogues are trapped in a sort of circle. This circle is unique. It describes the form of the relationship between the history of metaphysics and the destruction of the history of metaphysics. *There is no sense* in doing without the concepts of metaphysics in order to attack metaphysics. We have no language— no syntax and no lexicon—which is alien to this history; we cannot utter a single destructive proposition which has not already slipped into the form, the logic, and the implicit postulations of precisely what it seeks to contest. To pick out one example from many: the metaphysics of presence is attacked with the help of the concept of the *sign*. But from the moment anyone wishes this to show, as I suggested a moment ago, that there is no transcendental or privileged signified and that the domain or the interplay of signification has, henceforth, no limit, he ought to extend his refusal to the concept and to the word sign itself— which is precisely what cannot be done. For the signification "sign" has always been comprehended and determined, in its sense, as sign-of, signifier referring to a signified, signifier different from its signified. If one erases the radical difference between signifier and signified, it is the word signifier itself which ought to be abandoned as a metaphysical concept. When Lévi-Strauss says in the preface to *The Raw and the Cooked* that he has "sought to transcend the opposition between the sensible and the intelligible by placing [himself] from the very beginning at the level of signs," the necessity, the force, and the legitimacy of his act cannot make us forget that the concept of the sign cannot in itself surpass or bypass this opposition between the sensible and the intelligible. The concept of the sign is determined by this opposition: through and throughout the totality of its history and by its system. But we cannot do without the concept of the sign, we cannot give up this metaphysical complicity without also giving up the critique we are directing against this complicity, without the risk of erasing difference [altogether] in the self-identity of a signified reducing into itself its signifier, or, what amounts to the same thing, simply expelling it outside itself. For there are two heterogeneous ways of erasing the difference between the signifier and the signified: one, the classic way, consists in reducing or deriving the signifier, that is to say, ultimately in *submitting* the sign to thought; the other, the one we are using here against the first one, consists in putting into question the system in which the preceding reduction functioned: first and foremost, the opposition between the sensible and the intelligible. The *paradox* is that the metaphysical reduction of the sign needed the opposition it was reducing. The opposition is part of the system, along with the reduction. And what I am saying here about the sign can be extended to all the concepts and all the sentences of metaphysics, in particular to the discourse on "structure." But there are many ways of being caught in this circle. They are all more or less naive, more or less empirical, more or less systematic, more or less close to the formulation or even to the formalization of this circle. It is these differences which explain the multiplicity of destructive discourses and the disagreement between those who make them. It was within concepts inherited from metaphysics that Nietzsche, Freud, and Heidegger worked, for example. Since these concepts are not elements or atoms and since they are taken from a syntax and a system, every particular borrowing drags along with it the whole of metaphysics This is what allows these destroyers to destroy each other reciprocally—for example, Heidegger considering Nietzsche, with as much lucidity and rigor as bad faith and misconstruction, as the last metaphysician, the last "Platonist." One could do the same for Heidegger himself, for Freud, or for a number of others. And today no exercise is more widespread.

What is the relevance of this formal schéma when we turn to what are called the "human sciences"? One of them perhaps occupies a privileged place—ethnology. One can in fact assume that ethnology could have been born as a science only at the moment when a de-centering had come about: at the moment when European culture—and, in consequence, the history of metaphysics and of its concepts—had been *dislocated,* driven from its locus, and forced to stop considering itself as the culture of reference. This moment is not first and foremost a moment of philosophical or scientific discourse, it is also a moment which is political, economic, technical, and so forth. One can say in total assurance that there is nothing fortuitous about the fact that the critique of ethnocentrism—the very condition of ethnology—should be systematically and historically contemporaneous with the destruction of the history of metaphysics. Both belong to a single and same era.

Ethnology—like any science—comes about within the element of discourse. And it is primarily a European science employing traditional concepts, however much it may struggle against them. Consequently, whether he wants to or not—and this does not depend on a decision on his part—the ethnologist accepts into his discourse the promises of ethnocentrism at the very moment when he is employed in denouncing them. This necessity is irreducible; it is not a historical contingency. We ought to consider very carefully all its implications. But if nobody can escape this necessity, and if no one is therefore responsible for giving in to it, however little, this does not mean that all the ways of giving in to it are of an equal pertinence. The quality and the fecundity of a discourse are perhaps measured by the critical rigor with which this relationship to the history of metaphysics and to inherited concepts is thought. Here it is a question of a critical relationship to the language of the human sciences and a question of a critical responsibility of the discourse. It is a question of putting expressly and systematically the problem of the status of a discourse which borrows from a heritage the resources necessary for the deconstruction of that heritage itself. A problem of *economy* and *strategy.*

If I now go on to employ an examination of the texts of Lévi-Strauss as an example, it is not only because of the privilege accorded to ethnology among the human sciences, nor yet because the thought of Lévi-Strauss weighs heavily on the contemporary theoretical situation. It is above all because a certain choice has made itself evident in the work of Lévi-Strauss and because a certain doctrine has been elaborated there, and precisely in a *more or less explicit manner,* in relation to this critique of language and to this critical language in the human sciences.

In order to follow this movement in the text of Lévi-Strauss, let me choose as one guiding thread among others the opposition between nature and culture. In spite of all its rejuvenations and its disguises, this opposition is congenital to philosophy. It is even older than Plato. It is at least as old as the Sophists. Since the statement of the opposition—*physis/nomos, physis/technè*—it has been passed on to us by a whole historical chain which opposes "nature" to the law, to education, to art, to technics—and also to liberty, to the arbitrary, to history, to society, to the mind, and so on. From the beginnings of his quest and from his first book, *The Elementary Structures of Kinship* Lévi-Strauss has felt at one and the same time the necessity of utilizing this opposition and the impossibility of making it acceptable. In the *Elementary Structures,* he begins from this axiom or definition: that belongs to nature which is *universal* and spontaneous, not depending on any particular culture or on any determinate norm. That belongs to culture, on the other hand, which depends on a system of *norms* regulating society and is therefore capable of *varying* from one social structure to another. These two definitions are of the traditional type. But, in the very first pages of the *Elementary Structures,* Lévi-Strauss, who has begun to give these concepts an acceptable standing, encounters what he calls a *scandal,* that is to say, something which no longer tolerates the nature/culture opposition he has accepted and which seems to require *at one and the same time* the predicates of nature and those of culture. This scandal is the *incest-prohibition.* The incest-prohibition is universal; in this sense one could call it natural. But it is also a prohibition, a system of norms and interdicts; in this sense one could call it cultural.

> Let us assume therefore that everything universal in man derives from the order of nature and is characterized by spontaneity, that everything which is subject to a norm belongs to culture and presents the attributes of the relative and the particular. We then find ourselves confronted by a face, or rather an ensemble of facts, which, in the light of the preceding definitions, is not far from appearing as a scandal: the prohibition of incest presents without the lease equivocation, and indissolubly linked together, the two characteristics in which we recognized the contradictory attributes of two exclusive orders. The

prohibition of incest constitutes a rule, but a role, alone of all the social
rules, which possesses at the same time a universal character (p. 9).

Obviously there is no scandal except in the *interior* of a system
of concepts sanctioning the difference between nature and culture. In
beginning his work with the *factum* of the incest-prohibition, Lévi-
Strauss thus puts himself in a position entailing that this difference,
which has always been assumed to be self-evident, becomes
obliterated or disputed. For, from the moment that the incest-
prohibition can no longer be conceived within the nature/culture
opposition, it can no longer be said that it is a scandalous fact, a
nucleus of opacity within a network of transparent significations.
The incest-prohibition is no longer a scandal one meets with or
comes up against in the domain of traditional concepts; it is
something which escapes these concepts and certainly precedes
them—probably as the condition of their possibility. It could perhaps
be said that the whole of philosophical conceptualization,
systematically relating itself to the nature/culture opposition, is
designed to leave in the domain of the unthinkable the very thing
that makes this conceptualization possible: the origin of the
prohibition of incest.

I have dealt too cursorily with this example, only one among so
many others, but the example nevertheless reveals that language
bears within itself the necessity of its own critique. This critique may
be undertaken along two tracks, in two "manners." Once the limit of
nature/culture opposition makes itself felt, one might want to
question systematically and rigorously the history of these concepts.
This is a first action. Such a systematic and historic questioning
would be neither a philological nor a philosophical action in the
classic sense of these words. Concerning oneself with the founding
concepts of the whole history of philosophy, de-constituting them, is
not to undertake the task of the philologist or of the classic historian
of philosophy. In spite of appearances, it is probably the most daring
way of making the beginnings of a step outside of philosophy. The
step "outside philosophy" is much more difficult to conceive than is
generally imagined by those who think they made it long ago with
cavalier ease, and who are in general swallowed up in metaphysics
by the whole body of the discourse that they claim to have
disengaged from it.

In order to avoid the possibly sterilizing effect of the first way, the other choice—which I feel corresponds more nearly to the way chosen by Lévi-Strauss—consists in conserving in the field of empirical discovery all these old concepts, while at the same time exposing here and there their limits, treating them as tools which can still be of use. No longer is any truth-value attributed to them; there is a readiness to abandon them if necessary if other instruments should appear more useful. In the meantime, their relative efficacy is exploited, and they are employed to destroy the old machinery to which they belong and of which they themselves are pieces. Thus it is that the language of the human sciences criticizes *itself*. Lévi-Strauss thinks that in this way he can separate *method* from *truth*, the instruments of the method and the objective significations aimed at by it. One could almost say that this is the primary affirmation of Lévi-Strauss; in any event, the first words of the *Elementary Structures* are: "One begins to understand that the distinction between state of nature and state of society (we would be more apt to say today: state of nature and state of culture), while lacking any acceptable historical signification, presents a value which fully justifies its use by modern sociology: its value as a methodological instrument."

Lévi-Strauss will always remain faithful to this double intention: to preserve as an instrument that whose truth-value he criticizes.

On the one hand, he will continue in effect to contest the value of the nature/culture opposition More than thirteen years after the *Elementary Structures*, *The Savage Mind* faithfully echoes the text I have just quoted: "The opposition between nature and culture which I have previously insisted on seems today to offer a value which is above all methodological." And this methodological value is not affected by its "ontological" non-value (as could be said, if this notion were not suspect here): "It would not be enough to have absorbed particular humanities into a general humanity; this first enterprise prepares the way for others... which belong to the natural and exact sciences: to reintegrate culture into nature, and finally, to reintegrate life into the totality of its physiochemical conditions" (p. 327).

On the other hand, still in *The Savage Mind*, he presents as what he calls *bricolage* what might be called the discourse of this method. The *bricoleur,* says Lévi-Strauss, is someone who uses "the means at hand," that is, the instruments he finds at his disposition around him, those which are already there, which had not been especially conceived with an eye to the operation for which they are to be used and to which one tries by trial and error to adapt them, not hesitating to change them whenever it appears necessary, or to try several of them at once, even if their form and their origin are heterogenous—and so forth. There is therefore a critique of language in the form of *bricolage,* and it has even been possible to say that *bricolage* is the critical language itself. I am thinking in particular of the article by G. Genette, "Structuralisme et Critique littéraire," published in homage to Lévi-Strauss in a special issue of *L'Arc* (no. 26, 1965), where it is stated that the analysis of *bricolage* could "be applied almost word for word" to criticism, and especially to "literary criticism."

If one calls *bricolage* the necessity of borrowing one's concepts from the text of a heritage which is more or less coherent or ruined, it must be said that every discourse is *bricoleur.* The engineer, whom Lévi-Strauss opposes to the *bricoleur,* should be the one to construct the totality of his language, syntax, and lexicon. In this sense the engineer is a myth. A subject who would supposedly be the absolute origin of his own discourse and would supposedly construct it "out of nothing," "out of whole cloth," would be the creator of the *verbe,* the *verbe* itself. The notion of the engineer who had supposedly broken with all forms of *bricolage* is therefore a theological idea; and since Lévi-Strauss tells us elsewhere that *bricolage* is mythopoetic, the odds are that the engineer is a myth produced by the *bricoleur.* From the moment that we cease to believe in such an engineer and in a discourse breaking with the received historical discourse, as soon as it is admitted that every finite discourse is bound by a certain *bricolage,* and that the engineer and the scientist are also species of *bricoleurs* then the very idea of *bricolage* is menaced and the difference in which it took on its meaning decomposes.

This brings out the second thread which might guide us in what is being unraveled here.

Lévi-Strauss describes *bricolage* not only as an intellectual activity but also as a mythopoetical activity. One reads in *The Savage Mind,* "Like *bricolage* on the technical level, mythical reflection can attain brilliant and unforeseen results on the intellectual level. Reciprocally, the mythopoetical character of *bricolage* has often been noted" (p. 26).

But the remarkable endeavor of Lévi-Strauss is not simply to put forward, notably in the most recent of his investigations, a structural science or knowledge of myths and of mythological activity. His endeavor also appears—I would say almost from the first—in the status which he accords to his own discourse on myths, to what he calls his "mythologicals " It is here that his discourse on the myth reflects on itself and criticizes itself. And this moment, this critical period, is evidently of concern to all the languages which share the field of the human sciences. What does Lévi-Strauss say of his "mythologicals"? It is here that we rediscover the mythopoetical virtue (power) of *bricolage*. In effect, what appears most fascinating in this critical search for a new status of the discourse is the stated abandonment of all reference to a *center*, to a *subject*, to a privileged *reference*, to an origin, or to an absolute *archè*. The theme of this decentering could be followed throughout the "Overture" to his last book, *The Raw and the Cooked.* I shall simply remark on a few key points.

I) From the very start, Lévi-Strauss recognizes that the Bororo myth which he employs in the book as the "reference-myth" does not merit this name and this treatment. The name is specious and the use of the myth improper. This myth deserves no more than any other its referential privilege:

> In fact the Bororo myth which will from now on be designated by the name *reference-myth* is, as I shall try to show, nothing other than a more or less forced transformation of other myths originating either i n the same society or in societies more or less far removed. It would therefore have been legitimate to choose as my point of departure any representative of the group whatsoever. From this point of view, the interest of the reference-myth does not depend on its typical character, but rather on its irregular position in the midst of a group (p. 10).

2) There is no unity or absolute source of the myth. The focus or the source of the myth are always shadows and virtualities which are elusive, unactualizable, and nonexistent in the first place. Everything begins with the structure, the configuration, the relationship. The discourse on this acentric structure, the myth, that is, cannot itself have an absolute subject or an absolute center. In order not to short change the form and the movement of the myth,

that violence which consists in centering a language which is describing an acentric structure must be avoided. In this context, therefore it is necessary to forego scientific or philosophical discourse, to renounce the *epistémé* which absolutely requires, which is the absolute requirement that we go back to the source, to the center, to the founding basis, to the principle, and so on. In opposition to *epistèmic* discourse, structural discourse on myths— *mythological* discourse—must itself be *mythomorphic*. It must have the form of that of which it speaks. This is what Lévi-Strauss says in *The Raw and the Cooked*, from which I would now like to quote a long and remarkable passage:

> In effect the study of myths poses a methodological problem by the fact that it cannot conform to the Cartesian principle of dividing the difficulty into as many parts as are necessary to resolve it. There exists no veritable end or term to mythical analysis, no secret unity which could be grasped at the end of the work of decomposition. The themes duplicate themselves to infinity. When we think we have disentangled them from each other and can hold them separate, it is only to realize that they are joining together again, in response to the attraction of unforeseen affinities. In consequence, the unity of the myth is only tendential and projective; it never reflects a state or a moment of the myth. An imaginary phenomenon implied by the endeavor to interpret, its role is to give a synthetic form to the myth and to impede its dissolution into the confusion of contraries. It could therefore be said that the science or knowledge of myths is an *anaclastic*, taking this ancient term in the widest sense authorized by its etymology, a science which admits into its definition the study of the reflected rays along with that of the broken ones. But, unlike philosophical reflection, which claims to go all the way back to its source, the reflections in question here concern rays without any other than a virtual focus.... In wanting to imitate the spontaneous movement of mythical thought, my enterprise, itself too brief and too long, has had to yield to its demands and respect its rhythm. Thus is this book, on myths itself and in its own way, a myth.

This statement is repeated a little farther on (p. 20): "Since myths themselves rest on second-order codes (the first-order codes being those in which language consists), this book thus offers the rough draft of a third-order code, destined to insure the reciprocal possibility of translation of several myths. This is why it would not be wrong to consider it a myth: the myth of mythology, as it were." It is by this absence of any real and fixed center of the mythical or mythological discourse that the musical model chosen by Lévi-Strauss for the composition of his book is apparently justified. The absence of a center is here the absence of a subject and the absence of an author: "The myth and the musical work thus appear as orchestra conductors whose listeners are the silent performers. If it be asked where the real focus of the work is to be found, it must be replied that its determination is impossible. Music and mythology bring man face to face with virtual objects whose shadow alone is actual.... Myths have no authors" (p. 25).

Thus it is at this point that ethnographic *bricolage* deliberately assumes its mythopoetic function. But by the same token, this function makes the philosophical or epistemological requirement of a center appear as mythological, that is to say, as a historical illusion.

Nevertheless, even if one yields to the necessity of what Lévi-Strauss has done, one cannot ignore its risks. If the mythological is mythomorphic, are all discourses on myths equivalent? Shall we have to abandon any epistemological requirement which permits us to distinguish between several qualities of discourse on the myth? A classic question, but inevitable. We cannot reply—and I do not believe Lévi-Strauss replies to it—as long as the problem of the relationships between the philosopheme or the theorem, on the one hand, and the mytheme or the mythopoem(e), on the other, has not been expressly posed. This is no small problem. For lack of expressly posing this problem, we condemn ourselves to transforming the claimed transgression of philosophy into an unperceived fault in the interior of the philosophical field. Empiricism would be the genus of which these faults would always be the species. Trans-philosophical concepts would be transformed into philosophical naivetes. One could give many examples to demonstrate this risk: the concepts of sign, history, truth, and so forth. What I want to emphasize is simply that the passage beyond philosophy does not consist in turning the page of philosophy (which usually comes down to philosophizing badly), but in continuing to read philosophers *in a certain way.* The risk I am speaking of is always assumed by Lévi-Strauss and it is the very price of his endeavor. I have said that empiricism is the matrix of all the faults menacing a discourse which continues, as with Lévi-Strauss in particular, to elect to be scientific. If we wanted to pose the problem of empiricism and *bricolage* in depth, we would probably end up very quickly with a number of propositions absolutely contradictory in relation to the status of discourse in structural ethnography. On the one hand, structuralism justly claims to be the critique of empiricism. But at the same time there is not a single book or study by Lévi-Strauss which does not offer itself as an empirical essay which can always be completed or invalidated by new information. The structural schemata are always proposed as hypotheses resulting from a finite quantity of information and which are subjected to the proof of experience. Numerous texts could be used to demonstrate this double postulation. Let us turn once again to the "Overture" of *The Raw and the Cooked,* where it seems clear that if this postulation is double, it is because it is a question here of a language on language:

> Critics who might take me to task for not having begun by making an exhaustive inventory of South American myths before analyzing them would be making a serious mistake about the nature and the role of these documents. The totality of the myths of a people is of the order of the discourse. Provided that this people does not become physically or morally extinct, this totality is never closed. Such a criticism would therefore be equivalent to reproaching a linguist with writing the grammar of a language without having recorded the totality of the words which have been uttered since that language came into existence and without knowing the verbal exchanges which will take place as long as the language continues to exist. Experience proves that an absurdly small number of sentences... allows the linguist to elaborate a grammar of the language he is studying. And even a partial grammar or an outline of a grammar represents valuable acquisitions in the case of unknown languages. Syntax does not wait until it has been possible to enumerate a theoretically unlimited series of events before becoming manifest, because syntax consists in the body of rules which presides over the generation of these events. And it is precisely a syntax of South American mythology that I wanted to outline. Should new texts appear to enrich the mythical discourse, then this will provide an opportunity to check or modify the way in which certain grammatical laws have been formulated, an opportunity to discard certain of them and an opportunity to discover new ones. But in no instance can the requirement of a total mythical discourse be raised as an objection. For we have just seen that such a requirement has no meaning. (pp 15–16).

Totalization is therefore defined at one time as *useless,* at another time as *impossible.* This is no doubt the result of the fact that there are two ways of conceiving the limit of totalization. And I assert once again that these two determinations coexist implicitly in the discourses of Lévi-Strauss. Totalization can be judged impossible in the classical style: one then refers to the empirical endeavor of a subject or of a finite discourse in a vain and breathless quest of an infinite richness which it can never master. There is too much, more than one can say. But nontotalization can also be determined in another way: not from the standpoint of the concept of finitude as assigning us to an empirical view, but from the standpoint of the concept of *freeplay*. If totalization no longer has any meaning, it is not because the infinity of a field cannot be covered by a finite glance or a finite discourse, but because the nature of the field—that is, language and a finite language —excludes totalization. This field is in fact that of *freeplay*, that is to say, a field of infinite substitutions in the closure of a finite ensemble. This field permits these infinite substitutions only because it is finite, that is to say, because instead of being an inexhaustible field, as in the classical hypothesis, instead of being too large, there is something missing from it: a center which arrests and founds the freeplay of substitutions. One could say— rigorously using that word whose scandalous signification is always obliterated in French—that this movement of the freeplay, permitted by the lack, the absence of a center or origin, is the movement of *supplementarity*. One cannot determine the center, the sign which *supplements* it, which takes its place in its absence— because this sign adds itself, occurs in addition, over and above, comes as a *supplement*. The movement of signification adds something, which results in the fact that there is always more, but this addition is a floating one because it comes to perform a vicarious function, to supplement a lack on the part of the signified. Although Lévi-Strauss in his use of the word supplementary never emphasizes as I am doing here the two directions of meaning which are so strangely compounded within it, it is not by chance that he uses this word twice in his "Introduction to the Work of Marcel Mauss," at the point where he is speaking of the "superabundance of signifier, in relation to the signifieds to which this superabundance can refer":

> In his endeavor to understand the world, man therefore always has at his disposition a surplus of signification (which he portions out amongst things according to the laws of symbolic thought—which it is the task of ethnologists and linguists to study). This distribution of a *supplementary* allowance [*ration* supplémentaire]—if it is permissible to put it that way—is absolutely necessary in order that on the whole the available signifier and the signified it aims at may remain in the

relationship of complementarily which is the very condition of the use of symbolic thought (p.xlix).

(It could no doubt be demonstrated that this *ration supplémentaire* of signification is the origin of the *ratio* itself.) The word reappears a little farther on, after Lévi-Strauss has mentioned "this floating signifier, which is the servitude of all finite thought":

> In other words—and taking as our guide Mauss's precept that all social phenomena can be assimilated to language—we see in *mana, Wakau, oranda* and other notions of the same type, the conscious expression of a semantic function, whose role it is to permit symbolic thought to operate in spite of the contradiction which is proper to it In this way are explained the apparently insoluble antinomies attached to this notion.... At one and the same time force and action, quality and state, substantive and verb; abstract and concrete, omnipresent and localized—*mana is* in effect all these things. But is it not precisely because it is none of these things that *mana is* a simple form, or more exactly, a symbol in the pure state, and therefore capable of becoming charged with any sort of symbolic content whatever? In the system of symbols constituted by all cosmologies, *mana* would simply be a *valeur symbolique zéro*, that is to say, a sign marking the necessity of a symbolic content *supplementary* [my italics] to that with which the signified is already loaded, but which can take on any value required, provided only that this value still remains part of the available reserve and is not, as phonologists put it, a group-term.

Lévi-Strauss adds the note:

> Linguists have already been led to formulate hypotheses of this type. For example: "A zero phoneme is opposed to all the other phonemes in French in that it entails no differential characters and no constant phonetic value. On the contrary, the proper function of the zero phoneme is to be opposed to phoneme absence." (R. Jakobson and J. Lutz, "Notes on the French Phonemic Pattern," *Word*, vol. 5, no. 2 [August, 1949], p. 155). Similarly, if we schematize the conception I am proposing here, it could almost be said that the function of notions like *mana is* to be opposed to the absence of signification, without entailing by itself any particular signification (p. 1 and note).

The *superabundance* of the signifier, its *supplementary* character, is thus the result of a finitude, that is to say, the result of a lack which must be *supplemented*.

It can now be understood why the concept of freeplay is important in Lévi-Strauss. His references to all sorts of games, notably to roulette, are very frequent, especially in his *Conversations,* in *Race and History,* and in *The Savage Mind.* This reference to the game or freeplay is always caught up in a tension.

It is in tension with history, first of all. This is a classical problem, objections to which are now well worn or used up. I shall simply indicate what seems to me the formality of the problem: by reducing history, Lévi-Strauss has treated as it deserves a concept which has always been in complicity with a teleological and eschatological metaphysics, in other words, paradoxically, in complicity with that philosophy of presence to which it was believed history could be opposed. The thematic of historicity, although it seems to be a somewhat late arrival in philosophy, has always been required by the determination of being as presence. With or without etymology, and in spite of the classic antagonism which opposes these significations throughout all of classical thought, it could be shown that the concept of *epistèmè* has always called forth that of *historia,* if history is always the unity of a becoming, as tradition of truth or development of science or knowledge oriented toward the appropriation of truth in presence and self-presence, toward knowledge in consciousness-of-self. History has always been conceived as the movement of a resumption of history, a diversion between two presences. But if it is legitimate to suspect this concept of history, there is a risk, if it is reduced without an express statement of the problem I am indicating here, of falling back into an anhistoricism of a classical type, that is to say, in a determinate moment of the history of metaphysics. Such is the algebraic formality of the problem as I see it. More concretely, in the work of Lévi-Strauss it must be recognized that the respect for structurality, for the internal originality of the structure, compels a neutralization of time and history. For example, the appearance of a new structure, of an original system, always comes about—and this is the very condition of its structural specificity—by a rupture with its past, its origin, and its cause. One can therefore describe what is peculiar to the structural organization only by not taking into account, in the very moment of this description, its past conditions: by failing to pose the problem of the passage from one structure to another, by putting history into parentheses. In this "structuralist" moment, the concepts of chance and discontinuity are indispensable. And Lévi-Strauss does in fact often appeal to them as he does, for instance, for that structure of structures, language, of which he says in the "Introduction to the Work of Marcel Mauss" that it "could only have been born in one fell swoop":

> Whatever may have been the moment and the circumstances of its appearance in the scale of animal life, language could only have been born in one fell swoop. Things could not have set about signifying progressively. Following a transformation the study of which is not the concern of the social sciences, but rather of biology and psychology, a crossing over came about from a stage where nothing had a meaning to another where everything possessed it (p. xlvi).

This standpoint does not prevent Lévi-Strauss from recognizing the slowness, the process of maturing, the continuous toil of factual transformations, history (for example, in *Race and History*). But, in accordance with an act which was also Rousseau's and Husserl's, he must "brush aside all the facts" at the moment when he wishes to recapture the specificity of a structure. Like Rousseau, he must always conceive of the origin of a new structure on the model of catastrophe—an overturning of nature in nature, a natural interruption of the natural sequence, a brushing aside of nature.

Besides the tension of freeplay with history, there is also the tension of freeplay with presence. Freeplay is the disruption of presence. The presence of an element is always a signifying and substitutive reference inscribed in a system of differences and the movement of a chain. Free play is always an interplay of absence and presence, but if it is to be radically conceived, freeplay must be conceived of before the alternative of presence and absence; being must be conceived of as presence or absence beginning with the possibility of freeplay and not the other way around. If Lévi-Strauss, better than any other, has brought to light the freeplay of repetition and the repetition of freeplay, one no less perceives in his work a sort of ethic of presence, an ethic of nostalgia for origins, an ethic of archaic and natural innocence, of a purity of presence and self-presence in speech—an ethic, nostalgia, and even remorse which he often presents as the motivation of the ethnological project when he moves toward archaic societies— exemplary societies in his eyes. These texts are well known.

As a turning toward the presence, lost or impossible, of the absent origin, this structuralist thematic of broken immediateness is thus the sad, *negative,* nostalgic, guilty, Rousseanist facet of the thinking of freeplay of which the Nietzschean *affirmation*—the joyous affirmation of the freeplay of the world and without truth, without origin, offered to an active interpretation—would be the other side. *This affirmation then determines the non-center otherwise than as loss of the center.* And it plays the game without security. For there is a *sure* freeplay: that which is limited to the *substitution of given and existing, present,* pieces. In absolute chance, affirmation also surrenders itself to *genetic* indetermination, to the *seminal* adventure of the trace.

There are thus two interpretations of interpretation, of structure, of sign, of freeplay. The one seeks to decipher, dreams of deciphering, a truth or an origin which is free from freeplay and from the order of the sign, and lives like an exile the necessity of interpretation. The other, which is no longer turned toward the origin, affirms freeplay and tries to pass beyond man and humanism, the name man being the name of that being who, throughout the history of metaphysics or of ontotheology—in other words, through the history of all of his history—has dreamed of full presence, the reassuring foundation, the origin and the end of the game. The second interpretation of interpretation, to which Nietzsche showed us the way, does not seek in ethnography, as Lévi-Strauss wished, the "inspiration of a new humanism" (again from the "Introduction to the Work of Marcel Mauss").

There are more than enough indications today to suggest we might perceive that these two interpretations of interpretation— which are absolutely irreconcilable even if we live them simultaneously and reconcile them in an obscure economy—together share the field which we call, in such a problematic fashion, the human sciences.

For my part, although these two interpretations must acknowledge and accentuate their difference and define their irreducibility, I do not believe that today there is any question of *choosing*—in the first place because here we are in a region (let's say, provisionally, a region of historicity) where the category of choice seems particularly trivial; and in the second, because we must first try to conceive of the common ground, and the *différance* of this irreducible difference. Here there is a sort of question, call it historical, of which we are only glimpsing today the *conception, the formation the gestation, the labor.* I employ these words, I admit, with a glance toward the business of childbearing—but also with a glance toward those who, in a company from which I do not exclude myself, turn their eyes away in the face of the as yet unnameable which is proclaiming itself and which can do so, as is necessary whenever a birth is in the offing, only under the species of the non-species, in the formless, mute, infant, and terrifying form of monstrosity.

CHAPTER XI

Absent Meaning

Dan Sperber

Semiologists—I mean self-avowed ones—might feel that if the preceding chapters were aimed at them they have gone wide of the mark. Indeed, the cryptological and psychoanalytic conceptions were elaborated outside the semiological framework proposed by Ferdinand de Saussure:

'A language is a system of signs that express ideas, and is therefore comparable to a system of writing, to the alphabet of deaf-mutes, symbolic rites, polite formulas, military signals, etc. But it is the most important of all these systems.

'*A science that studies the life of signs within society* is conceivable; it would be a part of social psychology and consequently, of general psychology; I shall call it *semiology* (from Greek *sémeîon*, "sign"). It would show what constitutes signs, what laws govern them' (Saussure 1959: 16).

In a semiology thus conceived, the fundamental question is no longer 'What do symbols mean?' but 'How do they mean?' These two questions are clearly linked. Pre- or para-Saussurian semiologists who are concerned above all with the what-question support their analyses with hypotheses about the 'how'; conversely, the question 'how' presupposes the knowledge of 'what'. Saussurian semiology therefore does not *in principle* constitute a radical break, but rather a shift of interest within a semiological approach which existed in the West long before it was known as such. I say 'in principle' because in fact, Saussurian semiologists have completely left aside the what-question, and have studied not at all 'How do symbols mean?', but rather 'How do symbols work?' In this study they have established all unknowing, that symbols work without meaning. Modern semiology, and this is at once its weakness and its merit, has refuted the principles on which it is founded.

The study of symbolism under the heading of Saussurian semiology only developed fully after the Second World War, and especially in the works of Claude Lévi-Strauss, to which my discussion will be limited. The arguments I shall put forward may, it seems to me, be extended to other expressly semiological perspectives in so far as these are clear, which is not always the case.

Lévi-Strauss formed largely new views on symbolism which do not fall under my previous arguments. The critique of the semiological conception as I have developed it so far would therefore be unfair and paradoxical if it were not that the paradox, as I shall show, is not of my making, but that of the semiologists themselves. Unlike the views discussed above, those of the semiologists are not semiological at all; despite a terminology borrowed from linguistics, symbols are not treated as signs. The symbolic signifier, freed from the signified, is no longer a real signifier except by a dubious metaphor whose only merit is to avoid the problem of the nature of symbolism, not to resolve it.

In the cryptological and Freudian views of symbolism, an element became a symbol from the mere fact of receiving an interpretation. In the Freudian view and in some of the cryptological ones, over and above that, the interpretations belong to a single domain. Two different principles are the basis of the study of symbolism proposed by Lévi-Strauss. Firstly, an element never of its itself receives a symbolic interpretation, but only in so far as it is opposed to at least one other element. Secondly, there is not one unique domain of interpretation, but a set of domains (which Lévi-Strauss calls 'codes') in which symbolic oppositions are interpreted.

The import of these principles becomes clearer if we return to the example of Dorze butter.

Butter on the head is only symbolic in so far as it is opposed to butter as ordinarily consumed. In its alimentary use, butter is consumed melted, in limited quantities, and as a sort of sauce. In its ritual use, it is solid, used in large quantities, and by itself. The opposition is thus between a modest and discreet normal usage and an expensive and ostentatious ritual usage. Similarly, meals which accompany rituals are doubly opposed to daily meals: quantity on the one hand, and quality on the other; for foods of animal origin—butter and meat—take pride of place in them.

In the economic domain, ritual is marked by a generous expenditure without a view toward profit, and daily life, by a modest expenditure and by calculated investments. In the same area, normal participation in market activities is discreet (no patter to attract customers) and respectful of others (great care is taken not to disarrange stalls); the ceremonial tour of the market, by contrast, is done by dashing aside, violently if necessary, every obstacle on a route that does not respect the normal market pathways. In the sociological domain, there is the same opposition between established statuses that are known by all and which it is generally bad form to wax expansive about, and the period that marks a change of status in which it is proper, on the contrary, to attract public notice. In the physiological domain, there is an opposition between recommended seminal retention and fertile incontinence; and opposition between 'normal' constipation and purifying purge. Further data would allow us to add further oppositions in the same domain or in others to complete the accompanying table.

	Moderation	Excess
Culinary domain	Butter on food	Butter on head
	Food in limited quantities, especially of vegetable origin	Abundant food, especially of animal origin
Economic domain	Parsimony and search for profit	Expenditure and generosity
	Discreet and respectful market participation	Showy and brutal ritual in the market
Sociological domain	Modesty about established status	Ostentatious affirmation of change in status
Physiological domain	Constipation	Purge
	Seminal retention	Seminal expenditure

In such a table, the first term $X1$ of a row X is opposed to a second term $X2$, as the first term, $Y1$, of a row Y is opposed to a second term $Y2$, thus giving the canonical formula of structural analyses of symbolism:

$$X1 : X2 :: Y1 : Y2$$

which is read $X1$ is to $X2$ as $Y1$ is to $Y2$. Thus, for example, alimentary butter is to ritual butter as modesty about status is to the ostentatiousness of the rite of passage, etc. In a given ritual, or a particular text of oral tradition, only some of these oppositions are manifest, but a tacit reference to absent oppositions is made possible. The dichotomy message/interpretation (if we wish to maintain it) is therefore circumstantial and not absolute. It is a given ritual or myth that singles out an opposition by expressing it openly and that thus sets it up as the representative of homologous oppositions.

If we left it at that, the symbolic code would seem like a set of matrices similar to the one presented above. But three supplementary properties of symbolic oppositions prevent our being content with such an elementary model. Firstly, a particular element may enter into several oppositions; thus butter on the head is opposed not only to consumed butter, but also to foliage and mosses put on the head during funerary rituals. Secondly, an opposition may have, simultaneously, several values: thus the ritual use of butter is opposed to its use as food not only as is excess to moderation, but also as is cool to hot. Now this second opposition value that plays a fundamental role in Dorze symbolism is realised in a different way— indeed the reverse—in other realms. In the sociological domain, for example, seniors are colder than juniors; in the physiological domain, it is seminal retention which is colder than incontinence, etc. These oppositions inform Dorze symbolic life no less than do those presented in the preceding table. A given opposition therefore figures in several matrices of which it constitutes so to speak the axis of intersection. Thirdly, two homologous oppositions may also be in a relationship of reduction: e.g., take an opposition between two terms A and B. Each of these two terms may itself include two aspects, A1 and A2, and B1 and B2, which are opposed among themselves as A is opposed to B. Thus the alimentary use of butter has two forms, depending on whether it is used in an ordinary meal, where it is used in small quantities, or whether it is used in a ritual feast, in which case it is nearly force-fed. The first form is opposed to the second as the alimentary use of butter generally is opposed to its ritual use, following Figure 1.

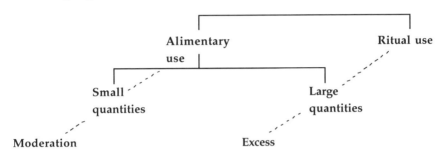

FIGURE 1

On the other hand, the ritual use of butter also has two forms, of which one is relatively moderate—and more common—in which only a piece of butter is placed on the head; the other—much more expensive—and reserved to young married women, in which butter is made into a veritable skullcap. The first form is opposed to the second as the alimentary use of butter is opposed to its ritual use in general, following Figure 2.

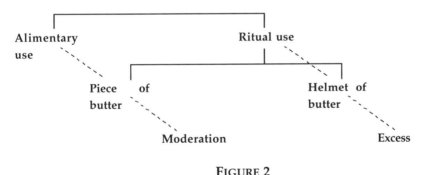

FIGURE 2

This sort of relationship between two oppositions, at once one of homology and of reduction, plays a fundamental role in the analyses of Lévi-Strauss, and further complicates the representation of symbolic systems. We have, thus, the four essential properties of symbolism following the structuralist view: an element does not take on symbolic value except in so far as it is opposed to at least one other element; a symbolic opposition is triply defined: (1) by its domain, (2) by its oppositional values, (3) by its level of reduction. The other properties of symbolism revealed by structural analysis only develop these four fundamental points.

This view, however, poses some serious problems. It most be said—following Lévi-Strauss himself—that the representation of these properties by means of tables, figures, etc., is a convenience of exposition; that the overall structure of the system remains essentially unknown and that we are far from being able to formalise it or explicate it; the model is vague and intuitive; this is a kind of frustration that every anthropologist, for the moment, must share. But above all: what guarantees that the structure outlined accounts for the properties of the object and does not derive simply from the systematising gaze of the analyst? And what *is* this object whose properties will thus be represented?

To the first question, Lévi-Strauss replies by a 'What does it matter?'; ' ...what does this matter', he says at the beginning of *Mythologiques,* 'for if the final aim of anthropology is to contribute to a better knowledge of objectified thought and its mechanisms, it is in the last resort immaterial whether in this book the thought processes of the South American Indians take shape through the medium of my thought or whether mine take place through the medium of theirs' (Lévi-Strauss 1969: 13). A response which I find enchanting, but not very satisfactory.

I accept that Lévi-Strauss' mind is a proper exemplar of the human mind, and I don't doubt that if, by his work, he revealed its mechanisms, science would have made a considerable leap forward. But just as observing an athlete does not lead to an understanding of muscular physiology, so it is very far from being the case that the exercise of an eminent thought may be its own explanation. A model of the human mind is not confirmed by the fact that it is the product of a human mind for, in that respect, all models—from the most pedestrian to the most fantastical—are equally valid. Yet I would hold it against myself were I to make Lévi-Strauss sound silly when it is possible to understand him in a completely different way: to consider *Mythologiques* as a deliberate exercise in explicit symbolic thought of which it matters little if it follows the same route as that of the Indians, as long as it reproduces and reveals—even imperfectly—the course of the unconscious. This way, the problem of what this intuitive model might be applicable to is posed in new terms; posed, but not resolved.

The anthropologist must locate the cultural elements that come under symbolic interpretation; so also must the native. He must group and articulate those elements that are to be interpreted together; he must look for and know how to find those elements without which the general articulation is impossible or incomplete; he must determine the abstract schemas by means of which an interpretation becomes possible; so also must the native. In short, the task of the anthropologist in his work, and that of the native in learning his culture, are comparable; with two qualifications. First, the task of the individual in his own culture is achieved in a way that is mostly unconscious; further, we may suppose that the individual does not start from zero, nor advance at random. He has at his disposal in an innate way, certain criteria for selection and data gathering, and certain organising principles for the mechanism which articulates them or, at the least, a learning strategy specifically adapted to the task. The anthropologist, on the contrary, must do it all explicitly and has at his disposal no criterion, no principle, no strategy specific to his objective.

That the anthropologist conceives criteria, principles, a strategy which proves to be efficient and permits him not only to articulate his materials but also to discover them—is this heuristics and not theory? To the extent that the object of the theory to be made is precisely another heuristic—the unconscious one of the native— the anthropologist is entitled to ask himself if the one is not an imperfect model of the other. The structuralist approach falsely presented as a methodology independent of its object is in fact such a heuristic, whose specific efficiency raises a theoretical issue.

So far, I have asserted, but certainly not demonstrated, the efficiency of the structuralist method. The table allowed us to show the principles of it, but does not, however, establish its validity. It is clear enough that symbolic phenomena depart from the ordinary, and that they do not depart just in any direction; therefore, there is always a non-symbolic term to which they can be opposed. Scarcely more remarkable is the fact that given an opposition, we find others that correspond to it. Excess and moderation, even if it is not just any excess or moderation, are general enough categories: they may be found to contrast in many domains without this being a great discovery. The same is true for most abstract symbolic oppositions found in the literature: up-down, cold-hot, feminine-masculine, right-left, nature-culture, etc. As in the case of Freudian symbolism, we are still at the level of a trivial party game. However, many societies do play this game, dividing things without laterality into left and right (see Needham 1973), and things without verticality into up and down. Thus the Dorze divide the whole universe into cool and hot and into senior and junior (see Sperber 1974), following principles I must have internalized intuitively since—I repeatedly tested this—I apply them as they do, without being able yet to make them explicit.

The reduction of symbolic oppositions is already a bit less expected. For example, that there are two modes of ritual use of butter, so be it. But that they are opposed as are excess and moderation -that is to say as are ritual use and alimentary use—is more interesting. But only a bit more, for though we could cite many analogous examples, we could foresee clearly neither the existence, nor the specific form, of a reduced opposition.

But the model considered entails other, more remarkable consequences. In the examples of symbolic oppositions given so far, one of the terms was marked with relation to the other. When a Dorze eats a normally buttered dish, no symbolism need be postulated. But if there is a large quantity of butter, this marked use points up the opposition between an ordinary meal and a feast. If butter is put on the head in a normal quantity, the opposition to culinary use is implicit; in turn, it takes the buttery skullcap of the young married woman to evoke the opposition between the two ritual uses whose second term only is marked. In other words, an element takes on its symbolic value to the extent that it departs from a norm, a norm which may, itself, be symbolic. If this departure is constitutive of symbolism, and not accessory or fortuitous, two consequences are foreseeable. Firstly, the direction of the departure should be relevant for, after all, there are at least fifty ways of not consuming butter normally. The existence of a series of departures operating in the same direction, and thus homologous among themselves, realises—but too vaguely—this first consequence.

Secondly, if the marked term of a symbolic opposition is located in a relevant direction, then in principle the reverse direction should also be relevant. It should determine a symbolic element opposed to the first, no longer this time, as a marked term to a non-marked term, but following a symmetrical inversion between the two terms located on both sides of a third, non-marked, term.

Take, again, the example of butter on the head. It is defined as a non-consumption of the food *par excellence*. Therefore it gives us occasion to look for the reverse—a case of consumption of the non-food *par excellence,* for example, coprophagy. But it would not suffice on the one hand to find a non-consumption of butter, and on the other, coprophagy, to be assured that contrasting them is not the ethnographer's own doing, but rather proceeds from Dorze symbolism itself. As butter on the head marks a social status, we would need to find that coprophagy, for example, marked a contrasting status.

We have seen that buttered dignitaries contrast with big sacrificers. Both are guarantors of fertility, do not cut their hair, cannot leave the country, etc. But while the position of dignitary is transitory, that of sacrificer is permanent. The one obliges its holder to make multiple gifts, while the other makes its holder receive them. The one is linked with public places, roads, forums and markets, the other with groves, forests, fields. The one makes a show, the other keeps himself apart from all agitation. The dignitary has a right to the most dramatic funerary rites in a public field; the sacrificer, alone among all the Dorze, has no other funerary rites than those at his home. Accession to the title of sacrificer does not include transition rituals, a tour of the market place or butter on the head. Yet—the sacrificer must swallow a part of the contents of the intestine of a slaughtered animal, that is to say, its wrapped-up liquid excrement, as opposed to the solid butter that the dignitary wears, open to the air, on his head. The sacrificer shows thereby—and this time the commentary is Dorze—what he is ready to swallow for the sake of his people. Inversely, the dignitary shows what food he is ready to give up.

Another thing. I knew that several Dorze rituals included a ceremonial tour (of the market place or of a public field), always oriented from right to left; therefore, I looked for one instance at least of a tour in the other direction, which would have clarified, contrastively, the status of the one who made the tour. For a long time, I was unsuccessful.

Furthermore, one of the last days of the big annual ritual at *Mask'al* ends with a very special sacrifice: the highest ranking dignitary slits the throat of a bull at the market place; all the spectators keep their distance. Scarcely does the animal begin to bleed, when the dignitary hurries away and all the spectators throw a hail of stones sometimes lasting for an hour, until an audacious person, braving the projectiles, goes up to the beast, which thereupon belongs to him. This inaccessible food suggested I should look, inversely, for a form of unusually easy access to food.

I was thus searching for two apparently unrelated symbolic elements. Aided by structuralist faith, here is what I found. Three years before my arrival in the field, the incumbent of a singular office—that of official beggar at the market—died, without an heir. This beggar (who, incidentally, was not particularly poor) could, the whole year round, demand foodstuffs of all the merchants without risking a refusal which would have brought them misfortune. The morning of the sacrifice outlined above, he too sacrificed a bull in the same place and, as soon as the animal was slaughtered, he rushed off, making a tour of the market place *from left to right,* under a volley of cow dung. Thus we have an opposition between the classical ceremonial tour, done from right to left and causing the merchants to flee the area, and a tour done in the other direction while fleeing the spectators. One between excessively easy access to all the commodities in the market, for a single individual, and excessively difficult access for all to a single slaughtered animal. One between a hail of hard projectiles deterring approach and a hail of soft projectiles forcing movement. A contrast between the dignitary, honoured provider of the community, and the official beggar, amply provided for but made ridiculous. Finally, there is a contrast between the ordinary role of each of these characters and their extraordinary role on this day: the one provided for becoming the provider, and the animal sacrificed by the provider being denied to the community.

These two cases suggest a turn about and confirm the connection between butter and excrement, at the same time showing that it should be made not under the sign of identity, but under that of symbolic inversion—the consumption of excrement opposed to the non-consumption of butter, and ritual anticlockwise tour of the market place with butter on one's head, opposed to a tour in the opposite direction with excrement on the body. Also possible is a return to the problem of exegesis: here is a set of facts that the natives abstain almost totally from commenting upon without thereby making it impossible to interpret. The third type of meaning envisaged by Turner, 'positional meaning' which derives from the relation of symbolic phenomena among themselves in a symbolic system, constitutes a primal principle of interpretation whereas the other two types of meaning—exegetical and operational—merely extend the object to be interpreted (cf. Turner 1967: 50–1).

Larger systems with fuller examples are to be found in *Mythologiques* and in other works, such as that which Marcel Detienne has devoted to the mythology of aromatics in Greece, *Les jardins d'Adonis* (1972). These works show not only the existence of systematic symbolic inversions, but also their relevance. They do not derive merely from an *a posteriori* organisation of already-assembled materials but, on the contrary, permit the *a priori* formulation of certain hypotheses and the discovery—in the field or in texts—of materials predicted by the analysis. From the point of view of the scholar who adopts such a method, this sort of inversion is too beautiful to be fortuitous, this sort of success too satisfying for him not carefully to concern himself with the systematic underlying properties that make it possible.

A personal conviction does not equal an argument, and we must consider the sceptic's reservations: 'Given the way you formulate your hypotheses, how can they be falsified? You only take account of your successes, not of your failures. When you fail, you don't question your general hypotheses, you only question their immediate application and you go off in another direction, guided as much or more by your flair as by your pseudo-theory. Other scholars before you have known how to winkle out and relate symbolic facts without mistaking their methods for that of the human mind itself. Conversely, several unimaginative structuralists have applied the principles you invoke to the letter, and have only come up with a string of sententious platitudes. If one were to give a structuralist a list of fifty words taken at random, he would be quick to see in them a pretty set of oppositions and structural inversions, and would set them out in elegant matrices, while another in his own way would arrive at an equally harmonious result which would be completely different. In sum, you have merely invented a party game which is a little more subtle than that of the cryptologists or the Freudians (and yet the latter have developed theirs since the texts you cite were published). But a theory? Even the outline of an hypothesis? Nonsense!'

These are not bad arguments. In any case, no worse than those commonly given in favour of the structuralist method. Thus it may be useful to answer them carefully.

First, we must distinguish two levels. On the one hand, the general principles that underlie the structuralist method, and on the other, the particular analyses which derive from it. These general principles—the sceptic is right—are not falsifiable, and therefore do not constitute a theory. Rather, it is a question, as I have already said, of a vague heuristic, or, of a reasoned flair, which amounts to the same thing. This heuristic works well. But since we do not know what symbolism would have to be like for it not to work, it does not tell us anything about what symbolism is not, nor consequently, about what it is.

If it is hard to conceive of a form of symbolism which would lie outside the scope of this heuristic, it is easy to think of other heuristics which cannot account for symbolism at all. We have seen several such examples in the preceding chapters. The structuralist method has at least the merit of giving every least element its place and thus of considerably enlarging the stock of relevant data. Suppose, for example, that we were content to explain butter on the head by saying that it visibly separates the participants in rituals of transition from the rest of the Dorze. In this way, one might account for the presence of a marker, but the fact that it is butter, that it is worn on the head, etc., remains completely arbitrary; a special hat, or a bit of red paint on the nose could serve as well. If we explain it as a symbolic equivalent of semen (in so far as this is an explanation), the presence of a whitish substance ceases to be arbitrary, but ten other substances could have done as well and—a consideration which is not a matter of indifference to the Dorze—most of them would be much less expensive. On the other hand, in the fragments of structuralist description I have offered, everything is based on the fact that it is butter which is at issue. Replace it with a hat or with wheat pap, and the analysis collapses.

If the stock of the relevant data is thus considerably enlarged, the price we pay for this enlarging is equally great. All previous analyses of symbolism articulate their data following the positive criteria of resemblance and contiguity (cf. Smith and Sperber 1971). In adding the negative criteria of opposition and inversion the structuralist gives himself the means of establishing many new relevant relationships and of including in his schemas—under one heading or another—any element at all. Moreover, as the criteria are applied in an intuitive and uncertain manner, the new instrument is much too powerful. The price of this success seems to be that the structuralist, from then on, cannot fail.

Thus it is, at least, on the level of general principles. This is what the sceptic is asserting when he says that from an arbitrary list of fifty words we can make one, or even several, structural descriptions. This is quite true, with one qualification: either the analyst will consider those fifty terms as the complete universe of his description, and not all the terms will be relevant, some only finding a place as redundant equivalents of others, or else he will consider them as a sample of a larger set and will manage to give relevance to each given element by bringing to bear hypothetical ones.

Imagine, then, two structural descriptions of such a list which would be different but equally good, in the sense that they both give relevance to each element. Now add a fifty-first element. For a given structural description, either this additional element will have a ready-made place, or else the new set must be the object of a new description. If the first fifty elements constitute a sample of a larger set which both descriptions must account for, and if one and not the other of these descriptions allows the accommodation of the new element, then this additional datum corroborates one description and falsifies the other.

In practice, structuralist descriptions of symbolism are never done on closed sets: either because the data are fragmentary (and when are they not?), or because the analyst is not initially working on the whole of his data but only on a fraction of it, checking or modifying his description as he goes along. Note that the position of the native *vis-à-vis* his own culture is identical: he is not confronted all at once by the whole set of myths, rites, etc., nor required to make an immutable representation of it. Thus, the analogy to a puzzle which is often made is misleading: in a well-made puzzle, all the pieces remain the same forever, and for each, there is only one 'solution'. Structural analysis allows several solutions but eliminates some as it goes along. There are good reasons for thinking that the native here again proceeds in the same way.

The example of an arbitrary list of fifty words invoked by the sceptic to make fun of the structuralist method turns back on him, for a first time. If it is true that several structural descriptions are possible, there are, in principle, good empirical arguments for preferring one description and throwing out another. Once a heuristic not only enlarges the stock of relevant data but also contains a criterion for evaluating the empirical import of differing descriptions, this heuristic incorporates not only know-how, but also actual knowledge which should then be explicated.

The example of the arbitrary list served, in the sceptic's mind, a further purpose to show that the method is applicable not only to symbolism but to anything at all, to the cultural as well as the accidental, to information as well as noise, in short, that it enlarges the stock of relevant data much too far. But here the sceptic has not reflected enough on the properties of symbolism and of any theory which could account for it. Or is he, too, a victim of the semiological illusion? Presented to the faithful as the ultimate message of their prophet, this arbitrary list would at once take on a symbolic value that would by extension apply to each of its elements. In fact, arbitrariness is one of the means of symbolic production: e.g., a collection of ordinary objects transformed into relics, pebbles tossed at random and interpreted by divination, surrealist experiments in automatic writing, etc. Symbolic thought is capable, precisely, of transforming noise into information; no code, by definition, would be able to do this. Any model of symbolism is inadequate if it is not capable of the same feat, and sceptic's example once again is turned against him.

In short, the structuralist works following intuitions which are partly explicit. The predictive value of his approach assures him that the structures he outlines do not derive solely from his systematising perception, but that they account—at least a little—for the properties of the object under scrutiny. Or, which amounts to the same thing, that his partially explicated intuitions more or less match the unconscious intuitions that are the basis of symbolism itself. Yet, if the anthropologist is reassured as to the value of his particular analyses, and ready, in principle, to put forward, on the basis of the success of his approach, some more general hypotheses, one would still like to know what object these hypotheses might be about.

Indeed, a system of homologies, oppositions and inversions is, in itself, mysterious enough. It is hard to see in what sense it explains or interprets symbolic phenomena. It organises them. But what is the role, what is the nature of this organization? To answer this question, one leaves oneself open to the reproach of having constructed a model without an object. The reply that Lévi-Strauss makes—i.e., that this object is a semiological system, a structure that articulates signs—does not satisfy me.

If we accept—for purposes of testing it—the hypothesis which states that the device underlying both the ethnographer's approach and symbolic thought generally is a code, the first question to be answered is, where are the pairs (message, interpretation) or (signifier, signified)?

The matrices we have outlined offer for each symbolic opposition, a surplus of possible interpretations. For the following equation:

$$\text{alimentary use of butter: ritual butter} :: x : y$$

the opposition $(x:y)$ may be replaced by all the values of the opposition of the two uses of butter: (moderation: excess), (hot: cold); and there are others. We might therefore consider the interpretation of one opposition as the set (or a subset, or one) of its values; the interpretation would be an abstract form of the opposition. When Lévi-Strauss suggests for the opposition (raw: cooked) and (nakedness: attire), the interpretation (nature: culture), it is definitely a case of an abstraction of this sort.

The opposition $(x: y)$ may also be replaced by the set (or the subset of one) of the oppositions that have the same value as (alimentary butter: ritual butter), for example, (commercial activity in the market: ceremonial tour), (constipation: purge). In this case, the interpretation would be of the same level of abstraction as the message, and the role of the shared abstract value would be to associate them. Thus, when Lévi-Strauss (1962) analyses so-called totemism by showing that the opposition between two animal totems refers back to the opposition between two human clans, the interpretation of an opposition in the zoological domain is an homologous opposition in the sociological domain. In this particular example, the value of the opposition may be nothing more than the distinctiveness between groups: a natural one between animal species, a cultural one between human clans. Or else more specific oppositional values may be used: aquatic animals opposed to terrestrial animals as a clan of fishers to a clan of hunters, for instance.

We may thus view symbolic matrices as sets of possible interpretations for each of the oppositions that figure in them; the choice of interpretation of a particular occurrence of a symbolic element would depend on contextual data. This model is analogous to that of a multi-lingual dictionary: we may consult it to find the meaning of a particular word (cf. the abstract value of a particular opposition), or to find a word having the same meaning in another language (cf. an opposition having the same value in another domain).

But Lévi-Strauss rightfully refuses to use these matrices as a set of terms among which to choose. For if at a given moment in the analysis an underlying opposition (abstract or not), homologous to a manifest opposition, takes on a particular importance, it neither exhausts nor even constitutes its interpretation. Firstly, the other homologies are kept in reserve and not abandoned, contrary to what happens in language when a choice is made between the meanings of an ambiguous word. Secondly, the underlying opposition which is focused upon does not substitute for the manifest opposition to which it is homologous, but rather is articulated to it, unlike what happens when an interpretation is substituted for a message.

Despite some statements to the contrary, symbolism conceived in this way is not a means of encoding information, but a means of organising it. A symbolic opposition must not be replaced by an interpretation, but placed in an organisation of which it constitutes a crucial element.

Thus, the problem for a Dorze is not to choose an interpretation for butter on the head according to the ritual context, but to organise his mental image of ritual and of social life in general in such a way that butter will find its place within it. The opposition of ritual use of butter to its alimentary use, the existence of homologous oppositions brought together by diverse rituals and texts, contributes to the formation of a coherent schema of Dorze ritual and social life. Butter will have served as an index for selecting some hypotheses which other indices corroborate. In other words, in contrast to what happens in a semiological decoding, it is not a question of interpreting symbolic phenomena by means of a context, but—quite the contrary—of interpreting the context by means of symbolic phenomena. Those who try to interpret symbols in and of themselves look at the light source and say, 'I don't see anything.' But the light source is there, not to be looked at, but so that one may look at what it illuminates. The same goes for symbolism.

The idea that symbolic elements organise the mental representation of systems of which they are parts is clearly suggested when, in the first chapter of *The Savage Mind*, Lévi-Strauss compares mythical thought to *bricolage*. The *bricoleur* gathers objects, various odds and ends of which he may always make something but never just anything; for each element, once one wishes to utilise it, suggests some plans and rejects others, just as each symbolic element suggests some interpretations not of itself, but of the set in which it finds its place. Of this symbolic *'bricolage'*, the very text of Lévi-Strauss gives an involuntary example for the author insists on using in it the notion of *signification* (translated in English in Lévi-Strauss 1966 as 'signification' but meaning nothing else than 'meaning') and can only do so by changing it: '[The *bricoleur*] interrogates all the heterogeneous objects of which his treasury is composed to discover what each of them could "signify" and so contribute to the definition of a set which has yet to materialise' (Lévi-Strauss 1966: 18 [the quotation marks around 'signify' are Lévi-Strauss' own]). And, contrasting 'concept' with 'signification' he says, 'Concepts thus appear like operators *opening up* the set being worked with and signification like the operator of its *reorganization*' (Lévi-Strauss 1966: 20). A definition which may work for symbolism, but surely not for *signification*.

And in *The Raw and the Cooked*: 'The layered structure of myth to which I draw attention... allows us to look upon myth as a matrix of meanings which are arranged in lines or columns, but in which each level always refers to some other level, whichever way the myth is read. Similarly, each matrix of meanings refers to another matrix, each myth to other myths. And if it is now asked to what final meaning these mutually significative meanings are referring—since in the last resort and in their totality they must refer to something—the only reply to emerge from this study is that myths signify the mind that evolves by making use of the world of which it is itself a part. Thus there is simultaneous production of myths themselves, by the mind that generates them and, by myths, of an image of the world which is already inherent in the structure of the mind' (Lévi-Strauss 1969: 341).

As these quotations show, for Lévi-Strauss meaning is not a concept, but a symbol, and he never uses it without 'bricolating' it a bit, without giving it a mytho-poetic quality it only acquires precisely in losing all precise meaning.

The same applies for the notion of language. In the four volumes of *Mythologiques*, Lévi-Strauss analyses a set of myths of the Indians of both Americas and shows that these myths are related to each other. Not only does the same thematic underlie them, not only are they developed on similar frames, but moreover, they maintain relations of structural proximity which only in part reflect either geographical or historical proximity. We might be tempted to see in these *Mythologiques* the description of a language of which each Indian society knows only bits which have finally been reassembled by Lévi-Strauss. A splendid metaphor which some accept to the letter: since myths arise from the human mind and form this language that no one speaks, then this human mind is the mind of no one, a metaphysical entity, similar to the Hegelian universal Mind whose inventor would be himself the incarnation of it—Hegel and Napoleon at one and the same time. I do not know how this interpretation could have been arrived at. In my view, Lévi-Strauss' purpose has less grandeur but more import.

Of his own culture and of neighbouring ones, the native generally knows more myths than does the anthropologist, and knows them better. The references are clear to him and few allusions escape him. To understand them, he has available a multitude of indices, for symbolism is an everyday affair. The anthropologist, on the contrary, must write everything down painfully, translate it all, verify it all. In the final analysis, he has only scraps at his disposal. Often he works on a colleague's cold materials, which speak little and don't answer at all. In these conditions, and because he doesn't see much, the anthropologist is entitled to look further afield.

He is entitled firstly, because he might suppose that the symbolisms of different peoples differ more in their representation than in their rules. When, for example, a myth includes an episode whose role is obscure, and the myth of another people, analogous to it in structure, develops more clearly a similar or inverse episode and clarifies its function, therein lies the basis of an hypothesis.

An example. I collected, in Dorze, a myth which may be summarised as follows: A man whose step-mother has emasculated him saves the daughter of a king by killing by fire the monstrous serpent to whom she has been given up. The king rewards him by giving him his daughter in marriage, but, having heard rumour about the misfortune of his son-in-law, he organises a public bathing party to reassure himself. Just as he joins the bathers, the hero sees a gazelle, and escapes by pretending to pursue it. When he is just at the point of killing it, Mariam, 'The Lady', appears before him, begs him to spare the animal, and in exchange, gives him new virility.

In this highly structured story, a detail nevertheless left me perplexed: why do all the narrators insist that the hero was emasculated by a step-mother who is never mentioned again? A dual hypothesis was suggested to me by a variant collected by Moreno among the Galla of Ethiopia. A young girl is disguised as a man and sent to war by her father, who is excessively proud of her. She attracts notice in combat and the king gives her his own daughter in marriage. But having been warned of the sex of his 'son-in-law' he organises a public bathing party to reassure himself. The heroine is saved *in extremis* by Mariam who lends her virility (Moreno 1935: 48–54).

A quick glance at these two texts reveals a dual inversion: on the one hand a father who elevates his daughter to manhood, and a step-mother who deprives her step-son of his, both departing from the norm according to which a girl, no matter how well loved, cannot succeed her father, while a step-son, no matter how hated, is nevertheless his father's heir and takes precedence over the children of a second wife. An inversion, on the other hand, between a victorious woman warrior, that is to say (in this cultural context), a woman who emasculates men, and a man emasculated far from the battlefield by a woman: two terms situated on either side of the norm that states that only men emasculate and uniquely in the context of battle.

Establishing this dual inversion is enough to reveal certain themes that are shared by Dorze and Galla symbolic systems. But, as far as I know, the Dorze do not know the Galla version and the hypothesis suggested by the comparison must be verified through examination of Dorze data alone. Among the Dorze, there is a status of killer which may be acquired either by killing a wild animal (a lion, leopard or rhinoceros, for example) and by cutting off its tail, or by killing a man in warfare and cutting off his penis. This status is the only one that is open to any man regardless of birth, and which is neither directly nor indirectly inherited. It is marked by the customary tour of the market place with butter on the head, and by spectacular funerary rites.

If we now return to the Dorze myth, we see that it is not concerned with warfare except by an underlying opposition between the domestic context of the castration of the hero and the military context which alone would be sanctioned by the norm. Neither does it concern real hunting, except that by killing a serpent by fire, which is a dual transgression of taboo, the hero places himself above it, and in attacking a gazelle, the hero places himself below it, taking each time for his target animals whose death does not give their killer the status of 'killer'. But as these oppositions suggest, it is not by chance that all these elements of the myth are placed in opposition to this central absent term formed by the status of killer and the warfare and hunting which are necessary to it. This absent term is in a way the very theme of the myth. The apparently gratuitous detail of the castrating step-mother evokes and doubly clarifies the status of killer—on the one hand by inversion, on the other directly, by showing that the killer *par excellence* is a non-heir who is in search of a penis: the principle of descent outside of descent. Many other endogenous data suggest this interpretation to the Dorze auditor, but the ethnographer only finds them because an exogenous datum—the Galla version, which is unknown to the Dorze—shows him the way.

It is never necessary, and it is even sometimes impossible, to formulate an hypothesis by means of only those data which would allow its validation. This distinction between two uses of materials is not limited to the study of symbolism. Here is a linguistic example of it. In the Marseillais dialect of French, the feminine form of the adjective is clearly marked by a suffix /e/, as in 'petite maison', where one hears the final 'e' of the adjective. The presence of this vocalic suffix allows a simple description of the phenomena of elision and liaison. In Parisian pronunciation, no vocalic suffix phonetically marks the feminine form, and the rules of elision and of liaison therefore seem more complex. But the example from Marseillais suggests to the linguist that he should hypothesise the existence in Parisian of an unpronounced vocalic suffix, corresponding to the famous 'silent e', which would greatly simplify his description. Other characteristics of Parisian will validate such an hypothesis (cf. Dell 1973, part 2) which is more obvious in Marseillais where it is based on immediately perceptible evidence and not on a phenomenon whose reality remains underlying—phonological, but not phonetic.

In any case, and even if the hypothesis is discovered by means of the data of Marseillais, it is only the data of Parisian which allow one to validate it. The reason is that even a Parisian who has never heard Marseillais may and must construct in his internalized the simple rules of elision and of liaison, and he can only do this by means of Parisian. Linguistics can only validate its hypotheses in terms of the data actually used by the native speaker, precisely because there are hypotheses about the mental mechanism of that speaker. Similarly, because the symbolic mechanism the Dorze use to interpret myth is a mental one, we cannot validate the model of it except by means of data that are available to them, even if other data have suggested the model in the first place.

However, the comparison of myths of different peoples has other justifications than its suggestive power. Indeed, when the anthropologist proceeds in this way, he is really only following the example of the natives themselves. The ethnographic literature shows that the men of one society often listen to the myths of their neighbours, and that they compare them to their own in order to create new ones.

Thus, the Dorze and the Galla belong to two language groups which are only distantly related. We can probably exclude the supposition that the myth in question derives from a hypothetical era when they had a common language, and that the two versions diverged at the same time as the languages did, if only because the episode with Mariam witnesses a much more recent borrowing from Ethiopian Orthodox Christianity. Two other hypotheses seem more realistic: either that the one group was inspired by the other at a time when they were more closely in contact, or that both were inspired, directly or indirectly, by the same third source. Now, what is striking, anyhow, is that the differences between the two versions are no less systematic than are the similarities. In other words, that the borrowing of a myth is not simply a departure which, with time, arbitrarily becomes more distant from its model, but rather it is a set of regular transformations: there is identity in the case of the three episodes of marriage with the king's daughter, the public bathing party, and the intervention of Mariam. There is paired suppression, in the Galla version, of the two episodes with the serpent and the gazelle—that is to say, of these two anti-hunts—which are replaced by exploits of warfare accomplished by an anti-warrior. There is transformation by inversion in the initial episode: young woman raised by a man and elevated to manhood status, as against young man deprived by a woman of his virility. In the one case, a positive abuse of a relation of descent; in the other case, a negative abuse of a relation of affinity, to the detriment of descent.

The fact of borrowing, in matters of symbolism, therefore has more than merely a comparative or historical interest. The systematic transformations which accompany these borrowings suggest hypotheses concerning the nature of symbolism itself, if only because they are related to inversions characteristic of a symbolic system viewed from the inside. Thus, the Dorze myth is in certain respects a transformation of the Galla one, and in other respects it is a transformation of the set of practices and rules that define the status of killer; and it is the first sort of transformation that allows the discovery of the second.

An hypothesis then comes to mind: the symbolic interpretation of myth and ritual which an individual may come to know in his own culture would consist in abstracting from them a more general structure that other myths and other rituals, opposed to them, would achieve as well, were it not that a second level of interpretation—this time ideological—dictates his adherence to the ones and his neglect or refusal of the others. Belief in myth and ritual would constitute not the first principle, but a second development of their symbolic value. If such an hypothesis were taken up, we could conceive that in moving from one culture to another, ideology would change radically, but symbolism only superficially; we could conceive that the individual object of symbolic interpretation is for a large part transculturally defined; that each culture gives it only a particular realisation, sufficient for the individual unconsciously to reconstruct the principle behind it, while the anthropologist, having available to him bits only, must assemble them on a broader scale in order to arrive at the same result.

The symbolisms of two related societies are certainly not identical, but it is possible that they overlap and that they differ more in their manifest forms than in the principles that underlie them. To the extent that these principles constitute the object of learning for the individual, as well as the object of study for the anthropologist, it matters little that they succeed by means of the same evidence.

This hypothesis is attractive. It is not very clear and lacks confirmation. One would have to establish, on the one hand, that these transcultural principles exist, and on the other, that it is really they that individuals internalize. Lévi-Strauss' work in *Mythologiques* bears only on the first point. He shows clearly, albeit in an intuitive fashion, that there are systematic relationships of transformation between myths separated in space and also differing in form. But these transformations are revealed in a *Gedankenexperiment,* and generally do not correspond to the actual transformations that would have accompanied direct borrowing. It is not even certain, nor asserted moreover, that they necessarily result from a series of borrowings for as is shown by some comparisons between Greek and Amerindian myths, for example, the same structure may appear in two parts of the world without our having to assume that they are related.

Although it is a mental experiment which by itself merely demonstrates its own possibility, *Mythologiques* suggests, nevertheless, a treasure trove of ethnographic hypotheses which concern Americanists and, also, two general theoretical hypotheses: firstly, that the logic of actual borrowing is the same as that of mental transformations; secondly, that the logic behind the formation of myths and the logic behind their transformations are the same.

A society's myths have two origins—one, the transformation of other myths, endogenous or exogenous, the other, the transformation into myth of data of another kind. Both are well attested, for example, in the Indo-European studies that Georges Dumézil has carried out. Imagine, for example, an historical narrative transmitted orally in a non-literate society. Unless a concerted effort were made to preserve it in its initial form, certain episodes would soon be forgotten, while others would be magnified; the whole—here impoverished, there enriched—would acquire a more regular structure, a greater symbolic import, a memorableness that the original did not have; in short, it is transformed into a culturally exemplary, psychologically salient object which, once adopted by a society, becomes—precisely—a myth (cf. Sperber 1973). This process of mnemonic and symbolic selection together is observable in a more condensed form in the transmission of rumours as well as in the remembering of personal experience (cf. Pierre Smith 1973). History itself—not that studied by professionals, but that retained by each of us—does not find itself any the less affected. Here is an example of it taken from Edmund Leach (Leach 1966a: 100):

'For a contemporary English schoolboy, the really memorable facts about English sixteenth-century history are details such as the following:
(a) Henry VIII was a very successful masculine King who married many wives and murdered several of them;
(b) Edward VI was a very feeble masculine King who remained a virgin until his death;
(c) Mary Queen of Scots was a very unsuccessful female King who married many husbands and murdered several of them;
(d) Queen Elizabeth was a very successful female King who remained a virgin until her death...'

Thus, the memorableness of a text seems to depend on a structure made up of homologies and inversions that the wear and tear of memory, and better still, oral transmission, confers upon it if it does not possess it to begin with. And we might, with Lévi-Strauss, admit 'that all literary, oral, or written creation can, at the beginning, only be individual. But once it is given over to oral tradition as the latter is produced among non-literate peoples, only structured levels that are based on shared foundations remain stable, while probabilistic levels will manifest an extreme variability, itself a function of the personalities of successive narrators. However, in the course of the process of oral transmission, these probabilistic levels run into each other. They thus wear each other down, progressively laying bare what one might call the crystalline core of the body of speech. Individual works are all potential myths, but it is their collective adoption actualises—if such should be the case—their "mythicism"' (Lévi-Strauss 1971: 560).

If the formation of myths consists precisely in giving them such a regular structure, once they have it, why transform them? Why not adopt, without changing a line, the neighbours' myths which—if they were good enough for them in this regard, should be good enough for others? Because this structure exists not only at the level of the isolated myth, but also—or especially—at that of the corpus of myths that are transmitted in a society, at the very level of the symbolism as a whole whose myths—properly so-called—are only one of its manifestations. The transformations have the effect precisely of integrating an exogenous myth into this ensemble; but this integration is never perfect. To improve it, it is still necessary to transform the endogenous myths as well. With the result that the search for an unattainable equilibrium is translated into constant change.

According to such a view, it is the same properties that make myths both memorable and transformable. The study of their transformations is not distinct from that of their own structure; they both uncover systematic relations of homology and inversion, both within and between myths, both within a corpus and between one corpus and another.

But if the anthropologist can view as similar these relations of internal or external transformations, they present themselves to the native under two vastly different lights. On the one hand, there are potential transformations between synchronically given elements of a corpus which the native may reconstruct mentally in an unconscious manner; on the other, there are actual transformations, diachronically arranged, and which, precisely because they really took place, are missing one of the terms so that they cannot be reconstructed in the mind.

It is in this sense that Lévi-Strauss, in *Mythologiques*, performs an artificial mental experiment: he treats as a synchronically given set myths which no one before him had ever envisaged *en bloc*, myths not found side by side in any culture, but only in Americanist libraries. Some critics argue from the artificiality of the object treated to the vacuousness of hypotheses about it. Others, on the contrary, argue from the strength of these hypotheses to the reality of the object, the existence of this famous language which would be constituted by myths across cultures. These attitudes both seem equally poorly founded to me.

Once again, it is not at all necessary that the materials that have led to the development of an hypothesis suffice to validate it, and so the object of *Mythologiques* may be artificial without its hypotheses therefore being empty. To corroborate them, it would be necessary to study mythology and symbolism within a society and not to look beyond except to the extent that its own members do. This is the direction of research that most of Lévi-Strauss' students are following today. We may ask ourselves then if it would not have been possible to begin there, to obviate an apparent detour. We may imagine a Lévi-Strauss who would have stayed for several years in one society and would have studied its myths from within to arrive at a similar view. It matters little. The study of myths has passed through the mental experiment of *Mythologiques* to its greatest benefit. It does not displease me that a rigourless discipline like ours can, as though in compensation, submit thus to the mark of individual genius.

The validity of a set of hypotheses is independent of the data that permitted its formulation; conversely, this validity does not guarantee that the set of these data constitutes an autonomous entity. We may accept the view of myths proposed by Lévi-Strauss without being bound to accept that the set of Amerindian myths is part of the selfsame language. Actually, if this were not the case, one would encounter an irresolvable paradox.

A grammar is a device that generates the sentences of the language it describes by means of given axioms and by the operation of rules, independently of all external input. All sentences, the whole language, are contained in its grammar. Inversely, according to Lévi-Strauss, myths are generated by the transformation of other myths or of texts which carry a certain mythicism; in other words, by a device that allows an infinite and non-enumerable set of possible inputs. No grammar therefore generates by itself the set of myths, any more than the mechanism of visual perception generates by itself the set of possible perceptions. The device that would generate myths depends on an external stimulus; it is thus similar to cognitive devices and opposed to semiological devices: it is an interpretative, and not a generative, system.

Lévi-Strauss has demonstrated the opposite of what he asserts, and myths do not constitute a language. He proposed the first elaborated alternative to semiological views of myth—and, beyond that of symbolism—all the while stating that he was, above all else, a semiologist.

Lévi-Strauss says that 'the universe of primitives (or those claimed to be such) consists principally of messages' (Lévi-Strauss 1964: 353–4). In fact, it is the universe of the French, and more generally, of Westerners, that consists of messages. In current usage, any object of knowledge has, perforce, a sense, a meaning—from the meaning of life to the meaning of the colour of leaves in the autumn. To say that a phenomenon has no meaning is to avow that nothing at all can be said of it. The Frenchman lives in a universe where everything means something, where every correlation is a relation of meaning, where the cause is the sign of its effect and the effect, a sign of its cause. By a singular inversion, only real signs—words, texts—are said, sometimes, to mean nothing at all.

But this semiologism, though it is found in other cultures as well, is in no way universal. For the Dorze, for example, the question 'What does that mean?' *(awa yusi?)* can only be asked about a word, a sentence, a text or a directly paraphrasable behaviour, such as a nod. Even when a natural phenomenon is considered as the effect of a supernatural will, it is not counted as meaning it. In short, if the Dorze universe 'consists principally of messages' they know nothing of it, nor do I.

The attribution of sense is an essential aspect of symbolic development in *our* culture. Semiologism is one of the bases of *our* ideology. For centuries, this semiologism has, tacitly and undividedly, dominated symbolic production. It is less surprising therefore that those whose work for the first time questions this domination expressly render it a first and last homage. If they feel a need to call themselves semiologists, it is to hide—from themselves as well as others—the fact that they have ceased to be such, that they don't know which sign to avow.

Soon it will be for semiology as it was for evolutionism. Once we saw that it was no longer necessary to take as gospel the declarations of the founders of contemporary anthropology or to see in the social forms they described the stages of a unilinear evolution, we realised at once that they had forged the conceptual tools for synchronic description of society and of culture. Similarly, when we strip the work of Lévi-Strauss of the semiological burden with which he has chosen to encumber it, we will then realise that he was the first to propose the fundamentals of an analysis of symbolism which was finally freed from the absurd idea that symbols mean. The argument may be summarised in this way: if symbols had a meaning, it would be obvious enough. All these learned terms—signifier and signified, paradigm and syntagm, code, mytheme will not for long hide the following paradox: that if Lévi-Strauss thought of myths as a semiological system, the myths thought themselves in him, and without his knowledge, as a cognitive system.

PART THREE:

LÉVI-STRAUSS RESPONDS

CHAPTER XII

Meaning and Use of the Notion of Model

Claude Lévi-Strauss

In his interesting paper, Mr. Maybury-Lewis takes me to task on two grounds. I am accused of misrepresenting the ethnographical data, at least in two instances. More generally, my methodological approach is said to be "morally" wrong. The first criticism has no real basis and results from his mistaking a theoretical reconstruction for a description of actual facts. As to the value judgment, it is, as such, irrefutable, and I can only try to clarify the line of reasoning which I have followed.

Let us first consider what I shall call, for brevity's sake, the Winnebago discrepancy (See *Structural Anthropology*, Vol. I [hereafter referred to as *S.A.*], pp. 133–135). Are we to believe that it can be overcome by admitting that one category of informants—those of the lower phratry—simply omitted the dual division because it was not contextually relevant? But it was not enough simply not to mention it. While they did away with it in their description of the ancient village, they introduced another dual division—admittedly not a social one, but not merely ecological either, since it emerges as a substitute for, and a transformation of, the other division.

To reconstruct the village layout, it would not be sufficient to put one diagram on top of the other, as if each offered a "true" picture, although in its way an incomplete one. In so doing, one would be doing the very thing for which I am reproached, i.e., "manipulating" models. The only empirical data given us consist of two drawings of the ancient Winnebago village, each of which bears a complementary relation to the other, if not the one suggested to us. These drawings not only present a fragmentary image of a total configuration (so that all we have to do is to supplement one with the other) but they also stand in opposition to each other, and this relation of opposition cannot be lightly dismissed since it is itself part of the ethnographical data.

In other words, if the distinction between the inhabited village and the cleared ground (as well as the one between the cleared ground and the surrounding woods) is not relevant in one diagram, why does it become so in the other? What we have here is nothing more than a curious fact, the true interpretation of which probably will never be known. This is all the more reason to follow each and every line of interpretation.

I have taken up one, which at least offers the advantage of being novel. What would be the theoretical consequences, if the social distinction between the two moieties, on the one hand, and the ecological (but also philosophical) distinction between cleared ground (pertaining to culture) and the wilderness beyond the timberline (pertaining to nature), on the other hand, should be recognized as two different codes, codes used to carry the same message, but at the cost of complementary distortions?

Let us recapitulate briefly. In the first place, a tribe whose social organization and religious thought are strongly marked with a principle of dual division displays another form of dualism, one which is no longer diametric but, as it were, concentric. In the second place, this concentric dualism manifests itself openly and in isolation in populations such as the Trobriand, where one can observe it independently from the other type. To object that the Trobriand have no dual organization in the classical sense of the term would therefore be to miss the point. For it is precisely the exclusive presence of the concentric dualism that permits its identification its definition as an ethnographic phenomenon. Thirdly, one could examine societies where the two types coexist in a particularly clear manner: Bororo, Timbia, and so many Indonesian groups. It is easier to present a syncretic model than to consider them one after the other. Three conclusions were reached: (1) where the two types coexist, there is a functional relation between them; (2) the concentric pattern is logically more essential than the diametric one; and (3) since this concentric pattern covers a ternary pattern, the latter can be said to underlie—at least in a latent manner—the diametric dualism itself.

It would then be futile to establish an empirical opposition between the two types of dualism. One of them could scarcely be reduced to a reflection of symbolic values in the village layout, with the other—the only "true" dualism—being said to involve the real segments of the social group. The latter type also has a symbolic value, and the former entails rights and obligations no less than the latter. What I have tried to do is to transcend these partial views of a selfsame reality, and put to the test a kind of common language into which the two forms of dualism could be translated. This would, I feel, enable us to reach—not on the level of observation, of course—a "generalized" interpretation of all the phenomena of dualism. I hope to have shown that such an interpretation is not only possible, since all the considered instances of dualism can be reduced, despite their apparent heterogeneity, to the various combinations of only five binary oppositions (*S.A.*, p. 160); but that this common language reveals an important and hitherto undetected fact. It is that social dualism exists not only in the form which we described but assumes and covers a triadic system, of which each individual case of dualism (taken in a broad sense, but including among other forms, dual organizations) should be considered as a simplification and as a limit.

Admittedly, this marks a departure from the thesis put forward in *Les Structures élémentaires de la parenté,* as I have myself taken care to explain (*S.A.*, p. 150). But it does not do away with the distinction between dyadic and triadic structures which occupied such an important place in that work, since, for practical purposes, that distinction remains as useful as it was. But it seems that—as mathematicians with whom the problem was discussed agreed—by treating dyadic systems as a special case of the triadic formula, the general theory of reciprocity becomes greatly simplified. Moreover, this manner of formulating the problem seems to be more convenient for the purpose of historical reconstruction, since there are cases when the triadic "core" appears to be not only logically more simple, but older than the dyadic "upper crust" which covers it.

Now let us get down to the supposed ethnographical distortions, and first to the question of the Bororo north-south axis. If its presence contradicted the observations of the Salesian Fathers to the extent that has been maintained, I would suspect that I misunderstood my informants, whose statements were quite clear in that particular respect. But (1) these observations were made in a different part of the Bororo country, where the villages were not necessarily structured in the same manner; (2) there are similar indications recorded in Colbacchini's first publications; and (3) Albisetti's more recent descriptions show something which looks like the north-south axis inside the men's house, dividing the sectors allocated to each moiety; then a north-south axis ideally present inside of each clan, and resulting in independently attested correlation between "lower" and west, on the one hand, and "higher" and east, on the other hand. Thus, the difference between the two accounts is that, in one case, the north-south axis has a positive existence inside the men's house, and a relative one outside; while in the other case, the north-south axis is objectively present both inside and outside.

In order to see there an insurmountable contradiction, one would have to postulate two things: first, that the Bororo social structure was perfectly identical throughout their vast territory; second, that the north-south axis, as recorded on the Rio Vermelho, did serve to separate the clans according to status distinction.

With regard to the first point, such a homogeneity does not seem very likely. The Bororo once occupied a territory as big as half of France; in historical times, it was still a quarter of the earlier area. The rate of growth and extinction could not be the same for each clan and in each village, especially when losses due to wars against or by neighboring tribes are taken into account. Each village was probably confronted with demographic problems of its own, and the number of clans and their distribution on the village circle must have varied considerably. The Salesians could hardly have given us a description of a situation which once existed in the whole territory. It did not even exist where they were working themselves, as their earlier, more empirical descriptions show. Rather, many years of patient work enabled them to construct an ideal formula, the theoretical model which was most suitable in accounting for numerous local variations. It is not surprising, then, if the actual pattern recorded at one time in a village is slightly different from that recorded at another time (in villages belonging to a distinct group). Finally, it is obvious that, when we work on the invaluable documents which the Salesian Fathers have left us after many years of painstaking reconstruction, we are not confronted with empirical data. Rather, we are manipulating a sociological model. Like it or not, this is what we all do when we engage in that type of discussion.

Will it be said that the two descriptions are incompatible and that one should have chosen between them, instead of using them both concurrently? Incompatibility would result if the terms *xobbuguiugue, xebbeguiugue* were given the same meaning in the earliest descriptions of the Salesians, in their later ones, and in my own; that is, if these terms always meant "superior" and "inferior" and connotated absolute differences. For, then, instead of having "superior" and "inferior" families inside each clan, the West clans would be absolutely inferior, the East clans absolutely superior, and it would be impossible to merge the two systems into one. But such was not the case on the Rio Vermelho, nor on the Rio das Garças, according to Colbacchini's earlier account. For him, as well as for me, the native terms referred to the topography and meant "uphill" and "downhill" for Colbacchini's informants, and "upstream" and "downstream" for mine. It just so happens that, in Bororo, as in many other languages, the same term has all three connotations. It was all the more easy for the Bororo to avoid equivocation when they had two couples of contrasted terms to express status distinction: between "great" and "small," on the one hand, and "red" and "black," on the other.

Was I wrong to write that two clans in each moiety represent the two legendary heroes of the Bororo? It is true that two clans belonging to one moiety do so at present and that, in the past, two clans of the other moiety did so. However, if this merging of a synchronic analysis with a diachronic analysis is an ethnographical mistake, does my critic not commit the same mistake when, in trying to explain the Winnebago discrepancy, he puts forth a mythical account according to which the lower phratry may once have held or shared the chieftainship—a story of exactly the same type as the Bororo one that I relied on?

This is not all. In neither case are we confronted with an opposition between the synchronic and the diachronic order. Here, the past referred to is mythical, not historical. And, as a myth, the content is actually given to the native consciousness. When the Bororo myth tells us about a time when two Tugare clans, instead of the two Cera clans, were connected with the cultural heroes, it may refer to past events. Of the truth of these events, we will remain forever ignorant. But we are made quite sure that, in the present, some kind of connection is felt to exist, between the dispossessed clans and the cultural heroes.

Coming now to the Winnebago, it is a mistake to attribute to me the notion that the Winnebago village actually comprised twelve clans distributed into three groups. This statement, as I made it, did not claim to be an ethnographical description of the Winnebago village as it existed in the past. It merely described a theoretical diagram, purporting to reorganize ethnographical data which, at the observation level, do not clearly exhibit those properties (or else, my undertaking would have been useless).

Thus, there is no claim that the Winnebago village was ever distributed into three groups of four clans each. What is being suggested here is quite different; namely, that on purely deductive grounds, the three cases taken from different societies may be treated as transformations one of the other under several conditions, one of them being that the Winnebago village be analyzed in such and such a way.

This inference being deductively drawn, it is highly gratifying that the ethnographical data should give it independent support. There is evidence in Radin's material that this interpretation of the village structure existed not only in the anthropologist's mind but also in the minds of some of the natives themselves. If it were imposed on us by the manifest content of the ethnographical data, there would be nothing to demonstrate—it would be sufficient to describe what one sees or what one is being told. On the other hand, a theoretical hypothesis which deviates from the manifest content of the ethnographical data is substantially upheld if we are to discover, in the latent content supplied by the myths, the religious representations, etc. Some data show a remarkable parallelism between the native categories, and they are arrived at by the way of theoretical reconstruction. In the Winnebago case, Radin says (1923, p. 241), "One informant . . . said . . . that the clans were arranged in three groups, one over which the Thunderbird clan ruled, another over which the Water-spirit ruled, and a third over which the Bear clan ruled." This is proof enough that a ternary system existed at least in a latent state. This is more than could be expected, especially as it comes from a part of the world where the operation of such ternary systems had remained hitherto unsuspected.

The argument that the ternary system would be irrelevant in consideration of the Winnebago marriage system appears, along these lines, out of order. The point made in Figure 13 of *S.A.* (p. 155) is that, even if the system should be considered as ternary, this would not affect the dualistic marriage system. As a matter of fact, the usefulness of the diagram lies in its enabling us to "see" the social structure either as ternary (sky, water, earth) or as binary (higher, lower). Also, the northwest-southeast axis, "spatial referent of Winnebago dualism," is not "omitted," since the diagram makes clear that marriage possibilities are between higher (= sky), on the one hand, and lower (= water + earth), on the other.

As to the village circle, which is claimed to be "irrelevant in a diagram of marriage relations," there are two comments to be made. In the first place—and contrary to what is maintained—the diagrams do not concern marriage relations alone. Rather, they are intended to show how marriage relations, social structure, village layout, religious representations, and so forth are all part of a system. The difference is that, in each case, they are assigned different functions; or—to express it in diagrammatic terms—they are permuted in different topological positions. To put it yet differently, what a given society "says" in terms of marriage relations is being "said" by another society in terms of village layout, and in terms of religious representations by a third, and so on.

In the second place (and to limit myself to the Winnebago ethnographical material which I have been reproached as having misrepresented), it is enough to refer the reader to Radin's enlightening comments on the relationship between village and clan structure. If there are Winnebago myths representing the whole tribe as having once consisted of one village, the overall social structure cannot be thought of as independent of the residential unit. Radin raises the question—wisely, I believe—whether the "band" or village, "setting off one group against another," is not an early form of social grouping, so that, as elsewhere in North America, village organization may have preceded the clan (Radin 1923, p. 184–185).

I shall not dwell at length on the discussion of the other diagrams since it follows the same erroneous line: that of confusing a theoretical analysis of models, intended to explain the ethnographical data (by reducing them to a small number of common factors) with an actual description of the data as they appear to the empirical observer. Many Southeast Asian societies make the useful and often true statement that women circulate, not men; this does not invalidate the truth (to be covered by a generalized model) that nothing would be changed in the formal properties of the structure, if the situation were described the other way around, as some tribes actually do. The "tripod" in Figures 13 to 15 (*S.A.*, pp. 155–158) only expresses the fact that, in an asymmetrical marriage system as well as in a symmetrical one, there is a rule of exogamy in operation; but that, in the first case, it creates a sociological opposition between the sexes, whatever group they belong to, while in the second case, the opposition exists between the groups, whatever sexes they include.

It is equally inaccurate to state that the east-west axis does not appear in the Bororo diagram. It is true that it does not appear where the natives put it, since it has been demonstrated that in so doing, they let themselves be mystified by their own system. For that reason, it has been represented, as it should, by the tripod, each branch of which bisects the three otherwise fully endogamous groups. On the other hand, the hypothesis that the north-south axis provides the unifying factor is admittedly weak. This is so, not because the existence of this axis results from an ethnographical error—a charge which has already been shown to be gratuitous (see p. 81, n. 1) because I have myself so qualified it, and have explained that it first requires a careful testing in the field.

Obviously, the Bororo diagram is not exhaustive—none of the diagrams are and none are meant to be. It nevertheless represents quite satisfactorily what is essential and was asked of us: on the one hand, a pair of moieties, on the other hand, a triad of endogamous groups. A diagram does not pretend to show everything, but only the functions which are recurrent in all the cases diagramatically exemplified (and despite the fact that these functions do not manifest themselves, each time, on the same level of social reality).

We reach here a major point of disagreement. Should the only conclusion of my paper be that disparate elements drawn from different societies can be represented in identical patterns, I would not consider such a demonstration devoid of sociological implications. For we may have found a way of showing that what appears superficially disparate may not be so, and that behind the bewildering diversity of empirical data, there may exist a small number of recurrent, identical properties, although they are combined differently.

To sum up, may I point out to what extent my critic remains the prisoner of the naturalistic misconceptions that have so long pervaded the British school. He claims to be a structuralist. He even claims to defend structuralism against my reckless manner of handling it. But he is still a structuralist in Radcliffe-Brown's terms in that he believes the structure to lie at the level of empirical reality and to be a part of it. When, therefore, he is presented a structural model which departs from empirical reality, he feels cheated in some devious way. To him, social structure is like a kind of jigsaw puzzle, and everything is achieved when one has discovered how the pieces fit together. But, if the pieces have been arbitrarily cut, there is no structure at all. On the other hand, if—as is sometimes done—the pieces were automatically cut in different shapes by a mechanical saw, the movements of which are regularly modified by a camshaft, the structure of the puzzle exists, though not at the empirical level (since there are many ways of recognizing the pieces which fit together). Its key lies in the mathematical formula expressing the shape of the cams and their speed of rotation. This information does not correspond in any perceptible manner to the puzzle as it appears to the player, but it alone can explain the puzzle and provide a logical method to solve it.

But Maybury-Lewis writes: "Social relations cannot be formally represented by symbols in the same way as mathematical relations can. Accordingly, sociological models are not manipulable in the sense that mathematical equations are." Should he not explain, first, what he means by "social relations"? (1960, p. 35). If he refers to concrete social relations, as seen by the empirical observer, we cannot but agree with Maybury-Lewis's statement, while remembering that already in primary school, we were taught the impossibility of adding pears to apples. But if a distinction is made between the level of observation and symbols to be substituted for it, I fail to see why an algebraic treatment of, say, symbols for marriage rules, could not teach us, when aptly manipulated, something of the way a given marriage system actually works, and bring out properties not immediately apparent to the empirical observer.

Of course, the final word should rest with experiment. However, the experiment suggested and guided by deductive reasoning will not be the same as the unsophisticated one with which the whole process had started; the latter will remain as alien as ever to the deeper analysis.

The ultimate proof of the molecular structure of matter is provided by the electronic microscope, which enables us to see actual molecules. This achievement does not alter the fact that henceforth the molecule will not become any more visible to the naked eye. Similarly, it is hopeless to expect a structural analysis to change our way of perceiving concrete social relations. It will only explain them better. If the structure can be seen, it will not be at the earlier, empirical level, but at a deeper one, previously neglected; that of those unconscious categories which we may hope to reach by bringing together domains which, at first sight, appear disconnected to the observer: on the one hand, the social system as it actually works, and on the other, the manner in which, through their myths, their rituals, and their religious representations, men try to hide or to justify the discrepancies between their society and the ideal image of it which they harbor.

To give, from the start, an absolute value to the distinction between those two domains is to beg the question. For the problem originally raised in my paper on dual organization (*S.A.*, Chapter VIII) is precisely that of the absolute value of such a distinction. The problem can be phrased in the following terms: Do these organizations always belong to the domain of real social segments, or are they not sometimes reduced to symbolic representations of this reality? If the descriptions of the Bororo social structure are correct, then, as I have shown elsewhere (*S.A.*, Chapter VII), dual organization among the Bororo belongs to the domain of symbolic representations, since its operative value is canceled, so to speak, by actual rules of endogamy. On the other hand, the concentric dualism of the Bororo village, opposing the profane circle to the sacred center, should be endowed with a higher coefficient of objective truth, since there is nothing in the system to contradict it, and since it is permitted to unfold all its consequences, on both the religious and the social levels.

But the same thing cannot be said of other examples of dual organization elsewhere. Hence the conclusion that actual social segments and symbolic representations may not be as heterogeneous as it seems. To some extent, they may correspond to codes whose functions and fields of application are permutable. Herein lies one's right to deal with social segments and symbolic representations as parts of an underlying system endowed with a better explanatory value, although—or rather, because—empirical observation never apprehends it as such.

CHAPTER XIII

Finale

Claude Lévi-Strauss

> *...lastly, all the chapters are prefaced by strange and mysterious epigraphs, which considerably enhance the interest of, and give character to, each part of the composition.*
>
> Victor Hugo, *Han d'Islande,*
> *Preface to the first edition*

If there is one conviction that has been intimately borne upon the author of this work during twenty years devoted to the study of myths...it is that the solidity of the self, the major preoccupation of the whole of Western philosophy, does not withstand persistent application to the same object, which comes to pervade it through and through and to imbue it with an experiential awareness of its own unreality. For the only remnant of reality to which it still dares to lay claim is that of being a 'singularity', in the sense in which astronomers use the term: a point in space and a moment in time, relative to each other, and in which there have occurred, are occurring or will occur events whose density (itself in turn relative to other events, no less real but more widely dispersed) makes possible its approximate definition, always remembering of course that this nodal point of past, present and probable events does not exist as a substratum, but only in the sense that phenomena are occurring in it, and in spite of the fact that these phenomena, of which it is the place of intersection, originate from countless other sources, for the most part unknown.

But why, it may be asked, should one have such reservations with regard to the subject when dealing with myths, that is, with stories which could not have come into being unless at some moment—even though, in most cases, that moment is beyond the reach of enquiry—each of them had been conceived and narrated in the first instance by a particular individual? Utterance is a function confined to subjects, and every myth, in the last resort, most have its origin in an individual act of creation. This is no doubt very true but, in order to achieve the status of myth, the created work must cease precisely to be individual and, in the process of generalization, must lose the essential part of those factors determined by probability with which it was infused at the outset, and which could be attributed to the particular author's temperament, talent, imagination and personal experiences. Since myths depend on oral transmission and collective tradition, the probabilist levels they include are continuously eroded, because of their lesser resistance to social attrition, than those levels which are more firmly organized, through corresponding to shared needs. It will be readily agreed, then that the difference between individually created works and myths which are recognized as such by a given community is one not of nature but of degree. In this respect, structural analysis can be legitimately applied to myths stemming from a collective tradition as well as to works by a single author, since in both cases the intention is the same: to give a structural explanation of that which can be so explained, and which is never everything; and beyond that, to seek to grasp, in varying degrees according to circumstances, another kind of determinism which has to be looked for at the statistical or sociological levels, i.e., in the life-story of the individual and in the particular society or environment.

Let us recognize, then, that all literary creative work, whether oral or written, cannot, at the outset, be other than individual. When it is immediately taken over by oral tradition, as is the case in communities without writing, only the structured levels will remain stable, since they rest on common foundations, whereas the probabilist levels will be subject to extreme variability resulting from the personalities of successive narrators However, during the process of oral transmission, these probabilist levels will rub against each other and wear each other down, thus gradually separating off from the bulk of the text what might be called its crystalline parts. All individual works are potential myths, but only if they are adopted by the collectivity as a whole do they achieve 'mythic' status.

It can be seen from this how far genuine structuralist interpretations differ from those practised by psychoanalysis or by schools of thought which claim to reduce the structure of a collective or individual work to what they mistakenly call its genesis. Not that I am unaware of the fact that every structure must have a genesis. In his recent and excellent little book on Structuralism, Piaget says I am unaware of this (p. 97), but his criticism seems to arise from a misunderstanding. It can be readily admitted that every structure has a genesis, provided we also recognize that—as Piaget's book demonstrates—each anterior state of a structure is itself a structure. 'It is not obvious why it should be unreasonable to think that the ultimate nature of reality is a constant process of construction instead of an accumulation of ready-made structures' (Piaget, p. 58). Indeed, but the process consists of structures which are undergoing transformation to produce other structures, so that *structure itself is a primordial fact.* Less confusion would have occurred in connection with the concept of human nature, that I continue to use, if it had been realized that I do not take it in the sense of a heap of completed and immutable structures, but rather with the meaning of matrices giving rise to structures all belonging to the same set, without necessarily remaining identical throughout any individual existence from birth to adulthood, or, in the case of human groups, at all times and in all places.

However, psychoanalysis and the so-called genetic schools of thought take a different view of genesis from that about which Piaget and myself might more easily reach agreement. Far from recognizing that, as Piaget puts it, 'in reality as in mathematics, every form is a content for the forms comprising it and every content is a form for the contents it contains' (p. 95), these people try to explain types of categories by reducing them to contents which are not of the same kind and which, through the operation of a remarkable contradiction, are supposed to modify their form from without. Genuine structuralism, on the contrary, seeks first and foremost to grasp the intrinsic properties of certain types of categories. These properties do not express anything external to themselves. Or, if it is felt that they really must refer to something external, that point of reference has to be the organization of the brain envisaged as a network whose various properties are expressed by the most divergent ideological systems in terms of some particular structure, with each system revealing, in its own way, modes of interconnection of the network.

But this philosophic caution, which makes it possible to avoid the pitfalls of reductionist interpretations, is also a strength. It supposes that each suggested new interpretation of a myth—and this means, for a start, my own interpretations—takes its place in sequence after already known variants of that myth (L.-S. 5, p. 240). But, it will be asked, does this not shut you off inside a circle where each form, having been immediately transformed into a content, requires to be explained by another form, thus creating an infinite regress? On the contrary, it follows from the preceding argument that the criterion of structural interpretation avoids this paradox, since only structural interpretation can account both for itself and for the other kinds. In so far as it consists in making explicit a system of relationships that the other variants merely embodied, it integrates them with itself and integrates itself with them on a new level, where the definitive fusion of content and form can take place and will therefore no longer lend itself to new embodiments. The structure of the myth, having been revealed to itself, brings to a close the series of its possible developments.

It can thus be seen how the elimination of the subject represents what might be called a methodological need: it corresponds to the scrupulous desire to explain no part of the myth except by the myth, and consequently to exclude the point of view of an arbiter looking at the myth from outside and therefore inclined to propose extrinsic causes for it. On the contrary, it must be recognized as a fact that behind each mythic system there loom others, which were the dominant factors in determining it; it is these other systems which speak through it and echo each other down the ages, if not indefinitely at least as far back as that irrecoverable moment in time, hundreds of thousands of years ago—or perhaps even longer ago still, as may one day be claimed—when mankind, in the beginning, produced its first myths. This is not to say that, at each stage of this complex development, the myth, in passing from one community to another, has not been modified by the proximity of different techno-economic infrastructures which exert an attraction on it. It has to adapt to their mechanisms, and I have shown again and again that, in order to understand the differential gaps between versions of the same myth belonging to different communities, sometimes close neighbours, sometimes geographically remote from each other, the infrastructure has to be taken into account.

Each version of the myth, then, shows the influence of a twofold determinism: one strand links it to a succession of previous versions or to a set of foreign versions, while the other operates as it were transversally, through the constraints arising from the infrastructure which necessitate the modification of some particular element, with the result that the system undergoes reorganization in order to adapt these differences to necessities of an external kind. But are only two possibilities: either the infrastructure is identical there with the kind of things which it is supposed to bring into play and, in that case, it is as inert and passive as the things themselves, and can engender nothing; or it belongs to the realm of lived-in experience and is therefore in a perpetual state of imbalance and tension: in this case, the myths cannot derive from it through a causality that wound very rapidly become tautological. They should be seen rather as constituting local and temporary answers to the problems raised by feasible adjustments and insoluble contradictions that they are endeavouring to legitimize or conceal. The content with which the myth endows itself is not anterior but posterior, to this initial impulse: far from deriving from some content or other, the myth moves towards a particular content through the attraction of its specific gravity. In each individual case, it alienates, in they process, part of its apparent liberty which, looked at from another angle, is no more than an aspect of its own necessity. The origin of this necessity is lost in the mists of time; it lies in the depths of the mind, and its spontaneous unfolding is slowed down, accelerated, deflected or bifurcated through the action of historical constraints which couple it, so to speak, with other mechanisms that its effects have to be reconciled with, but without involving a departure from its original direction.

The subject, while remaining deliberately in the background so as to allow free play to this anonymous deployment of discourse, does not renounce consciousness of it, or rather does not prevent it achieving consciousness of itself through him. Some people pretend to believe that the criticism of consciousness should lead, logically, to the renunciation of conscious thought. But I have never had any other intention than to further knowledge, i.e., *to achieve consciousness.* However, for too long now philosophy has succeeded in locking the social sciences inside a closed circle by not allowing them to envisage any other object of study for the consciousness than consciousness itself. This accounts, on the one hand, for the powerlessness of the social sciences in practice, and on the other for their self-deluding nature, the characteristic of consciousness being that it deceives itself. What structuralism tries to accomplish in the wake of Rousseau, Marx, Durkheim, Saussure and Freud, is to reveal to consciousness *an object other than itself;* and therefore to put it in the same position with regard to human phenomena as that of the natural and physical sciences, and which, as they have demonstrated, alone allows knowledge to developed. Recognition of the fact that consciousness is not everything, nor even the most important thing, is not a reason for abandoning it, any more than the principles professed a few years ago by the Existentialist philosophers obliged them to lead a life of debauchery in the cellars of Saint-Germain-de-Prés. Quite the opposite, in fact, since consciousness is thus able to gauge the immensity of its task and to summon up the courage to embark upon it, with the hope at last that it will not be doomed to sterility.

But this assumption of consciousness remains intellectual in character, that is to say it does not substantially differ from the realities to which it is applied; it is these very realities arriving at their own truth. There can be no question, then, of smuggling the subject in again, under this new guise. I could have no tolerance for a form of deceit in which the left hand slips under the table to restore to the worst kind of philosophy what the right hand claims to have taken from it above board, and which, through simply replacing the Self by the Other and by sliding a metaphysics of desire under the logic of the concept, deprives this logic of its foundation. By substituting for the Self on the one hand an anonymous Other, and on the other hand an individualized desire (individualized, because, were it not so, it would signify nothing), one would fail to hide the fact that they need only be stuck together again and the resulting entity reversed to recognize underneath that very Self, whose abolition had been so loudly proclaimed. If there is a point at which the Self can reappear, it is only after the completion of the work which excluded it throughout (since, contrary to what might be supposed, it was not so much the case that the Self was the author as that the work, during the process of composition, became the creator of an executant who lived only by and through it); then, it can and must take an overall view of the whole, in the same way as the readers who will peruse the text without having found themselves in the dangerous situation of feeling prompted to write it. This finale, headed by an epigraph which is unlike the preceding ones and is meant as a commentary on them, is itself in the nature of a commentary on a completed work, from which the writer is trying to deduce his own conclusions, now that his mission is over and he is again free to speak in the first person singular.

When I look back over my work, there is one thing that strikes me, and all the more sharply in that it was not intentional on my part. In beginning my enquiry with myths of the southern hemisphere, and gradually shifting it to the northern and western areas of the northern hemisphere, I have gone, as it were, against the grain of American history, since the peopling of the continent clearly took place for the most part in the opposite direction. Was this procedure useful or necessary, independently of the personal reasons which made it easier for me to deal with the myths of communities I had myself observed? I think so, but largely for a different reason, connected with the peculiar nature of ethnographical enquiry: the South American mythic corpus, being far less rich than the North American, is more appropriate for preliminary study, because it can be looked at as if from a distance: it is simplified, and its very poverty reduces it to its essential features. The North American corpus, on the other hand, appears so abundant, complex and detailed that, had I begun with it, my analysis might have been side-tracked. The investigation of South American sources, although apparently less rewarding, made it possible to save time. But I have often wondered whether, had I begun at the other end, the result would have been the same. I would probably not have chosen the same reference myth: the material used by the North American versions is so rich and varied that the myth does not stand out so sharply from the corpus. On the other hand, is it certain that since South America was peopled by way of North America, the South American versions of the reference myth represent more recent and defective forms? The contrary could be the case if the same myth, while being worked upon at length and transformed in North America, had preserved more of its initial freshness and simplicity in South America. If this is so, the sequence chosen corresponds to the sequence in reality. But it is very important that the order of ideas in these four volumes should not be seen as a linear programme. By means of myths introduced in the second volume, and following on from those presented in the first, we moved, in the third volume, from South America to North America, thanks to *inverted* myths with *identical* meanings....

But it is not on ethnographical grounds that my critics, for the most part; have chosen to attack me. They have usually raised methodological objections, some of which are so feeble that it would be unkind to mention the names of their originators. I propose to deal with them rapidly to clear the ground before moving on to more serious matters.

I have been accused of basing my analyses on summaries of myths, without first submitting the myths to textual criticism. Let me begin with the second point. No one with the slightest knowledge of the subject can have failed to notice that, in spite of the abundance of the material dealt with, it represents only a tiny fraction of the myths of both hemispheres that I might have used. Perhaps it is thought that I chose my documentation at random or according to personal convenience. Behind the thousand or so myths or variants of myths that I have commented on lie many others that I have examined, briefly analysed and have not included for various reasons, in which textual criticism had its part, but always kept in check by the conviction that, except in those cases where there is glaring evidence to prove the point, myths do not exist in 'good' and 'bad' versions; at any rate, it is not the analyst's business to decide the issue in the light of criteria foreign to the object he is studying: it would be truer to say that the myths criticize and select themselves, opening up, through the confused mass of the corpus, certain paths which would not have been the same, had one particular myth rather than another been the first to emerge. But not only have I, for my own enlightenment, constantly criticized my sources, without feeling the need to keep the reader informed of these preliminary phases of the enquiry, which were not his concern; also, whenever possible, that is, whenever the native text was available in languages for which there were also dictionaries and grammars, I have taken care to check the translation with the original, and this has sometimes enabled me...to throw light on certain points that were not clear in the version as printed.

As for the summaries which, I admit, have often given me more trouble than the actual commentaries, they have never been used as a basis for exegesis. They are intended for the reader and give him a general view of each myth, until such time as the discussion gradually brings in details and shades of meaning which could not be included in the body of the summary. I have too great a mistrust of summaries to admit that they could serve any other purpose; experience has taught me how impossible it is to grasp the spirit of a myth without steeping oneself in the complete versions, however diffuse they may be, and submitting to a slow process of incubation requiring hours, days, months—or sometimes even years—until one's thought, guided unconsciously by tiny details, succeeds in embracing the essential nature of the myth. The summary, as I use it, has no analytical function, but only serves as the starting-point for a synthetic account which enriches it with additional detail, until the complete myth has been successfully reconstituted and interpreted as an organic whole.

No less inadequate are those critics who claim to show that I am contradicting because I am supposed to have asserted, on the one hand, that the analysis of myths is endless and that the myths themselves are *interminable* (*RC*, p. 6), and on the other (*passim*) that the group of myths I have studied constitutes a closed syste. To argue in this fashion is to fail to understand the difference between the mythic discourse of any community, which, like any discourse, remains open-ended—every myth can have a sequel, new variants may appear or new myths come into being—and the 'language' (*langue*) brought into play by the discourse, and which, at any particular moment, forms a system. It is in relationship to itself, and considered as a discourse unfolding diachronically, that a mythology remains unclosed. But the open-endedness of this *parole*, in the Saussurian sense of the term, does not mean that the 'language' on which it depends is not closed in relation to other systems, also envisaged synchronically, rather in the way a cylinder might be said to be a closed surface, and would remain so, even if it were extended indefinitely through time at one end: an observer could claim to have seen round it and to be able to work out the formula for the calculation, at any moment, of the volume involved, even if he never succeeded in following it along its whole length.

Other critics have claimed that the method I use has shown a constant regression from one book to the next, and that this is evidence of its inadequacy. The argument has been applied to the first three volumes of this *Introduction to a Science of Mythology* on the curious ground that tables and diagrams, of which abundant use was made in the first volume, became less frequent in the second, and still more so in the third, before—as will now be pointed out—disappearing almost completely from this last volume. But these tables and diagrams are illustrations, not a means of proof, and their function is primarily explanatory. Once the reader has been sufficiently enlightened by their use, he does not need to have them inflicted upon him at every turn. If he finds it a useful exercise, as I myself have done throughout the work, he is free to take pencil and paper and, at every comparison of two or more myths, to convert into diagrammatic form the elucidation that I have thought fit to give in discursive prose in order to save time and space (a diagram never absolves one from the explanation, without which it would be unintelligible), and also, to be quite frank, to reduce printing costs. But throughout the whole process of analysis, I have never stopped drawing up such tables and diagrams for my own guidance, and as frequently as at the beginning, the only difference being that I no longer thought it useful to include them in the text. However, any attentive reader will notice that each time I compare two or more myths, I am describing, and commenting on, an implicit table or diagram in which the homologous terms of several syntagmatic chains are superimposed, item by item.

Some critics have gone further still in accusing me, rather inconsistently, of using symbols borrowed from the typographical language of logic and mathematics to compose formulae which, for them, are devoid of any validity or significance—although I discussed this point frankly at the outset, when I made it clear that these formulae are not instruments of proof but shorthand patterns or expressions—while at the same time reproaching me with having changed my ground between 1955, when I wrote an article welcoming the general introduction of mathematics into the social sciences, and the end of the overture to *The Raw and the Cooked*, where I confessed my inability to deal with myths in a logico-mathematical fashion. Such critics thus betray a total ignorance of matters about which they boldly claim to express opinions. My 1955 article dealt with the treatment of kinship systems by means of set theory, which was initiated by André Well in one of my books, and which quickly started a new trend; since 1949, so many volumes and articles have followed up this theme that there now exists what might be called a mathematics of kinship, to the inception of which I claim to have made no other contribution than to have formulated the problems in a style capable of attracting the attention of mathematicians and encouraging them to take over from anthropologists, who had reached a point where the complexity of the problems defeated their rudimentary methodology and brought them to a halt.

However, the study of myths raises much more difficult issues and which do not arise simply from the fact that, of this vast field, we can never hope to know more than certain fragmentary and partial aspects which, before they come into our ken, have already been subjected to all kinds of upheavals and phenomena of erosion. Each particular body of myth, even if we supposed it to be ideally intact, although reality offers no such example, can only be apprehended in a process of becoming and, for reasons already it carries along with it, and engenders in the course of its oral transmission, probabilist levels which, at best, will only make it possible to single out and define restricted areas where phenomena are completely determined. This state of affairs need not lead to discouragement, since it is not so very different from that which physicists have to deal with in studying the most stable and highly organized forms of matter. As one of them has written: 'At the beginning of the century physicists were busy pointing out that crystals are orderly arrays of atoms, ions or molecules. More recently, they have been just busy insisting that the order is limited, and that imperfections are always present because of impurities or native irregularities. Nevertheless, crystallography exists, and the prospects for the structural analysis of myths are not jeopardized by the knowledge that it can only fully operate on certain favourable aspects of its subject matter.

The difficulties in the way of a logico-mathematical treatment of myth, which can nevertheless be seen to be desirable and possible, are of a different order. They are linked in the first place with the problem of arriving at an unequivocal definition of the constituent elements of myths either as terms or as relations; according to the variants being considered and the different stages of the analysis, each term can appear as a relation and each relation as a term. Secondly, these relations illustrate types of symmetry which are different from each other, and too numerous to be described in the limited vocabulary of contrariness, contradiction and their opposites. This second difficulty is still further increased by the fact that the elements defined as such for the purposes of the analysis are, themselves, more often than not, complex entities that the analyst has been unable to break down for want of the appropriate techniques. Thus it is that mythological analysis, without always being fully aware of the fact, is dealing not so much with simple terms and relations as with bundles of terms and bundles of relations which it classifies and defines in an inevitably crude and clumsy fashion.

It was through being conscious of these obstacles that I felt unable to promise, for the structural study of myths, the same rapid progress on the logico-mathematical level as was accomplished twenty years ago in the study of marriage rules and kinship systems. Since then, both in France and the United States, mathematicians have drawn my attention to the fact that a recent development of their subject, known as category theory, might make it possible to treat myths by means of the same methods as are applied to kinship data; I have been given to understand that promising work along these lines has already been done on the basis of *An Introduction to a Science of Mythology*. The definition of categories, as systems formed both by a set of terms and by the set of relations between these terms, corresponds closely to that which can be given of myth, and the concept of morphism, which expresses nothing more than the existence of a relation between two terms without any indication of its logical nature, seems to overcome the same kind of dilemma as was solved for me twenty-five years ago when, after I had been told by a famous mathematician of the old school that he could not help me to clarify kinship problems because he was acquainted only with addition, subtraction, multiplication and division, and marriage could not be likened to any of these operations, a young mathematician to whom I have already referred by name, assured me that it was a matter of indifference to know what marriage might be, mathematically speaking, provided it were possible to define the relation between the different types of marriage.

The caution I expressed at the beginning of this new venture was, then, in no sense a recantation. It is to be explained by the emergence of new problems, the difficulty of which I realized at the outset, when I admitted that I was trying to blaze a trail in an area where 'everything, or almost everything, still remained to be done before there could be any question of genuine scientific knowledge'; I was incidentally convinced that others, helped perhaps by the fact that I had cleared the ground, would shoulder the task of solving these problems by the use of new logico-mathematical instruments, more finely tuned than those which have already proved effective in less complex areas.

It is true that, in order to imprison me within a contradiction of another kind, a prejudicial objection has been made to my openly expressed desire for the use of logico-mathematical instruments. These instruments, it is said, belong to the epistemological equipment of our own culture; in wishing to apply them to material deriving from different societies to improve such knowledge as we can have of these societies, I am said to display a naïve ethnocentrism and to be transposing, on to the level of knowledge, the ethnocentrism I claim to be breaking free from by seeking, in the underlying logic of the myths, the rules engendering the authentic discourse of each community. But—and I shall have occasion to return to this point)—cultural relativism would be puerile if, in conceding the richness of civilizations different from our own, and the impossibility of arriving at any moral or philosophical criterion by which to decide the respective values of the choices which have led each civilization to prefer certain ways of life and thought while rejecting others, it felt itself obliged to adopt a condescending or disdainful attitude towards scientific knowledge which, however harmful it may have been, and further threatens to be, in its applications, is nevertheless a mode of knowledge whose absolute superiority cannot be denied. It is true that scientific knowledge came into being, and has developed, with a total disregard for other modes of knowledge, because of their practical inefficiency in respect of the new aims which it had in view. For too long, this intellectual divide has, perhaps inevitably, caused us to lose sight of certain aspects of reality that are now almost forgotten, and that the forms of knowledge best adapted to them formulated in terms of genuine problems, which scientific knowledge brushed aside as being insignificant,whenin fact its initial lines of development did not allow it to understand the interest of these problems, and still less to solve them. Only during the last few years has science taken a different turn. By venturing into areas close to human sensibility, areas which may seem novel but which in fact it is only rediscovering, it is proving that, from now on, knowledge can progress only by broadening out to comprehend other forms of knowledge; and to comprehend should be taken here with the meaning of to understand and to include. It follows that true development of knowledge goes hand in hand with a gradual widening of the framework traditionally assigned to science: science now overlaps with, incorporates and in a sense legitimizes forms of thought that it previously considered as being irrational and beyond the pale. To adopt the viewpoint of scientific knowledge is therefore not equivalent to smuggling in the epistemological framework peculiar to one society to explain other societies; on the contrary, as I realized for the first time when I was studying the kinship systems of the Australian aborigines, it is to accept the fact that the newest forms of scientific thought may be on a par with the intellectual procedures of savages, however lacking the latter may be in the technical resources that scientific knowledge, during its intermediary phases, has allowed us to acquire. It is, therefore, at least on this particular level, to reconcile the undeniable fact of the progress of science with the possibility of recovering a great wealth of knowledge that scientific progress itself began by sacrificing; and finally, it is to take one's stand in an area where abstract thought and theoretical knowledge, as they go forward, realize that, through a retrograde movement in no way incompatible with their advance, they are simultaneously rediscovering the inexhaustible lessons of a realm of sensibility that they originally believed they should deny. Nothing could be more false than to postulate opposite types of knowledge, mutually irreducible throughout the ages, with a sudden and unexplained switch from one type to another. While it is true that seventeenth-century thought, in order to become scientific, had to set itself in opposition to that of the Middle Ages and the Renaissance, we are now beginning to glimpse the possibility that this century and the next, instead of going against the immediately preceding ones, might be able to achieve a synthesis of their thought with that of more remote times, whose themes, as we are now beginning to realize, were not entirely nonsensical.

Other criticisms are more philosophical in nature, and are based on the philosophical element that some readers claim to find in my books. But although, from time to time, I take the trouble to indicate briefly in passing the philosophical implications that seem to arise from my work, I attach no importance to this aspect of it. I am more concerned to deny in advance what philosophers might read into my statements. I do not set my philosophy in opposition to theirs, since I have no philosophy of my own worth bothering about, apart from a few homely convictions that I have come back to, less through the development of my own thought than through regressive erosion of the philosophy I was taught, and that I myself once taught. I am averse to any proposed philosophical exploitation of my work, and I shall do no more than point out that, in my view, my findings can, at best, only lead to the abjuration of what is called philosophy at the present time.

This negative attitude is dictated by circumstance. In reading the criticisms that certain philosophers formulate against structuralism, accusing it of demolishing the human person and its traditional values, I am just as flabbergasted as if they were to attack the kinetic theory of gases on the ground that, by explaining why hot air expands and rises, it endangered family life and the morality of the family hearth, whose warmth, being thus demystified, would lose its symbolic and emotional overtones. The social sciences, following the example of the physical sciences, must grasp the fact that the reality of the object they are studying is not wholly limited to the level of the subject apprehending it. These appearances are underlaid by other appearances of no greater value, and so on, layer by layer, as we look for the ultimate essence of nature which at each level escapes us, and will probably remain forever unattainable. These levels of appearance are not mutually exclusive or contradictory, and the choice of any one or of several depends on the problems one is dealing with and the various properties one wishes to perceive and interpret. The politician, the moralist and the philosopher are free to take up their abode on whichever storey they deem the uniquely honourable one and to barricade themselves in, but they should not try to shut away everyone else along with themselves and forbid us, when we wish to tackle problems different from theirs, to adjust the microscope and change the focusing so as to bring into view another, different object, behind the one in whose contemplation they are totally engrossed.

We have, indeed, to conclude that their object of study is not the same as ours, since several philosophers seem to agree in accusing me of having reduced the living substance of the myths to a dead form, of having abolished the meaning and frantically endeavoured to work out the syntax of 'a discourse which says nothing'. But seriously, if the myths really said what some people seem to expect from them, they would not repeat themselves endlessly throughout the world, and they would not produce unlimited series of variants around the same armatures. Those societies which, during hundreds of thousands of years, or even longer, depended on the myths for the solution of their theoretical problems, would not have been restricted to the technical procedures, forms of economic life and types of social institutions which, however varied they may have been, have nevertheless made it plausible to assert that the human condition has undergone greater change between the eighteenth and the twentieth cenruries than it did between the neolithic period and modern times. The fallacious complaint that the myths have been impoverished hides a latent mysticism, nourished in the vain hope of the revelation of a meaning behind the meaning to justify or excuse all kinds of confused and nostalgic longings, which are afraid to express themselves openly. I too, of course, look upon the religious field as a stupendous storehouse of images that is far from having been exhausted by objective research; but these images are like any others, and the spirit in which I approach the study of religious data supposes that such data are not credited at the outset with any specific character.

We have to resign ourselves to the fact that the myths tell us nothing instructive about the order of the world, the nature of reality or the origin and destiny of mankind. We cannot expect them to flatter any metaphysical thirst, or to breathe new life into exhausted ideologies. On the other hand, they teach us a great deal about the societies from which they originate, they help to lay bare their inner workings and clarify the *raison d'être* of beliefs, customs and institutions, the organization of which was at first sight incomprehensible; lastly, and most importantly, they make it possible to discover certain operational modes of the human mind, which have remained so constant over the centuries, and are so widespread over immense geographical distances, that we can assume them to be fundamental and can seek to find them in other societies and in other areas of mental life, where their presence was not suspected, and whose nature is thereby illuminated. In all these respects, far from abolishing meaning, my analysis of the myths of a handful of American tribes has extracted more meaning from them than is to be found in the platitudes and common places of those philosophers— with the exception of Plutarch—who have commented on mythology during the last 2,500 years.

But philosophers pay little attention to the concrete problems that ethnographers themselves have striven with in vain so long that they have practically given up all hope of solving them; these problems have cropped up one after the other at every turn in my analysis, which has proposed for them solutions as simple as they are unexpected. Being incapable, through ignorance, of recognizing and appreciating these problems, philosophers have preferred to adopt an attitude whose real motives, however, are much more dubious than if they were the mere consequence of a lack of information. Without being fully conscious of this reaction, they hold it against me that the extra meaning I distil from the myths is not the meaning they would have liked to find there. They refuse to recognize and to accept the fact of their deafness to the great anonymous voice whose utterance comes from the beginning of time and the depths of the mind, so intolerable is it for them that this utterance should convey something quite different from what they had decided in advance should be its message. In reading my work, they feel a sense of disappointment, almost of grievance, at being supernumeraries in a dialogue—far richer than any so far entered into with the myths— which has no need of them and to which they have nothing to contribute.

Whither, then philosophy, and in present circumstances, what can it possibly find to do? If the prevailing tendencies continue, it is to be feared that two courses only will be open to it. One, incumbent on the philosophers following in the wake of Existentialism—a self-admiring activity which allows contemporary man, rather gullibly, to commune with himself in ecstatic contemplation of his own being—cuts itself off from scienrific knowledge which it despises, as well as from human reality, whose historical perspectives and anthropological dimensions it disregards, in order to arrange a closed and private little world for itself, an ideological Café du Commerce where, within the four walls of a human condition cut down to fit a particular society, the habitués spend their days rehashing problems of local interest, beyond which they cannot see because of the fog created by their clouds of dialectical smoke.

The other possibility for philosophy, when it feels stifled in this confined space and longs to breathe a fresher air, is to make its escape into areas previously forbidden to it and where it is free to disport itself. Intoxicated with its new-found liberty, it gambols off, losing touch with that uncompromising search for truth which even Existentialism, the last embodiment of metaphysics in the grand style, still wished to pursue. Becoming an easy prey for all sorts of external influences, as well as a victim of its own whims, philosophy is then in danger of falling to the level of a sort of 'philosop'art' and indulging in the aesthetic prostitution of the problems, methods and vocabulary of its predecessors. To seduce the reader, woo his interest and win his custom, it flatters their common fantasies with shreds of ideas borrowed from a now antiquated but still respectable heritage, using them to produce surprise effects, more connected with the art of display than with the love of truth, and whose occasional felicities remain purely sensuous and decorative.

Between these two extremes, I may mention various phoney activities pursued by fishers in troubled waters: one example is that is "structuralism-fiction', which has recently flourished on the philosophico-literary scene, and whose productions, in relation to the world of linguists and anthropologists, is more or less equivalent to the contents of certain popular magazines flirting with physics and biology: a debauch of sentimentality based on rudimentary and ill-digested information. The question even arises whether this so-called structuralism did nor come into being to serve as an alibi for the unbearable boringness of contemporary literature. Being unable, for obvious reasons, to defend its overt content, this structuralism may be trying to find hidden justifications for it on the formalistic level. But if so, this is a perversion of the structuralist aim, which is to discover why works capture our interest, not to invent excuses for their lack of interest. When we give a structuralist interpretation of a work which has had no need of our help to find an audience, we are supplying additional reasons in support of a successful effect which has already been achieved in other ways; if the work had no intrinsic interest on the levels at which it is immediately open to appreciation, the analysis, in reaching down to deeper levels, could only reduce nothingness to further nothingness.

It is unfortunately to be feared—and here we have a link-up with another kind of philosophy—that too many contemporary works, not only in the literary field but also in those of painting and music, have suffered through the naïve empiricism of their creators. Because the social sciences have revealed formal structures behind works of art, there has been a rush to create works of art on the basis of formal structures. But it is not at all certain that these artificially arranged and conscious structures are of the same order as those which can be discovered, retrospectively, as having been at work in the creator's mind, and most often without any conscious awareness on his part. The truth is that the long-awaited renascence of contemporary art could only result, as an indirect consequence, from the clarification of the laws inherent in traditional works, and which should be sought at much deeper levels than those at which the analysis is usually content to stop. Instead of composing new music with the help of computers, it would be more relevant to use computers to try to understand the nature of existing music: to determine, for instance, how and why we need to hear only two or three bars by a particular composer to recognize his style and distinguish it from others. Once the objective foundations had been reached and laid bare, artistic creation, liberated from its obsessions and phantasms by this new awareness and now face to face with itself, might embark on a new development. It will only succeed in doing so if it first realizes that not every structure can automatically have significance for aesthetic perception because of the mere fact that every aesthetic signifier is the sensory manifestation of a structure.

The social sciences have, then, an ambiguous status in the mainstream of contemporary thought: sometimes, philosophers reject them out of hand; at other times, like writers and artists, they presume to appropriate them and, by carving off fragments according to the dictates of their fancy, produce compositions as arbitrary as collages, while imagining that this dispenses them from reflecting on, or practising, the social sciences, and above all from following the line which these sciences prescribe for themselves in the scrupulous search for truth.

They are, in fact, forgetting that the social sciences do not exist on their own or in their own right. Like the moieties in dualist societies studied by anthropologists, they are simultaneously united to, and subordinated to, the exact or natural sciences by a relationship of reciprocity, which does not exclude, but on the contrary implies, a constitutive dissymmetry. In the resulting dialogue, the social sciences have taken over from philosophy, which is doomed to stagnate unless it turns itself into reflection on scientific knowledge, an ambitious enough programme. The social sciences are no doubt comparable to the physical and natural sciences in the sense that neither achieves direct apprehension of reality, but only of the symbols in terms of which the mind perceives reality in accordance with the constraints and thresholds of our sensory system. However, there is a fundamental difference between them, arising from the twofold fact, firstly, that the physical and natural sciences operate on the symbols of phenomena while the social sciences operate on the symbols of phenomena which are themselves symbols in the first place, and, secondly, that, in the former instance, the adequate approximation of the symbol to the referent is demonstrated by the 'grip' exercised by scientific knowledge on the world around us, whereas the practical ineffectiveness of the social sciences—apart from the teaching of a problematical wisdom—does not allow us, at least for the time being, to assume any adequate correspondence between the representative symbols and the represented symbols.

Looked at in this perspective, the social sciences take on the appearance of a shadow theatre, the management of which has been left to them by the natural and physical sciences, because the latter do not yet know the location or the constitution of the puppets whose silhouettes are projected on to the screen. As long as this provisional or definitive uncertainty lasts, the social sciences will retain their peculiar and double function, which is to soothe the impatient thirst for knowledge by approximate suggestions, and to provide the natural and physical sciences with an often useful, anticiparory simulacrum of the truer knowledge which it will one day be their task to formulate. Let us beware, then, of too hasty analogies: it may be that the attempt to decode the myths has a resemblance to the work of the biologist in deciphering the generic code, but the biologist is studying real objects and he can check his hypotheses by their experimental consequences. We are doing the same thing as he is, the only difference being that social sciences worthy of the name are no more than the image-reflection of the natural sciences: a series of impalpable appearances manipulating ghostlike realities. Therefore, the social sciences can claim only a formal, not a substantial, homology with the study of the physical world and living nature. It is precisely when they try to come closer to the ideal of scientific knowledge that it becomes most obvious that they offer no more than a profiguration, on the walls of the cave, of operations that will have to be validated later by other sciences, which will deal with the real objects of which we are examining the reflections. Neither philosophy nor art can, then. give in to the illusion that they have only to try to commune with the social sciences, often with predatory intent, to achieve their own redemption. Both of them, often so contemptuous of scientific knowledge, ought to realize that, in appealing to the social sciences, they are entering into a dialogue with the physical and natural sciences, and thus rendering homage to them, even if, for the time being, the homage is indirect.

None of the objections that I have just briefly reviewed goes to the heart of the problems that these volumes try to elucidate. A much more serious one, worthy of greater attention, has been made by certain linguists who reproach me with having, only in exceptional cases, taken into account the diversity of the languages in which all these myths were first conceived and formulated, although not invariably recorded. Even though I have referred to the original language in a few instances where it was not too difficult to do so, I cannot claim to be linguistically competent, and even among the specialists there is probably no one capable of undertaking the comparative philological study of texts originating in languages which, although all American, differ as much among themselves as those of the Indo-European, Semitic, Finno-Ugrian and Sino-Tibetan families.

Philological analysis has to be resorted to in the case of the dead languages, where the meaning of each term can only be determined by looking at it in several contexts. The situation is not exactly the same when the stories have been taken down directly from informants still speaking their language and who were able to clarify a good many doubtful or ambiguous points. In most cases, unfortunately, there is no original text, and the myth is known only in translation, or even through several successive translations made by interpreters capable of understanding a foreign language and who made versions in their mother tongue, which was not always that of the person recording the story.

Hic Rhodus, hic salta: if, in spite of the decisive part played by philology in Professor Dumézil's outstanding works, from which I have learned so much, I had made it a preliminary condition that I would study the myths only in the original languages, my project would have been unrealizable, not only by me, since I am not a philologist with expert knowledge of the Amerindian languages, but by anyone else. I had therefore to commit myself to a double wager, first in making do with such instruments as I could improvise, not of course as a substitute for philological study, the lack of which will always remain obvious, but to offset to some extent the impossibility of having recourse to philology; then in deciding to await the result before coming to a conclusion about the fundamental problem. The result is now available; I myself at least am convinced that this enquiry, which was undertaken in the face of limitations serious enough to make it theoretically unfeasible, has on the contrary proved most fruitful. This is an accomplished fact we must now argue from, even if at first sight it seems to constitute a mystery, which calls for explanation.

The key to the enigma is, I think, to be found in the myth creation process revealed by my study, and which it alone could demonstrate clearly by being carried through to its conclusion. If, as is shown by the comparative analysis of different versions of the same myth produced by one or several communities, *conter* (to tell a story) is always *conte redire* (to retell a story), which can also be written *contredire* (to contradict), it is immediately understandable why it was not absolutely essential, for the purposes of the rough sorting out I had in mind, to study the myths in the originals, instead of in a translation or a series of translations. Properly speaking, there is never any original: every myth is by its very nature a translation, and derives from another myth belonging to a neighbouring, but foreign, community, or from a previous myth belonging to the same community or from a contemporaneous one belonging to a different social sub-division—clan, sub-clan, descent group, family or brotherhood—that some listener tries to plagiarize by translating it in his fashion into his personal or tribal language, sometimes to appropriate it and sometimes to it, and therefore invariably distorting it. A particularly striking instance of this phenomenon is supplied by the Hupa myth about the origin of fire that the demiurge is said to have tried initially, and unsuccessfully, to produce by percussion, and then by inventing the first fire-drill. The person who recorded this story states specifically that it was produced with the intention of giving the lie to a myth belonging to a neighbouring tribe and which asserted that the first fire had been obtained by theft (Goddard, p. 197; cf. above, p. 158).

These oppositional relationships between the myths, which can only rarely be observed at their actual inception, are brought out strongly by comparative analysis. Therefore, the reason why philological study of the myths is not an absolute precondition is to be found in what might be called their diacritical nature. Each of their transformations results from a dialectical opposition to another transformation, and their essence lies in the irreducible fact of translation *by and for* opposition. From an empirical point of view, every myth is simultaneously primary in relation to itself, and derivative in relation to other myths; it does not exist *in* a language and *in* a culture or sub-culture, but at their point of articulation with other languages and other cultures. Therefore a myth never *belongs to its language,* but rather represents an angle of vision on to *a different language,* and the mythologist who is apprehending it through translation does not feel himself to be in an essentially different position from that of the native narrator or listener. I pointed out this aspect of the problem at an early stage in my research when I emphasized that 'the substance of the myth is neither in the style nor in the form of the narrative, nor in the syntax, but in the *story* that it tells' (L.–S. 5, p. 232).

This is not to say, of course, that a knowledge of the original language, supposing the text to be available, is superfluous, and that philological study would not make it possible to arrive at a more exact and complex definition of meanings, to correct mistakes and give more depth and scope to the interpretation: these are tasks for the people who come after me. But once all these advances and corrections have been made, it will no doubt be seen that, except in exceptional circumstances, philological study adds extra dimensions to the myth and gives it more substance and character, but does not essentially affect the semantic content. The gain will be rather on the literary and poetic side; it will make it easier to appreciate the aesthetic properties of the text, whose message—given the fact that translation allows the myth to be understood as myth—will hardly be modified.

Contemporary philosophy, being imbued with a mysticism that is rarely openly and more often concealed under the appellation of humanism, and always hoping to discover a gnosis that would allow it to mark out for itself a private area inaccessible to scientific knowledge, has taken fright on seeing mythology, which it wanted to be full of hidden meaning, reduced to what some people take to be the vacuity of a series of translations without any original text. This is to fail to see that the same might be said about an area where, however, mystical aspirations and sentimental outpourings are given fairly free rein; I am referring to music. The truth is that the comparison between mythology and music, which was the *leitmotif* of the overture' to this work, and which was condemned as arbitrary by many critics, was based essentially on this common feature. The myths are only translatable into each other in the same way as a melody is only translatable into another which retains a relationship of homology with it: it can be transcribed into a different key, converted from major to minor or vice versa; its parameters can be modified so as to transform the rhythm, the quality of tone, the emotive charge, the relative intervals between consecutive notes, and so on. Perhaps, in extreme cases, it will no longer seem recognizable to the untutored ear; but it will still be the same melodic form. And it would be wrong to argue, as some people might be inclined to do, that in music at least there is an original text: famous composers have proceeded in the way I have just described; starting from the works of their predecessors, they have created works stamped with the mark of their own style, which it is impossible to confuse with any other. Research into the recognition of forms, which is henceforth feasible thanks to computers, would no doubt make it possible, in many instances, to discover the rules of conversion that would show styles of popular music or those of different composers to correspond to various states of the same transformational group.

But while one can always, and almost indefinitely, translate one melody into another, or one piece of music into another piece, as in the case of mythology one cannot translate music into *anything other than itself* without falling into the would-be hermeneutic verbiage characteristic of old-fashioned mythography and of too much musical criticism. This is to say that an unlimited freedom of translation into the dialects of an original language forming a closed system is bound up with the radical impossibility of any transposition into an extrinsic language.

The fundamental nature of myth, as it has been revealed by my enquiry, confirms, then, the parallel between mythic narrative and musical composition that I indicated at the beginning. Now that my study has been brought to a close, it would seem that the relationships between them can be formulated more clearly and convincingly. I propose to assume, as a working hypothesis, that the field open to structural study includes four major families of occupants: mathematical entities, the natural languages, musical works and myths.

Mathematical entities consist of structures in a pure state, free from any embodiment. In this respect, they are in a correlational and oppositional relationship to linguistic phenomena which, as Saussure showed, exist only through their double embodiment in sound and sense, and arise in fact from the intersection of these two phenomena.

This axis having been established, with mathematical entities and linguistic phenomena at the two poles, it is immediately obvious that the other families, in relation to it, occupy positions on a different axis, transversal to the first. In the case of music, the structure which is, so to speak, detached from the sense, adheres to the sound; in the case of mythology, the structure is detached from the sound and adheres to the sense. As far as mythology is concerned, this is precisely what I have tried to demonstrate in the preceding pages in connection with the problem of translation.

Let us postulate, then, that mathematical structures are free in relation to both sound and sense; and that linguistic structures, on the contrary, are concretized in their union. Musical and mythic structures, being less completely embodied than the latter, but more so than the former, are biased, in the case of music, in the direction of sound (without sense) and, in the case of myth, in the direction of sense (without sound). This way of looking at the relationships between them has several consequences.

In the first place, if music and mythology are each to be defined as language from which something has been subtracted, both will appear as derivative in relation to language. If this supposition is correct, music and mythology become by-products of a structural shift which had language as its starting-point. Music no doubt also speaks; but this can only be because of its negative relationship to language, and because, in separating off from language, music has retained the negative imprint of its formal structure and semiotic function: there would be no music if language had not preceded it and if music did not continue to depend on it, as it were, through a privative connection. Music is language without meaning: this being so, it is understandable that the listener, who is first and foremost a subject with the gift of speech, should feel himself irresistibly compelled to make up for the absent sense, just as someone who has lost a limb imagines that he still possesses it through the sensations present in the stump. It is the same in the case of myth: the shift which takes place in the direction of sense explains how the myth, when reduced—or raised—to the status of a pure semantic reality, can, as a vehicle of meaning, become detached from its linguistic base, with which the story it tells is less intimately connected than ordinary messages would be.

So far, I have defined the relationships between music and mythology as if they were perfectly symmetrical. It is obvious, however, that there is a dissymmetry because, unlike music which borrows only the sound element from natural language, myth needs the whole of language to express itself. The comparison I have just suggested only remains valid if we see each myth as a score, which, for its performance, requires language to serve as orchestra, unlike music, the means of realization of which are the singing voice (produced in physiological conditions totally different from those required for speech) and instruments.

It cannot be claimed, then, that myth is as completely free from language as music, since it remains involved with it. However, its relative detachment expresses itself, in the mythic narrative, by attempts to recapture sound, attempts comparable to the impulse that leads the listener to try to give sense to a musical work. The myth is attracted towards sense, as if by a magnet: and this partial adhesion creates a potential void with regard to sound that the narrator feels the need to fill by various devices, such as vocal effects or gestures which diversify, modulate and reinforce his speech. Sometimes he chants or intones the myth, sometimes he declaims it; and his recitation is almost always accompanied by stereotyped formulae and gestures. In addition, he imagines the scenes vividly, and he knows how to make them equally present to his listeners: he sees them as if they were happening there and then, he relives them and communicates his experience with appropriate mimicry and gesticulation. It can even happen that the myth is recited by several voices and thus becomes a theatrical performance. The defective relationship to sound is thus compensated for by a redundancy of verbal formulae, repetitions, de capos and refrains. Alliterations and paronomasia produce a wealth of assonance and recurrent verbal sounds which excite the ear, as the meaning invested in music by the listener excites his intellect. Something remains, then, of the disparity recognized at the beginning of this paragraph, in spite of the re-establishment of symmetry at the cost, however, of an inner torsion. In music, the coalescence of a global metaphorical significance around the work makes up for the missing aspect, whereas the myth reintroduces sound by metonymical means. In the one case, the sense restored to music corresponds to *the totality* of the sound; in the other, sound is added as part of the sense....

. . .

The apparent digressions I have allowed myself in the preceding pages have a part to play in this finale. They show that, contrary to what certain critics have said, I do not underestimate the importance of the emotions. I merely refuse to give in to them and to abandon myself, in their presence, to the kind of mysticism which proclaims the intuitive and ineffable character of moral and aesthetic feelings, and even sometimes asserts that they heighten awareness, independently of any apprehension of their object by the intellect; on this basis it has been said that, in describing and analysing 'savage thought', I have misunderstood and misrepresented its true nature because, in the account I give of it, 'the aesthetic faculty as well as the emotions have practically disappeared' (Milner, p. 21).

Any reader with a modicum of sensitivity, who has gone through my books from *The Elementary Structures of Kinship* to this *Introduction to a Science of Mythology*, by way of *Tristes Tropiques* and *The Savage Mind*, will realize the inaccuracy of this statement. Certainly, none of these works is lacking in feeling. On the other hand, it is true that I try to discern, behind emotional phenomena, the indirect effect of changes occurring in the normal course of the operations of the intellect, instead of accepting intellectual operations as being secondary in relation to emotional phenomena. It is only those operations that we can claim to explain, since they are of the same intellectual nature as the activity which is endeavouring to understand them. Emotions not deriving from intellectual operations would be strictly unknowable as mental phenomena. In postulating the existence of such emotions as a basis for intellectual operations, in relation to which they would have the privilege of priority in time, we would merely be deluding ourselves with empty words (since meaning, by definition, lies beyond), and substituting magic formulae for the exercise of reason. Any phenomenon of the life of the emotions which does not reflect, on the level of consciousness, some important event hindering or accelerating the work of the understanding, is not a matter for the social sciences; it belongs rather to biology, and its discussion must be left to others.

In various quarters, but mainly in England, I have been accused of reducing the intensely lived experiences of individual subjects to emotionally neutral symbols, like those used by mathematicians, whereas the thought of communities without writing is said to have recourse to concrete symbols, highly charged with emotional values. It is added that the gap is unbridgeable, given the stance I have assumed. My preceding remarks about the nature of musical emotion prove the contrary, but it remains to be established that the same type of interpretation can apply to phenomena more relevant to anthropological research, and especially to ritual. I have been challenged with the impossibility of linking up ritual chiefly with the operations of the intellect (Beidelman, p. 402), on the grounds that— in the words of another author who shares the same point of view—

> the symbols and their relations... are not only a set of cognitive classifications for ordering the universe...They are also, and perhaps as importantly, a set of evocative devices for arousing, channelling and domesticating powerful emotions such as hatred, fear, affection, grief.

They are also informed with purposiveness and have a 'conative'
aspect. In brief, the whole person and not just the mind... is
existentially involved in life and death issues (V. W. Turner, 3, pp. 42-
3).

This may well be so; but when it has been said, and pious lip
service has been paid to the importance of the emotions, we have not
advanced one step nearer an explanation of how the strange
activities characteristic of ritual, and the symbols relating to them,
can produce such fine results.

Anthropologists mainly concerned with ritual start from a fact
which, in itself, is undeniable: like the Ndembu studied by Turner,
some societies 'have remarkably few myths, and compensate for this
by a wealth of item-by-item exegesis... There are no short-cuts
through myth and cosmology to the structure... of religion. One has
to proceed atomistically, and piecemeal...' (V. W. Turner 3, p. 20).
However, when the matter is presented in this way, no account is
taken of the fact that mythology exists in two clearly different
modalities. Sometimes it is explicit and consists of stories which,
because of their dimensions and internal organization, rank as works
in their own right. Sometimes, on the contrary, the mythic text is
fragmentary, and is made up, as it were, only of notes or sketches;
instead of the fragments being brought together in the light of some
guiding principle, each remains linked to a particular phase of the
ritual, on which it serves as a gloss, and it is only recited in
connection with the performance of ritual acts.

But, just as a novel and a collection of essays, in spite of being
conceived differently, both belong to literature, explicit mythology
and implicit mythology are two different modes of an identical
reality: in both cases, we are dealing with mythic representations.
The error of contemporary theoreticians of ritual arises from the fact
that they do not distinguish between these two modes of existence of
mythology, or do so only incidentally. So, instead of taking as a
whole the problems raised by mythic representations, whether
explicit or implicit, and making a separate study of ritual, they draw
the dividing line between explicit mythology on the one hand,
arbitrarily reserving the name mythology for it, and, on the other,
the glosses or commentaries on ritual, which belong to the category
of myth, but which they link up with, and confuse with, ritual proper.
Having mixed up the two categories inextricably, they find

themselves dealing with a hybrid entity about which anything can be said: that it is verbal and non-verbal, that it has a cognitive function and an emotional and conative function, and so on. By endeavouring at the outset to give a specific definition of ritual distinguishing it from mythology, they leave in the former all sorts of elements which rightly belong to the latter, and get everything thoroughly confused.

If we wish to study ritual in itself and for itself, in order to understand in as an entity separate from mythology and to determine its specific characteristics, we should on the contrary begin by removing from it all the implicit mythology which adheres to it without really being part of it, in other words, those beliefs and representations which are connected with a philosophy of nature, in the same way as the myths; and when trying to bring out 'the non-verbal language of ritual symbols' (V. W. Turner 3, p. 39), we should avoid putting ourselves, like Leach (3, 4), in the position of asserting simultaneously that the concrete symbols of primitive thought are steeped in emotional values, and that the function of ritual is to ensure the transmission and communication of a complex set of information about the natural world, which is exactly the opposite. Besides, all these commentators, who see the emotional aspect of ritual as being central to it, and who expatiate on the anguish created by taboos, make one think irresistibly of some anthropologist from another planet who, in his monograph on earth-dwellers, might describe the superstitious terror which prevents motorists from crossing the symbolic limit marked simply by a line along the road, and even from infringing the taboo ever so slightly; he might also give a horrifying account of the penalty, which is collision with another vehicle... But we have no feelings of this kind; we respect the white line as part of our everyday routine without attributing any emotional value to it. As is the case with so many ritual actions, performance is automatic on the part of the people involved, because they are only aware of it as an intrinsic part of their conception of the world.

This is not to say that I underestimate the specific nature of ritual, or—although I feel that the point is often exaggerated—the anxiety states that may prompt ritual actions when they are not, on the contrary, caused by these actions. The initial question of which causes which was left undecided, after a famous controversy between Malinowski and Radcliffe-Brown, it will become clearer later why both theories can be disregarded. Be that as it may, the very fact that the study of ritual obliges one to discuss its relationship with anxiety proves that the comments I am about to make had to be preceded by my preliminary remarks about anxiety or anguish in the broadest sense, without reference to the particular circumstances in which it occurs. These remarks were prompted by the attempt to define the reciprocal relationships between mythology and music, and I shall therefore begin by considering whether ritual can be given a place in the total system I indicated.

We have seen that myth, which has articulate language as its vehicle, remains bound to language; only music, defined as a system of sounds, breaks completely free. This is mainly true in the case of instrumental music; vocal music, which was probably the earliest form, is comparable in this respect to myth: vocal music also has articulate language as its vehicle, although in each particular case the signifying function is out of phase, being always above or below the linguistic level proper. From this point of view, it can be said that the respective fields of articulate language, vocal music and myth intersect. In the area where they overlap, they have an affinity which is demonstrated by the fact that myths are often chanted or sung. The affinity gradually diminishes, and eventually disappears, as we move from pure vocal music to singing or chanting with an instrumental accompaniment, and finally to pure instrumental music, which is outside language. The same gradation can be observed, on the hither side and the far side of myth, between explicit mythology, which is literature in the full sense of the term, and implicit mythology in which fragments of discourse are bound up with non-linguistic actions, and lastly pure ritual which, in its extreme forms, can be said to lose all contact with language, since it consists either of sacred formulae—incomprehensible for the uninitiated, or belonging to an archaic tongue that is no longer understood, or even of utterances devoid of any intrinsic meaning, such as are often used in magic—or of physical movements or of the selection and handling of various objects. At this point, ritual, like music at the other extreme of the system, moves right outside language, and if we wish to understand its distinctive nature, we have obviously to consider this pure form, not the intermediary states.

How, then, are we to define ritual? We can say that it consists of words uttered, gestures performed and objects manipulated, independently of any gloss or commentary that might be authorized or prompted by these three forms of activity, and which would belong not to ritual itself but to implicit mythology. This being so, to discover the distinctive properties of ritual we should not compare, it with mythology, particularly since the comparision would hardly be possible as 'regards gestures (these are not totally absent from myth, but... they have a metonymical function, instead of the metaphorical role they play in ritual), and totally impossible as regards objects. On the other hand, the three forms of activity are present in everyday life, the problem posed by the nature of ritual can then be formulated as follows: firstly, why, in order to achieve the results aimed at necessary to utter words perform gestures and manipulate objects; secondly, in what way do these operations, as carried out in ritual, differ from similar operations which also occur in daily life; in other words, and without raising the question of content, which would inevitably bring us back to mythology—thus giving rise to the illusion that we were defining ritual when in fact we were talking about the accompanying myth—we can ask three questions, the answers to which must underlie any theoretical interpretation of ritual. What distinctive manner of speech is used in ritual? What gestures? And what special criteria govern the choice of ritual objects as well as their manipulation?

As regards gestures and objects, all observers have rightly noted that, in ritual, they are given a function additional to their practical use, and which sometimes replaces that use. gestures and objects serve in *loco verbi;* they are a substitute for words. Each is a global connotation of a system of ideas and representations; by their use, ritual condenses into a concrete and unitary form procedures which otherwise would have had to be discursive. The gestures are not being performed, or the objects manipulated, as in ordinary life, to obtain practical effects resulting from a series of operations, each following on from the preceding through a causal link. Instead, ritual uses gestures and things to replace their analytical expression (L.-S. 9, pp. 203–204) The performance of gestures and the manipulation of objects are devices which allow ritual to avoid speech.

This observation faces us immediately with a paradox, since, in fact, there is a great deal of speech in ritual. Whenever a ritual ceremony has been recorded and transcribed in its entirety, as has been the case in North America among the Iroquois, the Fox, the Pawnee, the Navajo and the Osage, and also in Africa and Polynesia, we see, that the complete text, which may take several days to recite, may fill a whole volume, sometimes a very large one. But here we are again, we must refrain from asking what the ritual words *are saying*, and restrict ourselves to the question of *how they are saying*. On this point, there is a twofold observation to be made, and it applies both to the choice and manipulation of objects and to the performance of gestures. In all cases, ritual makes constant use of two procedures: parcelling out and repetition.

Parcelling out, in the first place; within classes of objects and types of gesture, ritual makes infinite distinctions and ascribes discriminatory values to the slightest shades of difference. It has no concern for the general, but on the contrary goes into great detail about the varieties and sub-varieties in all the taxonomical categories, whether it be those of minerals, animals and plants, or those, for which it is itself largely responsible, of raw materials, forms, gestures and objects. The same type of gesture takes on a different role and a different meaning, and its place in the ritual is altered, according to whether it is performed from right to left, high to low, or inside to outside. The same is true of speech. As early as 1949, in studying a particular rite, I emphasized that each procedure was described with extreme minuteness, and broken down into as many minimal sequences as could be found through the most pernickety analysis. It is probably not without significance in this connection that when some Navajo Indians were given a movie-camera by anthropologists and asked to make films, they produced works all of which had the common feature of giving more importance to the movements of the actors from one place to another than the chief activity intended as the subject and defined in the title: the actors were shown in great detail walking along with a view to doing something, much more than actually doing it; the promoters of the experiment rightly saw a parallel between this feature and certain Navajo stories, which they referred to as myths, but which are in fact songs chanted during the rites, and made up interminable sequences enumerating the various ways of walking in the minutest detail, and describing the inner feelings experienced by someone in the course of such peregrinations. The observers were also surprised to see that the Indians could do the montage of their films with greater rapidity than any technician would have been capable of; they cut and rejoined the lengths of film apparently at random, but it later turned out that, without checking, they were able to remember some particular image from among the thousands or tens of thousands that had been photographed (Worth-Adair, pp. 23-30). It is well known that Navajo ritual is exceptionally rich and varied, and that it plays an important part in the individual life-cycle and the collective life of the community. It is not surprising, then, that they should have transposed the process of fragmentation, combined with the capacity to perceive the smallest distinctive units, to the material discourse recorded on the film, in order to produce a form of presentation different from that to which they were traditionally accustomed.

At the same time as ritual indulges in these subtleties, emphasizing the slightest phases of procedures so that their performance, through its infinite attention to detail, is carried to aberrant lengths, and gives the impression of 'slow motion' camera-work marking time to the point of stagnation, it uses another, no less striking device: at the cost of considerable verbal expenditure, it goes in for a riot of repetition: the same formula, or formulae similar in syntax or assonance, are repeated at short intervals, and are only operative, as it were, by the dozen; the same formula must be repeated a great many times running, or alternatively, a sentence containing a very slight meaning is sandwiched, and almost concealed, between accumulations of identical and meaningless formulae. The Iroquois and Fox rituals provide striking examples of such repetitions of the same formulae: thrice, thrice, four times, once, thrice... during a single phase of the ritual, the same formula may be uttered consecutively in blocks of ten, twelve, twenty and twenty-five repetitions.

At first sight, the two devices of parcelling out and repetition are in opposition to each other: in the one case, it is a question of finding differences, however small, between operations which could seem identical, and in the other, of repeating the same statement indefinitely. But, in fact, the first procedure is equivalent to the second, which represents, so to speak, its extreme development. Differences which have become so small as to be infinitesimal tend to disappear in quasi-identity; and this brings us back to the reference to cinematographic film, which breaks movement down into such small units that consecutive shots are hardly distinguishable one from another and appear to be repetitions, so that a film editor has to use markers to make sure of getting his cuts right, unless he happens to be a Navajo Indian, that is, someone long accustomed, through the practice of ritual, to distinguishing the limit-values of identity and differentiation.

What, we may now ask, are the fundamental reasons which cause ritual to resort systematically to the complementary procedures of parcelling out and repetition? G. Dumézil's famous studies of archaic Roman religion throw light on the problem, and allow us to suggest a solution. Dumézil distinguishes two categories of Roman gods: the major divinities, who are few in number, arranged in a triad of distinctive oppositions and each in charge of an aspect of the order of the world, thus forming a functional set, whose relationship with other functional sets reconstitutes the total structure of the universe and human society; and a pleiad of minor divinities, who are numerous enough to be assigned to the various phases of ritual or to the successive, and minutely distinguished, stages of some aspect or other of practical life, such as the periods and successive operations characteristic of agriculture and cattle-breeding with their accompanying rites, and also perhaps the incidents of childbirth.

It would be easy to make similar observations about the cults of Ancient Mexico or of various areas of South-East Asia and Africa. Only the major divinities can be directly related to the myths. How are we to explain, then, this opposition between major divinities, few in number and each corresponding to a major segment of the universe and society, and minor divinities numerous enough for each of them to be entrusted with particular responsibility for a concrete aspect of practical life?

The two categories result from the movement of thought in two different and complementary directions. The fluidity of the real is such that it constantly tends to escape through the mesh of the grid that mythic thought has placed over it so as to bring out only its most contrasting features. Ritual, by fragmenting operations and repeating them unwearyingly in infinite detail, takes upon itself the laborious task of patching up holes and stopping gaps, and it thus encourages the illusion that it is possible to run counter to myth, and to move back from the discontinuous to the continuous. Its maniacal urge to discover the smallest constituent units of lived experience by fragmentation and to multiply them by repetition, expresses the poignant need of a guarantee against any kind of break or interruption that might jeopardize the continuance of lived experience. In his sense, ritual does not reinforce, but runs counter to, mythic though, which divides up the same continuum into large distinctive units separated by differential gaps.

On the whole, the opposition between rite and myth is the same as that between living and thinking, and ritual represents a bastardization of thought, brought about by the constraints of life. It reduces, or rather vainly tries to reduce, the demands of thought to an extreme limit, which can never be reached, since it would involve the actual abolition of thought. This desperate, and inevitably unsuccessful, attempt to re-establish the continuity of lived experience, segmented through the schematism by which mythic speculation has replaced it, is the essence of ritual, and accounts for its distinctive characteristics that were brought out by the analysis conducted in the preceding pages....

The fact that ritual constantly has recourse to non-verbal means of expression, such as gestures and material symbols, is to be explained by the increasingly difficult struggle—as thought progresses along these perpendicular axes and so moves away from their common origin—to maintain diagonal connections between them. Almost everywhere, the foundation myths of ritual express the need to slow down, hold back and reunite these divergent impulses. There are myths which say that, for ritual to be invented, some human being must have abjured the sharp, clear distinctions existing in culture and society; living alongside the animals and having become like them, he must have returned to the state of nature, characterized by the mingling of the sexes and the confusion of degrees of kinship; a status of chaos which—contrary to the evidence of practical experience—is said immediately to cause the creation of rules for the benefit of a chosen individual and the edification of his kinsfolk, in other words, the reverse of the interminable and fruitless road, at the entrance to which ritual itself struggles in vain.

Thus, while myth resolutely turns away from the continuous to segment and break down the world by means of distinctions;

contrasts and oppositions, ritual moves in the opposite direction: starting from the discrete units that are imposed upon it by this preliminary conceptualization of reality, it strives to get back into the continuous, although the initial break with lived experience effected by mythic thought makes the task forever impossible. Hence the characteristic mixture of stubbornness and ineffectiveness which explains the desperate, maniacal aspect of ritual. Hence, too, on the other hand (and this may be why, in spite of what has just been said, men have never given it up, although they ought to have been enlightened by its failure or its vacuity), what might be called the 'senatorial' function of magic, a complicated and, unlike mythic thought, essentially irrational activity, but one which has proved indispensable, since it introduces into any moderately serious undertaking an element of deliberation and reflection, pauses and intermediary stages, and acts as a tempering factor even in war.

Contrary to the assertions of old-fashioned naturalism, ritual does not arise, then, from a spontaneous reaction to reality: it turns back towards reality, and the anxiety states which prompt it, or which it causes—and which therefore, it is said, accompany it in either case—do not express (supposing they exist) an immediate relationship between man and the world, but the reverse: in other words, a lurking thought in the human mind, starting from a conceptualized and schematic vision of the world, that immediate datum of the conscious mind, will be unable to find its way back to reality. When Turner (I, p. 7) states that religious rites 'create or actualize the categories by which man apprehends reality, the axioms underlying social structure and the laws of the moral or natural order', he is not fundamentally wrong, since ritual does, of course, refer to these categories, laws or ritual does not create them, and endeavours rather, if not to deny them at least to obliterate, temporary, the distinctions and oppositions they lay down, by bringing out all sorts of ambiguities, compromises and transitions between them. Thus, I was able to show in another context how a rite such as sacrifice is in diametrical opposition to totemism as a system of thought, although both are concerned with the same empirical material: animals and vegetables, in the one case doomed simply to destruction or to be eaten, and in the other given an intellectual significance which may rule out their consumption as food, or limit it in various ways.

In the particular case of ritual... the emotional aspect is not a primary datum. Man does not feel, indeed cannot feel, anxiety in the face of the circumstances of pure and immediate living, except when some internal and organic disorder is part of these circumstances. When this is not so, and certainly in the case of ritual, the anxiety is of quite a different order; it is not existential, but rather epistemological. It is connected with the fear that the segmentation effected on reality by discrete thought in order to conceptualize it will, as was pointed out earlier; make it impossible to recover contact with the continuity of lived experience. It is, then, an anxiety which, far from moving from life to thought, as the functionalists believe. proceeds in exactly the reverse manner, and results from the fact that thought, merely by being thought, creates an ever-increasing between the intellect and life. Ritual is not a reaction to life; it is a reaction to what thought has made of life. It is not a direct response to the world, or even to experience of the world; it is a response to the way man thinks of the world. What, in the last resort, ritual seeks to overcome is not the resistance of the world to man, but the resistance of man's thought to man himself.

It has already been said that laughter expresses an unhoped for gratification of the symbolic faculty, since a witticism or a comic anecdote spares it the trouble of making a long, roundabout effort to link up and unify two semantic fields. On the other hand, anguish—a persistent constriction of the internal organs, and thus morphologically in opposition to the external and spasmodic relaxation of the muscles in laughter—appears, we said, as the contrary emotional state, resulting from an unavoidable frustration of the symbolic faculty. But, in either case, the symbolic faculty, whether gratified or inhibited, inevitably comes between the world as it is thought and the world as lived experience.

I am not, then, ignoring emotional states in assigning them their true position—or, what amounts to the same thing, the only position in which they are comprehensible—a position which does not precede the apprehension of the world by thought, but on the contrary is posterior and subordinate to it, and which is seen to be theirs, once we have grasped the contradiction, inherent in the human condition, between two inevitable obligations: living and thinking.

   It is true that states which may be comparable to anguish can be observed in animals, and that we can, from inner experience, recognize something animal-like in anguish, so much so indeed that it, more than anything else, can give us the experience of being reduced below the human level and put in touch again with our original animal nature. It will be agreed that the symbolic faculty is essentially human. It might be thought, then, that intellectualist interpretations are invalidated from without by animal ethology, and from within by subjective observation. But, on reflection, they can be seen, on the contrary, to be confirmed from both sources. If it is possible to imagine animals in contrasting states, so that they move, without any transition, from an unthinking enjoyment of existence, during which they are entirely relaxed, to sudden crises of anxiety caused by a noise, a scent or a shape, so that they can be seen, from one second to the next, tensing their nerves and their muscles for flight, this is surely because, in them, the disproportion is infinitely greater than it is in man, between powerful and efficient physical resources and the symbolic faculty; they are not entirely lacking in this faculty, but it is rudimentary, and therefore exposed to frequent and more serious frustrations through the problems of life in the wild, so that these frustrations reach an intensity comparable to what we might feel, if a creaking noise in the night made us suspect that thieves had broken into a lonely house where we were asleep. But the same type of occurrence, which provokes a ready-made response in the animal, creates a global state of inhibition in man. In a fraction of a second, a thousand painful possibilities and anticipatory images of the various fates that may be in store for us and of the ways we might avoid them, invade the mind and fight for precedence in the consciousness, which is dominated by a sense of urgency and yet paralysed by the complexity of the problems facing it, and by the lack of time in which to synthesize all the elements effectively.

   It follows, then, that the interpretation of anguish I proposed earlier is not wrong; what is wrong is the constant use made by zoologists—and too often, after them, anthropologists—of the concept of ritual to characterize the stereotyped behaviour patterns noticeable in numerous animal families on various occasions, such as the mating season and encounters between individuals of the same sex; because of their complexity and their detailed and hieratic character, the term 'ritualization' has been applied to them. In spite of appearances, these features make them the opposite of ritual, through proving that they consist of ready-prepared mechanisms, which remain inactive and latent until they are automatically set in motion by the occurrence of a particular type of stimulus.

It has been rightly emphasized that the effect of ritualization is 'to sharpen the messages and reduce them to a discontinuous code' (Bronowski, p. 377). Therefore, the term 'ritualization' is an inaccurate borrowing from human behaviour since, in man, ritual fulfils the opposite purpose of reconstituting the continuous by means of practical operations, on the basis of the speculative discontinuity which provides the starting-point. The difference between the discontinuous of the intelligence and that of instinctive behaviour patterns, lies in the richness of the former and the poverty of the latter, since the complexity of the intellectual operations involved in the one has as its counterpart in the other only patterns which, however complex, are pre-programmed in the organism, instead of being produced , as ideas by the understanding.

It is no doubt legitimate to try to explain man in general to some extent by means of observations on mammals, insects and birds: the gap between the animals and man is so incommensurably greater than the differences between men that makes the latter differences negligible. On the other hand, and for the same reason, it would be radically impossible to explain the differential gaps between human groups, such as the so-called primitives and civilized societies, or between several so-called primitive societies, by comparing the customs peculiar to any one of these groups with animal behaviour patterns, either generic or specific. To find an area in which it is plausible to make some comparison between what I may call the respective soul-states of humans and animals, one has to look elsewhere.

A man accustomed to driving a car controls this supplementary power by means of a nervous system adapted to the more modest function of controlling his body. We see here, then, the same disproportion as in the animal between a symbolic faculty whose capacity for synthesis is remarkably limited in relationship to the problems that it may have to solve, and the enormous physical resources available for the solution of the problems.

A man is driving at speed along an open road; there is nothing special to attract his attention; he falls into a state of blissful, dreamy absentmindedness and trusts to his automatic reactions as an experienced driver for the carrying out of slight and precise movements that he no longer need control consciously, since they have become second nature to him. But if suddenly, some object that he has carelessly thrown on to the seat and forgotten about, falls out of place, producing an unexpected noise that cannot be confused with the hum of the engine or the familiar vibrations of the car body, his attention is immediately alerted, his muscles begin to tense, his whole being is seized with feverish anxiety through fear of some incomprehensible mishap that could in a fraction of a second, lead to disaster. In no less short a time, his mind reels off the list of possible explanations, his defence mechanisms spring into action and his memory is called upon to function: the effect is then linked with its cause, and the occurrence is understood as the insignificant matter it is. It was nothing of any importance, and yet, for a moment, the nervous system of an ordinary human body has had to cope with the risks inherent in the enormous surplus of power bestowed on it by the engine. One sometimes reads in the newspapers that drivers, at the wheel, behave like animals; as can be seen, there is another sense too, an intellectual not a moral one, in which the use of a machine produced by human inventiveness, paradoxically takes man back to the animal condition: his symbolic capacity, although incomparably greater than that of an animal, is, as it were, minimized by his being in charge of an artificial body whose physical power is far in excess of that of his natural body. It is in such a situation, which has nothing to do with ritual, that the messages become impoverished, schematic and discontinuous, and call for an all-or-nothing answer.

But the resemblance goes no further. At the same distance from ritual, the animal acts out its myths, and man thinks his; and the universality of the binary code is demonstrable only at the point of common origin of these divergent tendencies: in a code reduced to its simplest expression, i.e., in the elementary choice between a yes-answer and a no-answer. In the animal, the two possibilities, which are controlled from without, come into play to release or inhibit a chain of pre-programmed actions; in man, on the contrary, the all-or-nothing response marks the lower limit at which, through the effect of a paralysis felt throughout the organism, the resources of a combinatory system rooted in the understanding seize up and cancel each other out; this same combinatory system puts on, in the form of myths, a parade of ideas no less fantastic than the indescribably poetic performance that the genius of the species, during the mating season, imposes on bower-birds.

This conception of the understanding as the source of an autonomous activity, which is subject in the first place to its own constraints, is criticized by all those who imagine that a display of fine feelings can be a substitute for the search for truth, and who do not hesitate, in the defence of what they call the freedom, spontaneity and creativity of the subject, to enter into unnatural alliances, for instance with certain trends in contemporary linguistics, whose philosophical and methodological bias is nevertheless contrary to theirs; after the successful analysis of language in the preceding phase of linguistics, the present practitioners are tackling the complementary problem of the synthesis of utterance, and are moving still further in the direction of determinism. It would be irrelevant, in this context, to discuss the specifically linguistic controversies to which this change of approach has given rise; in any case, I feel they are hardly my concern since, as early as 1945, I applied transformational rules to sociological data and artistic works, with the conviction that I was respecting the teachings of structural linguistics, the same form of linguistics as is now declared to be out of date by people who do not even realize that it has been given a natural and objective status through the discovery and the cracking of the genetic code: the universal language used by all forms of life, from micro-organisms to the higher mammals, as well as by plants, and which can be seen as the absolute prototype, the model of which is echoed, on a different level, by articulate language: the model itself consisting, at the outset, of a finite group of discrete units, chemical bases or phonemes, themselves devoid of meaning but which, when variously combined into more complex units—the word of language or triplets of nucleotides—specify a definite meaning or, definite chemical substance. Similarly, the words of language or the triplets of the genetic code combine in turn to form 'sentences', that life compose; in the molecular form of DNA, this form being the bearer of a differential meaning, the message of which specifies such and such a protein of a given type as can be seen, when Nature, several thousand million years ago, was looking for a model, she borrowed in advance, and without hesitation, from the human sciences: this is the model which, for us, is associated with the names of Trubetskoy and Jakobson.

Technical discussions among linguists are one thing; it is quite a different matter when certain philosophers make illegitimate use of such discussions, through the naïve illusion that linguists, in shifting attention from the language code to the process of utterance, are re-erecting the statue of a free, creative subject which was overthrown by their sacrilegious predecessors: it is rather like imagining that the way in which people make love relieved them of the constraints of the genetic code. But if the genetic code did not exist, they would not 'make' anything at all, and only because it exists do they have the very limited possibility of bringing it into play, with small variations independent of their consciousness and their will. Language in its entirety is potentially pre-existent to any utterance that is selected from it, as all the genomes are potentially pre-existent to the particular individuals that other individuals, through the effect of chance or elective affinities, come together to create.

When linguists emphasize that language, even when reduced to a finite set of rules, can be used to generate an infinite number of statements, they are putting forward a thesis which, although approximate, is nevertheless legitimate from the strictly operational point of view, since the wealth of possible combinations is such that, in practice, it is as if the relative formula had absolute validity. The situation is not the same when philosophers try to draw metaphysical inferences from this methodological principle. Strictly speaking, a finite set of rules governing a finite vocabulary, used to produce sentences the length of which is not definitely limited but which at least in the spoken language, rarely if ever exceeds a certain extent, can only generate a discourse which is itself finite, even if successive generations, each consisting of millions of speakers, do not exhaust the possible combinations.

The fact that a finite set of rules can generate a practically infinite series of operations is interesting, but no more so than the fact that individuals endlessly different from each other are engendered through the operation of a finite genetic code. By shifting the centre of interest from the finite nature of the code to the infinite number of operations, the philosophers seem to believe that, when it is a question of human thought, the code becomes secondary in comparison with the relatively indeterminate nature of its effects: as if, to study and understand the human make-up, it were less important to know that each individual has a heart, lungs, a digestive tract and a nervous system, than to pay particular attention to certain statistical fluctuation, such as the fact that one individual is five foot ten inches and another six feet, or that one has a rather round, and another a rather long face, etc. Such details, however interesting in their explanation might be, are not of prime importance, and biologists, quite rightly, do not pay much attention to them, being content to conclude provisionally that every gene does not determine a characteristic with strict accuracy, but only the approximate boundaries between which the characteristic will vary according to external contingencies.

As in genetics, the practically unlimited number of possible utterances, that is, of verbal combinations, is in the first place a consequence of the fantastic range of elements and rules that can be brought into play. The statisticians tell us that two pairs of chromosomes determine the four possible genomes, and that n pairs of chromosomes will give a corresponding potential total of 2^n genomes which, in the case of man, is 2^{23}. All things being equal , the probability of two parents giving birth to two identical children is, then, of the order of $(1/2^{23})^2$, or one chance in millions of millions. The combinatory system of language is richer still than that of life, so that even if it is admitted to be theoretically finite, there is no possibility whatever, within observable limits, of the recurrence of two identical statements of a certain length, even if we leave out of account the diachronic changes which take place, independently of the conscious awareness or intentions of the speakers concerned, through the effect of the grammatical and phonological mutations involved in the evolution of language, and of the biological mutations and other accidents, such as the crossing, overlapping and translocation of chromosomes, involved in the evolution of life, with the result that, after a certain lapse of time, the same sentences and that the same genome cannot reappear, for the simple reason that the range of genetic and linguistic possibilities has altered.

But we can also see the fundamental reasons for the epistemological perversion resulting from the change of perspective advocated by the philosophers; disregarding their primary duty as thinkers, which is to explain what can be explained, and to reserve judgment for the time being on the rest, they are chiefly concerned to construct a refuge for the pathetic treasure of personal identity. And, as the two possibilities are mutually exclusive, they prefer a subject without rationality to rationality without a subject. But although the myths, considered in themselves, appear to be absurd narratives, the interconnections between their absurdities are governed by a hidden logic: even a form of thought which seems to be highly irrational is thus contained within a kind of external framework of rationality; later, with the development of scientific knowledge, thought interiorizes this rationality so as to become rational in itself. What has been called 'the progress of consciousness' in philosophy and history corresponds to this process of interiorizing a pre-existent rationality which has two forms: one is immanent in the world and, were it not there, thought could never apprehend phenomena and science would be impossible; and, also included in the world, is objective thought, which operates in an autonomous and rational way, even before subjectivizing the surrounding rationality, and taming it into usefulness.

Through the acceptance of these postulates, structuralism offers the social sciences an epistemological model incomparably more powerful than those they previously had at their disposal. It reveals, behind phenomena, a unity and a coherence that could not be brought out by a simple description of the facts, 'laid out flat', so to speak, and presented in random order to the enquiring mind. By changing the level of observation and looking beyond the empirical facts of the relations between them, it reveals and confirms that these relations are simpler and more intelligible than the things they interconnect, and whose ultimate nature may remain unfathomable, without this provisional or definitive opacity being, as hitherto, an obstacle to their interpretation.

Secondly, structuralism reintegrates man into nature and, while making it possible to disregard the subject—that unbearably spoilt child who has occupied the philosophical scene for too long now, and prevented serious research through demanding exclusive attention—involves other consequences that have not been sufficiently noted, and the implications of which ought to have been understood and appreciated by those who criticize linguists and

anthropologists from the point of view of religious faith.
Structuralism is resolutely teleological; finality, after being long
banned by a form of scientific thought still dominated by mechanism
and empiricism, has been restored to its true place and again made
respectable by structuralism. The believers who criticize us in the
name of the sacred values of the human person, if they were
consistent with themselves would argue differently: they ought to be
putting the question: if the finality postulated by your intellectual
method is neither in the consciousness nor in the subject, since you
attempt to locate it on the hither side of both, where can it be, except
outside them? And they would call upon us to draw the logical
consequences... The fact that they do not do so, shows that these
timorous spirits attach more importance to their own selves than to
their god.

However, it should not be assumed that I am trailing my coat,
since this would be inconceivable on the part of someone who has
never felt the slightest twinge of religious anxiety. Structuralism is
attentive, of course, to the purely logical arguments put forward by
mathematicians to reveal the inadequacy and the contradictions of
the Neo-Darwinism that is still accepted by most biologists
(Moorhead-Kaplan). But even the clumsy, slow, obstinate,
anonymous drive by which we might be tempted to explain the fact
that, since its creation thousands of millions of years ago, the
universe, and man with it, are, to quote the cautious terms used by
Piaget (see above, p. 6-7), 'in a state of constant construction', would
not provide any common ground with theology. Although
structuralism does not herald any reconciliation of science with faith
and argues still less in favour of any such reconciliation, it feels
better able than the naturalism and empiricism of previous
generation to explain and validate the place that religious feeling
has held, and still holds, in the history of humanity: religious feeling
senses confusedly that the hiatus between the world and the mind,
and between causality and finality, does not correspond so much to
things as they actually are as to the limit beyond which knowledge
strains in vain to reach, since its intellectual and spiritual resources
will never be commensurable with the dimensions of the essence of
the objects it studies. We cannot overcome this contradiction, but it is
not impossible that we shall more easily adjust to it, now that the
astronomers have accustomed us to the idea of the expanding

universe. If an explosion, a phenomenon that sensory experience allows us to perceive only during a fraction of a second, and without being able to distinguish any of its details because of the suddenness and rapidity with which it occurs, can be the same thing as cosmic expansion, which appears infinitely slowed down in comparison with the scale of the phenomena in which we live our daily lives, and which we cannot imagine but can only translate into the abstract formulae of mathematics, then it does not seem so incredible that a project conceived in a flash by a lucid consciousness, together with the appropriate means for its realization, might be of the same kind, on an infinitely reduced scale, as that obscure drive which, over millions of years and with the aid of tortuous and complicated devices, has ensured the pollinization of orchids, thanks to transparent windows allowing the light through to attract insects and guide them towards the pollen enclosed in a single capsule; or has intoxicated them with the secretions of the flower so that they wobble, lose their balance and slide down an artfully directed slope or fall into a little pool of water; or again sets a trap, the mechanism of which is touched off unwittingly by the insect so that it is held for the necessary length of time against the pollen; or deceives it by giving the flower a shape reminiscent of the female insect, so that the male attempts a sterile copulation which results in genuine fertilization for the plant; or places a tiny trigger so that the foraging bee inevitably bumps against it with its head, thus releasing a sticky capsule of pollen that, all unknowingly, it will carry off to another flower....

Nothing could seem more unacceptable, then, than the compromise suggested by Sartre (p. 89), when he says he is prepared to allow structure a place in the practico-inert, provided we recognize that 'this thing outside man is at the same time material worked upon by man, and bearing the trace of man'. He goes on to say further:

> You will not find, in nature, oppositions such as those described by the linguist. In nature there are only independent forces. The material elements are linked to each other and act upon each other. But this link is always external. It is not a matter of internal links, such as that which posits the masculine in relation to the feminine, or the plural in relation to the singular, that is, of a system in which the existence of each element conditions that of all the others.

These dogmatic assertions leave one bewildered. As if the opposition between, and complementarily of, male and female, positive and negative, right and left—which, as has been known since 1957, have an objective existence—were not written into biological and physical nature and did not bear witness to the interdependence of forces! Structuralism, unlike the kind of philosophy which restricts the dialectic to human history and bans it from the natural order, readily admits that the ideas it formulates in psychological terms may be no more than fumbling approximations to organic or even physical truths. One of the trends of contemporary science to which it is most sympathetic is that which, validating the intuitions of savage thought, already occasionally succeeds in reconciling the sensory with the intelligible and the qualitive with the geometrical, and gives us a glimpse of the natural order as a huge semantic field, 'in which the existence of each element conditions that of all the others'. It is not a type of reality irreducible to language but, as the poet says, 'a temple in which living pillars from time to time emit confused words'; except that, since the discovery of the genetic code, we know that the words are neither confused nor intermittent.

Binary distinctions do not exist solely in human language; they are also found in certain animal modes of communication: for instance, the chirring of crickets uses a simple reversion of rhythm (x, y/y, x) to alter the nature of the message from a warning cry from male to male to a mating call from male to female (Alexander). And what better illustration of the interdependence of forces could one ask for from nature than the marvellously geometrical evolution of flower forms from the Triassic to the end of the Tertiary, which shows a development from amorphous structures at the beginning, first to two-dimensional radial symmetry then to four or five detector-units arranged on the same plane, then to three-dimensional structures and lastly to bilateral symmetry, all of which involved a complementary development of the pollinating insects, constantly adjusting to botanical evolution through a process one would have no hesitation in calling dialectical, were it taking place in the realm of thought.

In another area closer to man, communication usually appears to us to be at the opposite extreme from hostility and war. And yet it would seem that a hormone, whose function in mammals is to ensure communication between the cells during certain physiological processes, is identical with acrasin, which brings about the social aggregation of the amoebae; the basic cause of this phenomenon is, apparently, the attraction of the protozoa to bacteria on which they feed, and which secrete acrasin. This represents a remarkably dialectical transition from communication as a form of sociability to the conception of sociability itself as the lower limit of predatoriness (Bonner). In the lower organisms at least, social life is the result of a chemical threshold high enough to allow individuals to attract each other, but just below the level at which, through an excess of desire, they would begin eating each other. While awaiting further progress in biochemistry, we can leave it to the moralists to decide whether there are any other lessons to be drawn from these observations.

When, in *La Pensée sauvage* (*The Savage Mind*), I interpreted the names we give to birds as indicating that their various species, taken as a whole, appear to us as a sort of metaphorical counterpart of human society, I did not realize that an objective relation of the same type actually exists between their brains and ours. It would seem that mammals and birds, in evolving from their common source, the reptiles, followed two divergent paths as regards the development of the brain and arrived at complementary solutions. In the higher mammals, intellectual operations take place in the cortex, which surrounds the extensive area occupied by various components of the striatum. In birds, on the contrary, as if through the effect of a topological transformation, the same operations (using a code simpler than, but of the same type as, the one programmed in the cortex) are carried out by the upper part of the striatum, which constitutes almost the whole mass of the brain, and which partly surrounds a rudimentary cortex lodged in a furrow at the top (Stettner-Matyniak). In so far as a metaphor always consists of referring to a total, implied semantic field by means of a complementary part of the whole, we can say, then, that in the field of possible cerebral organizations, the mammalian brain and the bird brain present a metaphorical image of each other.

The structuralist ambition to link up the sensory with the intelligible and to reject any explanation which sacrifices one aspect for the benefit of the other is also encouraged by the work of those who, like D'Arcy Wentworth Thompson following on from Dürer..., have been able to establish a term-by-term correspondence between abstract and intelligible relationships on the one hand, and, on the other, living forms—that one would have otherwise thought to be indistinguishable except through aesthetic intuition and long practical familiarity with forms of the same type—and chief among which is the human face, usually thought to be a visible expression of the personality, and its qualities of character and feeling. And what forester could say exactly how he identifies a tree from a distance? Yet only about a thousand instructions are needed to programme a computer to draw trees which, according to variations in the parameters, can be recognized by a botanist as firs, willows or oaks... Differences which might have been thought to be of a purely qualitative nature can be reduced, then, to the operation of a few simple mathematical properties.

Stereochemical theory reduces the range of smells—which one would have thought inexhaustible and indescribable—to seven 'primary odours' (camphoraceous, musky, floral, pepperminty, ethereal, pungent and putrid) which, when variously combined like the constituent elements of phonemes, produce sensations, both indefinable and immediately recognizable, such as the smells of roses, carnations, leeks or fish. According to the same theory, these sensory values can be related to the corresponding simple or complex geometrical forms of the odorous molecules, each of which fits into the olfactory receptor-site specialized to receive it through having a similar form (Amoore; Grive). The theory has not yet been generally accepted (Wright), but it may well be elaborated and refined through comparison with the chemistry of taste, which explains the sensation of sweetness by a change of form of one of the proteins of the body, through contact with certain molecules. Information about this geometrical change, when relayed to the brain, is expressed by the recognition of the appropriate sensation (Lambert). Bird-songs illustrate the opposite situation. Their inexpressible beauty eludes all attempts at description in acoustic terms, since the modulations are so rapid and complex that the human ear cannot perceive them, or does so only fragmentarily. But their hidden richness is directly seen in geometrical form in the oscillograms that have been made of them; expressed as graphs, the songs of the different species can be completely apprehended as incredibly delicate and refined shapes (Greenwalt), as if they were extraordinary masterpieces, in ivory or some other precious material, turned on a lathe.

In fact, structural analysis, which some critics dismiss as a gratuitous and decadent game, can only appear in the mind because its model is already present in the body. I have already mentioned... the exhaustive research that has been done on the mechanism of visual perception in various animals, from fish to cats and monkeys. It shows that each cell in the appropriate area of the cortex continues the processing already begun by several types of retinal or ganglion cells, each of which reacts to a particular stimulus: the direction of movement, the size of the moving object, or the relative rapidity of the movement of small objects, and so on. Consequently, in the first place the eye, and then the brain, do not react to objects which are independent of each other, and independent of the background against which they are seen. What we might call the raw material of immediate visual perception already consists of binary oppositions: simple and complex, light and dark, light on a dark background and dark on a light background, upward and downward, straight and slanting movement, etc. (Pfeiffer; Hubel; Michael). Structuralist thought, by following procedures that have been criticized as being too intellectual, rediscovers, then, and brings to the surface of the consciousness, profound organic truths. Only its practitioners can know, from inner experience, what a sensation of fulfilment it can bring, through making the mind feel itself to be truly in communion with the body.

The preceding remarks do not amount to a still less are they; meant as the preliminary outline of philosophy; I hope they will be taken for what they are: the free-ranging, intellectual musings, tinged with confusion and error, that the subject indulges in, during the short time when, having been released from one task, he does not yet know in what new one he will again dissolve his identity. As I cast a last look over the outcome of eight years' labour, which will soon be as foreign to me as if it had been the work of someone else, I think I can understand, and to some extent excuse, the mistrust with which it has been received in various quarters reaction is to be explained, I should say, by the doubly paradoxical nature of the undertaking. If any result emerges from it, it is, in the first place, that no myth or version of a myth is identical with the others and that each myth, when it appears to give gratuitous emphasis to an insignificant detail, and dwells on it without any stated reason, is in fact trying to say the opposite of what another myth said on the same subject: no myth is like any other. However, taken as a whole, they all come to the same thing and, as Goethe says about plants: 'their chorus points to a hidden law'.

The second paradox is that a work I know to be packed with meanings appears to some as the elaboration of a form without meaning. But this is because the meaning is included, and as it were compressed, within the system. Those who cannot enter into it through lack of knowledge of the immense anthropological storehouse represented by the native cultures of the New World are doomed to grasp nothing of its inner significance; seen from the outside, this significance cancels itself out. It is not surprising, then, that the philosophers do not feel themselves to be involved; they are not involved, in fact, because the scope of the undertaking is beyond their apprehension, whereas, being more directly concerned, semiologists may be interested in the form and anthropologists in the content.

I myself, in considering my work from within as I have lived it, or from without, which is my present relationship to it as it drifts away into my past, see more clearly that this tetralogy of mine, now that it has been composed, must, like Wagner's, end with a twilight of the gods; or, to be more accurate, that having been completed a century later and in harsher times, it foresees the twilight of man, after that of the gods which was supposed to ensure the advent of a happy and liberated humanity. At this late hour in my career, the final image the myths leave me with and—not only individual myths but, through them, the supreme myth recounted by the history of mankind, which is also the history of the universe in which human history unfolds—links up with that intuitive feeling which, in my early days and as I explained in *Tristes Tropiques*, led me to see in the phases of a sunset, watched from the point in time when the celestial spectacle was set in place until, after successive developments and complications, it finally collapsed and disappeared into the oblivion of night, the model of the phenomena I was to study later and of the problems of mythology that I would have to resolve: mythology, that huge and complex edifice which also glows with a thousand iridescent colours as it builds up before the analyst's gaze, slowly expands to its full extent, then crumbles and fades away in the distance, as if it had never existed.

Is this image not true of humanity itself and, beyond humanity, of all the manifestations of life: birds, butterflies, shell-fish and other animals, as well as plants and their flowers? Evolution develops and diversifies their forms, but always in view of their ultimate disappearance, so that, in the end nothing will remain of nature, life or man, or of his subtle and refined creations, such as languages, social institutions and customs, aesthetic masterpieces and myths, once their firework display is over. My analysis, by proving the rigorous patterning of the myths and thus conferring on them the status of objects, has thereby brought out the mythic character of those objective realities: the universe, nature and man which, over thousands, millions or billions of years, will, when all is said and done, have simply demonstrated the resources of their combinatory systems, in the manner of some great mythology, before collapsing in upon themselves and vanishing, though the self-evidence of their own decay.

The fundamental opposition, the source of the myriad others with which the myths abound and which have been tabulated in these four volumes, is precisely the one stated by Hamlet, although in the form of a still overoptimistic choice between two alternatives. Man is not free to choose whether to be or not to be. A mental effort, consubstantial with his history and which will cease only with his disappearance from the stage of the universe, compels him to accept the two self-evident and contradictory truths which, through their clash, set his thought in motion, and, to neutralize their opposition, generate an unlimited series of other binary distinctions which, while never resolving the primary contradiction, echo and perpetuate it on an ever smaller scale: one is the reality of being, which man senses at the deepest level as being alone capable of giving a reason and a meaning to his daily activities, his moral and emotional life, his political options, his involvement in the social and the natural worlds, his practical endeavours and his scientific achievements; the other is the reality of non-being, awareness of which inseparably accompanies the sense of being, since man has to live and struggle, think, believe and above all, preserve his courage, although he can never at any moment lose sight of the opposite certainty that he was not present on earth in former times, that he will not always be here in the future and that, with his inevitable disappearance from the surface of a planet which is itself doomed to die, his labours, his sorrows, his joys, his hopes and his works will be as if they had never existed, since no consciousness will survive to preserve even the memory of these ephemeral phenomena, only a few features of which, soon to be erased from the impassive face of the earth, will remain as already cancelled evidence that they once were, and were as nothing.

Paris, October 1967 — Lignerolles, September 1970